Journey to Recovery

A Comprehensive Guide to Recovery from Addiction and Mental Health Problems

By: Dr. Dawn-Elise Snipes

Artwork and Cover Design by Mireia Carré Ferrer

Recovery & Resilience Publishing
1633 W. Main St. #902
Lebanon, TN 37087
RecoveryandResilience.org

First Printing: 2015

ISBN: 978-0-9862563-0-1

Recovery & Resilience Publishing
1633 W. Main St. #902
Lebanon, TN 37087

RecoveryandResilience.org

Ordering Information: Special discounts are available on quantity purchases by corporations, associations, educators, and others. For details, contact the publisher at the above listed address.

CONTENTS

Introduction

If you are reading this book, then addictions and/or mental health issues are probably affecting you or someone you care about. Please realize that, just like you are not a psychologist after passing Psychology 101, you will likely not be "recovered" after reading one book. This book is designed to walk you through a series of activities which will help you learn more about yourself and how the health of your mind and body, and your preferences, choices and thoughts impact every aspect of your life. You will be able to identify issues and aspects that may need to be dealt with in greater depth.

Many people struggling with addictions also have mental health issues such as depression or anxiety. Likewise, many people with depression or anxiety may have an addiction. We refer to this as a co-occurring disorder. Some people will try to argue that symptoms of depression and anxiety are caused by drug use, and once you are clean and sober those symptoms will go away. While this may be true for some, these symptoms that are still present in early recovery can cause a relapse. After all, how long will someone stay clean and sober if they are constantly depressed or anxious. **Regardless of whether you self-medicated a mental health issue with your addiction, or your addiction caused your mental health issues, BOTH need to be addressed**.

It is also important to remember that mental health issues and addictions occur along a continuum. You may drink, but not be an alcoholic. You may have sex, but not be a sex addict. There will be days that you feel depressed or blue, but are not "clinically depressed." The crucial difference between being "clinically depressed" and not is that to be diagnosable, the behaviors or symptoms have to cause significant distress in your life over a period of time, usually at least 2 weeks. Does that mean you just ignore the symptoms on the days you are stressed out or depressed but not "diagnosable?" No, absolutely, positively not. It is important to figure how to deal with your symptoms when they arise to prevent them from becoming worse. In the first couple of chapters you will learn what addiction and different mental health issues look like, tips for living with these issues and treatments available to assist you. Identify what things you have tried in the past that have worked. When you are having an "off" day, try doing some of those things. Don't wait until you are so anxious you cannot think straight, or too depressed to move. It is far easier to prevent problems than to treat them

Another thing you will notice early in the book is that you are not required to embrace the 12-step philosophy. There are many different paths to recovery. 12-Step programs do work for many people, but not everyone. You will learn about multiple options. You are encouraged to develop sober social supports, but that may or may not include the 12-Step Program. That being said, remember that your addictive behaviors helped you numb, and avoid negative feelings for so long that it will be virtually impossible to identify and work through all of your "blind spots" on your own. To that end it is strongly recommended that you either have a sponsor, hire a recovery coach and/or participate in group or individual counseling

How to use this book.

This book can be used as a self-help workbook, or in addition to group or individual therapy. Since not everyone is ready or willing to work on the same things at the same time, each chapter can be used by itself. The goal is each chapter is to provide you with some useful knowledge and help you apply it to your current situation and recovery process. Additionally, you will find additional resources including videos and worksheets at http://RecoveryandResilience.org/JTR

If you are working with a therapist, recovery coach or sponsor, share the activities with him or her.

If you are a therapist or recovery coach, most of the activities in the book can serve as the foundation for group discussion.

In Appendix 1 you will find a blank template for creating a treatment plan. As you work through the exercises in this book, you may want to use that to keep you focused.

Chapter 1: Understanding Addiction

Did you know that more than 90% of people either have an addiction or are related to someone who does? That is a staggering number. Our culture has morphed over the years to value material possessions (greed), keeping up appearances (envy/pride), power and control (anger), immediate gratification and quick fixes (sloth/gluttony) and lust. While The Seven Deadly Sins was (in my opinion) a good movie, it certainly is not healthy as the foundation for a society. As a result of these priorities, many people are at a higher risk for depression, anxiety and addiction. Even though addiction did exist in the 1950s (nobody talked about it), it was not as prevalent or severe as it is today.

In the 1950's there was more of an emphasis on family values and many people had the luxury of having family dinners where people actually sat down and talked. Without computer games and television to occupy their time and tell them what they "should" think, people of the days gone by actually lived much more mindfully. There was less pressure to have the most expensive car, the biggest house, or the most powerful job. Today, people work 16 hour days to try to get a promotion to prove they are important or special. They work three jobs so they can have the biggest house. They obsess over celebrities, believing that being rich and famous is the path to complete happiness. All of this adds to their depression and anxiety/stress. They spend huge amounts of energy trying to get approval from others, instead of appreciating themselves for who they are, and being grateful for what they have.

This emphasis on "like me for what I can do, not for who I am," teaches you that unless you are the best, brightest, richest and most powerful, you are not worthy of love. Since there is almost always someone better, brighter, richer or more powerful, you are pretty much doomed to feel unlovable, empty, depressed and/or scared. To try to escape this awful feeling, you may frantically search for something to fill the hole inside---in many cases this is addiction. Food, alcohol, money, drugs, in many cases these things fill that void by giving you a temporary feeling of happiness or fulfilment.

Activity: It's All About Priorities

How are some of society's values are negatively impacting you today.

Placing a High Value on Material Possessions

How is this present in your addiction or current situation? _____

_____

Why might this be a problem in recovery? _____

_____

Needing Power and Control

How is this present in your addiction or current situation? _____

_____

Why might this be a problem in recovery? _____

_____

Quick Fixes/Looking for the Easy Way

How is this present in your addiction or current situation? _____

_____

Why might this be a problem in recovery? _____

_____

Lust/Sex/ Focus on Pleasure

How is this present in your addiction or current situation? _____

_____

Why might this be a problem in recovery? _____

_____

Always Wanting More/Being Envious of What Others Have

How is this present in your addiction or current situation? _____

_____

Why might this be a problem in recovery? _____

_____

Activity: Like Me for Who I Am

In what ways have you felt unworthy of love or not good enough? _____

_____

_____

What messages did you (or do you still) hear that tell you that you that you can only be loved for what you do, not who you are. Said another way, love has strings attached.

_____

_____

What are 3 reasons that you are worthy of love and good enough?

1. _____

2. _____

3. _____

What is Addiction

Addiction is the continued use of a person, activity or substance in order to escape from negative feelings, despite experiencing negative consequences as a result of use. These behaviors develop as a last-ditch effort to survive unbearable misery or physical pain. All of your other coping skills have been overwhelmed, yet, somewhere, deep inside, you do not want to die. You just have to make the pain stop. What causes this pain is different for everyone. What seems to be the same is that, over time, you have come to believe that the addiction is your best friend. It stops the pain when nothing else can. It never abandons you. It never judges you or adds to your stress. (Or, at least it seems that way.)

Addictions are a solution to a problem, a bad solution, but a solution. For that reason, you probably have substitute or "back up" addictions. When you cannot access your addiction of choice, you probably use something else to help you escape, or lash out at anyone or anything that stands between you and your addiction. You can be addicted to just about anything that produces pleasure or distracts you. While it is easy to see the connection between using drugs or alcohol and feeling better, other addictive behaviors like obsessing over a person, exercise, shopping or gambling can also not only distract your mind, but also usually has a pleasurable result.

Addictions (even behavioral ones) also mess with your brain chemistry. Whatever it is that you are doing to get the rush/relief/escape causes your brain to rapidly burn through happy chemicals. While it feels great at the moment, you are using up your reserves. At a certain point, your happy chemicals run out and the only way to get the rush is through the addiction. But wait…at a certain point that does not even work anymore, so you start doing riskier things or using harder drugs, or both---sometimes just to feel normal. While this is a very oversimplified explanation of what is happening during the addiction process, you can see that a large part of recovery is allowing your brain to rest, recover and rebalance. This process takes anywhere from a few weeks to a couple of years depending on the amount of damage. The great news is that your brain (and body) can recover.

As a side note, some people actually begin their addiction when something happens to trigger a mental health issu e. All of the same happy chemicals that get mucked up in addiction are the ones that can go wonky and cause things like depression, anxiety and schizophrenia. When you feel bad, you want relief, so you may have self-medicated with your addiction. This is why it is important to not only address the addiction and coping behaviors, but also make sure you are addressing any mental health issues such as anxiety, depression, grief, anger or schizophrenia.

Who Develops an Addiction?

While we do not yet understand why some people develop addictions and others do not, we have identified several risk factors. That is, if you have these risk factors, you may be more vulnerable to developing an addiction. Among them are genetics, an unstable family environment, a family history of substance use or mental health issues, a lack of rewards for positive behaviors, early use of drugs, childhood trauma, and any event or situation that completely overwhelms a person's capacity to cope. That is the kicker---whatever it is, completely overwhelmed your capacity to cope. This means that at any point in your life, an addiction can develop—after a divorce, a death, job loss or after the onset of mental health issues or physical illness.

Think about stressful times in your past. Some days it is easier to deal with what life throws at you than others. If you are at a point of being exhausted and overwhelmed, and then a crisis occurs, you may not be able to cope as well with those added demands. If, up until that point, you had learned some pretty effective coping skills you are much more prepared to deal with the crisis. If you began your addictions early in life it is likely that you used the addiction to escape because you did not have the skills to cope, therefore, you may not have developed the same tools/coping skills as someone who had the benefit of a relatively healthy childhood. Your recovery journey may be a bit longer and more challenging, but very do-able. You will have to learn the skills to cope that most of us learned in middle and high school.

So why do people develop addictions early in life? Having parents with an addiction, for instance, makes you four times more likely to develop an addiction. There are a couple of reasons for this. First, addicted parents cannot teach healthy coping skills or provide the unconditional love and support needed by a child. This means that when you had problems, your parents may not have been any better equipped to handle them than you were. Additionally, addicted parents are often so overwhelmed with their own problems, that they lack the ability and energy to be aware of their children's issues. As a child, when you were struggling, depressed, or going through adolescence, they may not have noticed your pain. Recovery involves developing a support system that can provide that love and support, develop effective coping skills to deal with life on life's terms, and to become aware of your moods and maladies, so you can do something to address them instead of simply avoiding them with your addiction.

Thirdly, it is not uncommon for people develop addictions as a way of self-medicating undiagnosed mental health issues like anxiety, depression or bipolar disorder. Since there is a genetic component to mental health issues, if someone in your family has a mental health issue, then you are more likely to have that same issue. It is important to remember that mental health problems can begin at any age. The average age people start developing symptoms of things like bipolar disorder or schizophrenia is in their mid-20s. When the symptoms begin, it often makes coping with day to day life a lot harder. Initially people may self-medicate, because they do not realize they have a problem. However, it does not take long before the body becomes dependent upon the addiction. Effective treatment must deal with the mental health issues by rebalancing the brain chemicals causing the symptoms, AND deal with the addiction by rebalancing the brain chemicals that were disrupted by the addiction and teaching healthier ways of dealing with the mental health issues and stressors prompting the self-medication.

Another factor that can lead people to desperately search for something that makes them feel good is a lack of rewards for positive behaviors. Throughout this book you will learn that people do not do things unless the benefit outweighs the cost. Would you study hard for a test that had no impact on your grade? When you were young, you did things to get approval from your parents. (If you like to learn, look up "Kohlberg's Stages of Moral Development," and "Erickson's stages of psychosocial development" to help you understand why children seek approval) If you did not get approval, you may have tried harder for a while, but then, eventually, you probably gave up. Going back to society's message that "You are loved for what you can do, not who you are" you can see that, if you failed to receive approval, you probably started to feel like you were unlovable. You couldn't do anything right. Your addiction may have comforted you and made you think you felt okay for a while.

Early use of drugs also increases a person's risk for developing addictions later in life. The young brain is even less equipped to deal with the impact of alcohol and other drugs, especially in addition to hormones and everything else. This means that the young person abusing drugs may experience a more devastating withdrawal, than an adult. The consequence is that they are even more desperate to use again to feel better. Recreational use quickly turns to abuse. Over the past two decades, most of my patients have basically stopped social and emotional development at the point that addiction became a major part of their life. They quit giving a crap about anything and just wanted to be involved in their addiction. It was the only thing that made them feel good. It helped them forget…

Finally, your social environment is almost as critical as your family environment. You probably remember a time in your life when you thought your peers knew everything, and your parents, pastors or teachers knew nothing. If those peers regularly engaged in addictive behaviors, then you were more likely to do the same, if for no other reason, than to fit in. Once those behaviors are started, they are very hard to stop.

The question you are now asking is "Do I have an addiction?" As you work through the following activity, if you answer yes to any of these, you may have, or be developing an addiction.

Activity: Do I Have an Addiction

✓ Have you tried to cut down and failed? Yes No

✓ Do you spend more time thinking about, or engaging in the activity than you intend? Yes No

✓ Do you continue to engage in the behavior even though it has directly or indirectly caused you multiple problems (health, relationship, financial, legal, etc.)? Yes No

✓ Do you get angry or defensive if someone expresses concern about your behavior? Yes No

You are Not the Addiction

One thing that you may struggle with is the term "addict." Behaviors you learned in the past, which have brought you pleasure or eliminated pain, will probably always remain in your "toolbox;" however, **these are simply behaviors**. They were the only way you found to survive the pain, until now.   **You are a person**. If you stop doing the addictive behaviors, you are still a person… Heck, you are a happier, healthier person. You wouldn't say I'm a cancer, or I'm an AIDS. Those are diseases, issues, disorders, but you wouldn't define yourself by them.

Some people have difficulty letting go of the term, addict, and stopping their addictive behaviors, because if they are not an addict, then who are they and what do they do? If they are not an alcoholic, what are they? I encourage you to view your addiction and mental health symptoms as behaviors and conditions… You are a person who has an addiction or a person with depression. Above all you are a person.

Activity: Who am I

Before you started your addiction, who were you? _____

_____

When you find other ways to cope with life on life's terms, who will you be? _____

_____

What Now?

The next few sections focus on honesty—being honest with yourself about what you do, why you do it, how it is impacting you and what (if anything) you want to change. Like ripping a bandage off of an infected wound, getting honest with yourself may hurt like hell. However, once you clean the wound and figure out what you are dealing with, you will be able to start trying to figure out what to do next. Think about it....

You feel like crap and go to see the doctor. She asks you about your symptoms. You answer her questions honestly, because lying might not give her the information she needs to make an accurate diagnosis. She runs a few tests, then comes back, tells you what is wrong, what may have caused it and what the course of treatment will be. Likely you feel a sense of relief—hope that you will start feeling better. Why? Because you have faith that the doctor knows what she is talking about, faith the medicine will work and faith in yourself that you will have the discipline to follow her directions. Some of this will start sounding familiar in the next few sections....

Right now you feel like crap. You are your own doctor though. The next few activities are your "tests" to figure out what you are dealing with---addiction, anxiety, depression, all of the above??? The majority of people with addictions also have some degree of mental health issues. Whether the addiction caused the mental health issues, or the mental health issues existed first is really pretty irrelevant. Either way, your brain chemicals need to be balanced out. The first step is to be honest with yourself. It is a humbling experience; however, once you have identified the scope of your problems, you can start making them better (hope, courage, discipline). Remember, other people have had similar issues and found happiness.

It is important during these first few weeks to find other people who may have the same symptoms, and who are finding that recovery is possible. InTheRooms.org is one place you can meet these people online. 12-Step, SMART Recovery, Celebrate Recovery and Recovery and Resilience (R&R) meetings are also good places. Unfortunately, there is still a stigma surrounding mental illness and addiction. People do not often chat about their recovery in the break room or after a worship service. While not everyone will find "meetings" to be their cup of tea, it is certainly a good place to start meeting people who understand.

Defining the Problem

In an addiction, you may have spent so much time trying to figure out how to get the substance, getting the substance and recovering from the substance that you formed a relationship with the substance. Remember your first love? How you felt the butterflies in your stomach and excitement when she or he would walk in the room? How he or she was all you could think about all day? How your day was planned around trying to spend as much time with the person as possible?

In a normal relationship when this preoccupation started interfering with other areas of your life, you would be able to refocus your attention and take care of business. In an addiction, you cannot get refocused in one or more areas of your life because of your preoccupation (obsession) with the addiction. When you began to have major problems in your life as a result of the addiction, but continued to use anyway, you had developed an addiction.

Activity: Defining Addiction

Complete the table below for each of the addictive behaviors you identified. Note: If you have been in jail or in a hospital, use the 6-months before being confined.

I have used more than intended, spent more money than intended or spent more time than intended engaging in this behavior.

Examples of how this is true for you over the last 6 months _____

_____

I have been unsuccessful at stopping or significantly reducing my use of this behavior.

Examples of how this is true for you over the last 6 months _____

_____

My tolerance has increased. I have needed more of the same substance or activity or have started combining substances or activities to get the same high.

Examples of how this is true for you over the last 6 months _____

_____

In the past 6 months I have engaged in risky behaviors to get the substance, engage in the activity or increase the "rush."

Examples of how this is true for you over the last 6 months _____

_____

In the past 6 months I have spent more time than intended thinking about use, planning to use, using or recovering from this behavior.

Examples of how this is true for you over the last 6 months _____

_____

In the past six months I have been spending more time engaging in this behavior and less time with friends, family, in work or school activities or pursuing interests.

Examples of how this is true for you over the last 6 months _____

_____

In the past six months I have experienced emotional or physical issues because of using or withdrawing from use.

Examples of how this is true for you over the last 6 months _____

_____

Many patients try to rationalize that they are "fine" because they are not using their drug or activity of choice. My response is usually, "You are right. You are F.I.N.E. (F***ed up, Insecure, Neurotic and Emotional) You are in early recovery. What I want to know is if you are dealing with all of that, or just avoiding it by some other means."

If you are addicted to one thing, and stop doing it without addressing whatever it is you were trying to escape from (anger, resentment, depression, grief, loss, low self-esteem, unhealthy relationships...), then you will likely simply choose another addiction--chaotic relationships, sex, food, smoking etc. You are starting to feel something and may think you need to distract yourself. As is often said, "One of the best things about recovery is that you start to feel things again. One of the worst things about recovery is that you start to feel things again."

Activity: Reasons for Use

Circle the reasons you have used your escape behaviors, and write in any others.

To reward yourself	To relax or calm down	As a social activity
To help you sleep	To avoid feeling physical withdrawals	To help you be romantic
Boredom	Peer pressure	To help you do something that is unpleasant
To help you be funny	To help you feel less sad	

Other: _____

Identify two things you can start doing today to achieve the same goals you circled above.

_____

_____

Activity: Identifying and Exploring Escape Behaviors

Place a mark by each of the behaviors which you use to escape/distract yourself/get a rush and give examples

Breaking the Law _____

What is the benefit of this behavior for me besides just helping me escape? _____

_____

What are the drawbacks for this behavior? _____

_____

How can I avoid using this behavior as an escape/substitute addiction? _____

_____

Creating Drama _____

What is the benefit of this behavior for me besides just helping me escape? _____

_____

What are the drawbacks for this behavior? _____

_____

How can I avoid using this behavior as an escape/substitute addiction? _____

_____

Drugs and/or Alcohol _____

What is the benefit of this behavior for me besides just helping me escape? _____

_____

What are the drawbacks for this behavior? _____

_____

How can I avoid using this behavior as an escape/substitute addiction? _____

_____

Exercise _____

What is the benefit of this behavior for me besides just helping me escape? _____

_____

What are the drawbacks for this behavior? _____

_____

How can I avoid using this behavior as an escape/substitute addiction? _____

_____

Food/Eating _____

What is the benefit of this behavior for me besides just helping me escape? _____

_____

What are the drawbacks for this behavior? _____

_____

How can I avoid using this behavior as an escape/substitute addiction? _____

_____

Gambling _____

What is the benefit of this behavior for me besides just helping me escape? _____

_____

What are the drawbacks for this behavior? _____

_____

How can I avoid using this behavior as an escape/substitute addiction? _____

_____

Internet _____

What is the benefit of this behavior for me besides just helping me escape? _____

_____

What are the drawbacks for this behavior? _____

_____

How can I avoid using this behavior as an escape/substitute addiction? _____

_____

Pornography _____

What is the benefit of this behavior for me besides just helping me escape? _____

_____

What are the drawbacks for this behavior? _____

_____

How can I avoid using this behavior as an escape/substitute addiction? _____

_____

Relationships _____

What is the benefit of this behavior for me besides just helping me escape? _____

_____

What are the drawbacks for this behavior? _____

_____

How can I avoid using this behavior as an escape/substitute addiction? _____

_____

Risk Taking/Adrenaline _____

What is the benefit of this behavior for me besides just helping me escape? _____

_____

What are the drawbacks for this behavior? _____

_____

How can I avoid using this behavior as an escape/substitute addiction? _____

_____

Sex _____

What is the benefit of this behavior for me besides just helping me escape? _____

_____

What are the drawbacks for this behavior? _____

_____

How can I avoid using this behavior as an escape/substitute addiction? _____

_____

Shopping _____

What is the benefit of this behavior for me besides just helping me escape? _____

_____

What are the drawbacks for this behavior? _____

_____

How can I avoid using this behavior as an escape/substitute addiction? _____

_____

Work _____

What is the benefit of this behavior for me besides just helping me escape? _____

_____

What are the drawbacks for this behavior? _____

_____

How can I avoid using this behavior as an escape/substitute addiction? _____

_____

Part of accepting that you have an addiction involves understanding that your addiction did not start overnight. For some reason, life has overwhelmed your ability to cope. People often ask "Why me? I had a great childhood." "How could this happen? I am a [doctor, lawyer, cop…] how could I have an addiction?" "I have not experienced major trauma, so what pain am I supposedly trying to escape from?" My response to these questions is often, "I do not know." (Which, by the way, does not usually make my patients too happy.) Unfortunately, nobody really knows why some people will develop addictions and other people will not.   The important thing is to understand that you have developed unhealthy behaviors, and they need to change. The next few exercises will help you identify the progression of your addiction, and, in the present, what makes it worse, what makes it better and what triggers you to want to use.   This will help you understand the function of, and address your addictive behaviors.

Activity: Jellenik Curve & Understanding Your Addiction Progression

Some people are still not convinced that they may have a problem. "I am not as bad as_____" or "I only drink on the weekends." The point is not how bad someone else is, or how often you are engaging in the behavior. The point is that you are experiencing problems in one or more areas of your life because of use. No, you may not be as bad as _____. Everyone's bottom is different. The point at which the behavior hurts more than it helps is your bottom.

Addiction follows a fairly predictable path. Part of this is because, as you use your addiction to escape problems, the problems never get solved---they only get worse, and your brain chemistry becomes progressively "wonky." Place a check next to each of the following statements that describes your behaviors as your addiction progressed.

- ☐ Started with occasional drinking/gambling/internet porn/exercise etc. in order to get relief/escape/relaxation, or to "fit in"

- ☐ Things keep getting worse, so relief drinking/gambling/internet porn/exercise becomes more constant. You cannot really imagine going without it.

- ☐ Need more of the substance/activity to get the same high. (Gamble more, buy more expensive things, get more attention from people, watch more extreme porn, start pushing your body to its limits)

- ☐ Your family or friends started expressing concern

- ☐ Started having blackouts/losing track of time while engaging in the behavior

- ☐ The urge to use/do the behavior became more urgent

- ☐ Began feeling guilty for using. You know what you are doing is causing you problems, but didn't want to or know how to stop.

16

☐ Unable to discuss problems. You didn't feel like anyone would understand

☐ Harder to stop using when others do, or adhere to self-imposed limits (i.e. only spending $100 at the mall, or 1 hour online or at the gym)

☐ Starting to fail to keep promises. You chose the addiction instead of helping your friend move or going to your kid's recital.

☐ Dramatic and/or aggressive behavior began as people started to question your behavior. The addiction is your obsession. It is all you think about. It is what makes you feel better. You believe the people who are questioning you are judging you. Nobody judges you when you are using.

☐ Efforts to control the behavior/use fail repeatedly

☐ Loss of other interests

☐ You begin to avoid family and friends --- They do not understand. You feel like they are judging you. You may feel a guilty, angry, resentful toward them

☐ You begin to have resentments (which you later look back on as unreasonable)--- Example: After I spent all my money at the bar, you did not give me money to fix my car, so I couldn't get to work and lost my job.

☐ You start having problems at work, with money, and begin to neglect your diet, sleep and general health

☐ Your intoxication/use periods become longer (days or weeks instead of hours)

☐ Your thinking becomes impaired---judgment is bad, memory is lost

☐ You start acting in ways that are contrary to your values so you could use

☐ You start feeling afraid, anxious and/or paranoid for no identifiable reason

☐ You begin feeling completely defeated

If this sounds familiar, then you probably have an addiction. **Remember, addiction is a lifestyle and a physical condition, not just a substance or activity.** It has taken a toll on your relationships, your mood and your health. Addiction is rarely something you wake up one morning and decide—"Hey, I don't think I will do that anymore." And badda-bing you are cured. Your body has to have time to recover. This includes your brain getting rebalanced. You probably have some relationships to mend. You may need to change residences or jobs. You most certainly have to work on becoming mindful or what you are feeling and choosing healthy coping skills. You are beginning your recovery journey.

How Did I Get Here

Now that you have identified the progression of your addiction (Jellenik Curve) and the ways you try to cope when you cannot access your addiction of choice (Identifying and Exploring Escape Behaviors Activity), it is time to figure out how you got here. Your autobiography can help you identify irrational or faulty thinking patterns, symptoms of mental health or physical issues, and the characteristics of your relationships that may be contributing to the problem. You will learn more about that in later chapters. For now, it is important to just start getting it down on paper. You can write it in paragraph form, or as a timeline. Whatever makes sense to you.

Activity: Your Autobiography

On several separate sheets of paper, write your autobiography. Start with your first memory and answer the following questions for that age and every year thereafter to the present. Generally you should aim to write at least one page per year---so if you are 40 and your first memory is when you were 4, keep a pencil sharpener handy.

1. What is your first memory and how old were you (first memory)?

2. Who did you live with?

3. Where did you live? What was it like (happy, scary…)

4. What do you remember about your parents/caregivers during this time?

5. What was your typical day like? What did you enjoy doing (sports, hobbies)?

6. Who was important in your life at this time (family, teachers, friends, coaches...)

7. What significant events occurred during this year (good and bad)?

8. What was school/work like? Did you have any difficulties?

9. Did you experience significant depression, anger or anxiety? If so, how did you deal with it? Do you know what caused it?

10. Did you start using/ engaging in your addictive behavior during this year? If so, what were you using/doing? How much? How often? Why?

Now, for *every year after this*, go back and answer the same questions. If your first memory was in second grade, then do this again for third, fourth, etc. up to present day.

Activity: Analyzing My Autobiography

Review your autobiography and look for patterns---good ones and bad ones. Think about ways you can enhance the good patterns that helped you feel content, loved,   relaxed or happy. Then, examine the negative patterns. Sometimes, changing those   patterns means choosing to not let those things or people bother you. Sometimes it means finding a healthier way to achieve the same goal.

Do you see any patterns? ___Yes ___No

If so what were/are they? _____

_____

What could you do now to change unhealthy patterns? _____

_____

Were you constantly trying to get acceptance? ___Yes ___No

If so, from whom (yourself, parents, friends…) _____

_____

How can you start accepting yourself? _____

_____

Were you constantly trying to be loved? ___Yes ___No   If so, by whom?

If you had been loved, what would have been different? What would have it looked like?

_____

_____

What can you do to make that happen now? _____

_____

_____

Were you constantly trying to get power?   ___Yes   ___No

If so, why? _____

_____

What could you do differently now? _____

_____

Were you constantly trying to get freedom?   ___Yes   ___No

If so, free from what or whom?   _____

_____

What could you do differently now? _____

_____

Were you self-medicating depression, anger, anxiety, ADHD?   ___Yes   ___No

If so, what were you self-medicating?   _____

_____

What were your symptoms? _____

_____

What made it worse? _____

_____

What made it better? _____

_____

What could you do differently now? _____

_____

What are the Consequences of Addictions and Mental Health Issues

Not everyone is in a bad place when they start using. Some people use drugs, gamble or engage in other behaviors recreationally. As the "happy chemicals" in your brain got used up, and other coping skills became overwhelmed, the addictive behaviors were used to help you feel better. It is easy to quickly get withdrawn into an addiction-focused world. At that point, development of coping skills and healthy social supports stops.

Much like an infection in a wound that is not treated, whatever is causing the pain in your life, whether it be addiction, mental health issues or both, continues to fester. This creates a vicious downward spiral. You are overwhelmed and in pain, so you use to stop the pain. Whatever is causing the pain continues to worsen. When you sober up, the problem, and the pain is worse, so you use again. Some of these issues may have existed before your use even started, or at least before the addiction took over; however, the addiction inevitably made them worse.

Now it is time to look at the consequences of your addiction and mental health issues, because it is the impact of these consequences that you face each time you sober up----which usually leads to crawling back into the bottle (or addiction). The other reason to examine these consequences is because you may be holding yourself hostage for things you cannot (or could not) control. Identifying the consequences of your behaviors and figuring out what you can and cannot control, you will have a clearer picture of the problem and can make a better recovery plan. That is, you can figure out what crappy things happened because of your actions or choices, and which ones were simply out of your control. Returning to the analogy of a physical illness, if you get sick, there are some symptoms that will likely happen regardless of what you do. If you have a cold, you will likely get a runny nose and a cough. You cannot control that. It is simply how the bug behaves. However, if you continue to workout at the gym and do not take your medicine, you could not only get other people sick, but also develop pneumonia (both potentially preventable and controllable outcomes).

For most addicts, something happens that pushes them from recreational use to abuse and addiction. Sometimes, as in the case of a loss or a trauma or onset of mental health problems, this is an uncontrollable event. Other times, as in a divorce, it may have been preventable, but these things happen. They are awful, and there is usually some fallout. Unlike getting a common cold, you may not know how to identify warning signs that something may be wrong---that your coping skills are failing. It may seem like your world suddenly came crashing down. You were left feeling hopeless and helpless, and just wanted to be happy and have some relief.

Activity: Consequences of Co-Occurring Disorders

In the following activity, give examples of how addiction and mental health issues have impacted your life in each area. If they have not impacted your life in that area, leave it blank for now---You may remember something later. For each consequence, indicate how concerned you are about this particular issue. 1= not at all to 10= Very concerned.

My addiction and/or mental health issues have impacted me emotionally by increasing my:

Anger   Level of Concern: _____

Example of how it has impacted you: _____

_____

Anxiety   Level of Concern: _____

Example of how it has impacted you: _____

_____

Depression   Level of Concern: _____

Example of how it has impacted you: _____

_____

Grief   Level of Concern: _____

Example of how it has impacted you: _____

_____

Irritability   Level of Concern: _____

Example of how it has impacted you: _____

_____

Guilt   Level of Concern: _____

Example of how it has impacted you: _____

_____

Impatience   Level of Concern: _____

Example of how it has impacted you: _____

_____

Envy   Level of Concern: _____

Example of how it has impacted you: _____

_____

Lack of Motivation   Level of Concern: _____

Example of how it has impacted you: _____

_____

Regret   Level of Concern: _____

Example of how it has impacted you: _____

_____

My addiction and/or mental health issues have impacted me legally by causing:

Problems with the law   Level of Concern: _____

Example of how it has impacted you: _____

_____

My addiction and/or mental health issues have impacted me mentally by causing:

Increased confusion, Inability to Concentrate   Level of Concern: _____

Example of how it has impacted you: _____

_____

Decreased ability to deal with stress   Level of Concern: _____

Example of how it has impacted you: _____

_____

Difficulty Making Decisions   Level of Concern: _____

Example of how it has impacted you: _____

_____

Memory Problems   Level of Concern: _____

Example of how it has impacted you: _____

_____

Paranoia/Increased suspiciousness   Level of Concern: _____

Example of how it has impacted you: _____

_____

My addiction and/or mental health issues have impacted me at work by:

Workaholic/overachiever or under involvement at work   Level of Concern: _____

Example of how it has impacted you: _____

_____

Frequent job changes or losses   Level of Concern: _____

Example of how it has impacted you: _____

_____

Difficulty getting along with co-workers   Level of Concern: _____

Example of how it has impacted you: _____

_____

My addiction and/or mental health issues have caused or worsened the following physical symptoms/issues:

Blackouts   Level of Concern: _____

Example of how it has impacted you: _____

_____

Changes in eating/weight   Level of Concern: _____

Example of how it has impacted you: _____

_____

Dental Problems   Level of Concern: _____

Example of how it has impacted you: _____

_____

Heart Racing   Level of Concern: _____

Example of how it has impacted you: _____

_____

Kidney Problems   Level of Concern: _____

Example of how it has impacted you: _____

_____

Liver Problems/Hepatitis   Level of Concern: _____

Example of how it has impacted you: _____

_____

Migraines/Headaches   Level of Concern: _____

Example of how it has impacted you: _____

_____

Pain   Level of Concern: _____

Example of how it has impacted you: _____

_____

Stomach Problems   Level of Concern: _____

Example of how it has impacted you: _____

_____

Sleep Problems   Level of Concern: _____

Example of how it has impacted you: _____

_____

My addiction and/or mental health issues have impacted my social life and other relationships leading to:

Loss of healthy friends   Level of Concern: _____

Example of how it has impacted you: _____

_____

Isolation from family   Level of Concern: _____

Example of how it has impacted you: _____

_____

Withdrawal from others   Level of Concern: _____

Example of how it has impacted you: _____

_____

Friends who use me   Level of Concern: _____

Example of how it has impacted you: _____

_____

Loneliness   Level of Concern: _____

Example of how it has impacted you: _____

_____

Lack of interest in anything but the addictions   Level of Concern: _____

Example of how it has impacted you: _____

_____

Behavior or emotional problems in children   Level of Concern: _____

Example of how it has impacted you: _____

_____

Review this with your counselor, coach or sponsor. Those areas that you marked as an 8 or above are where you are ready to work. Pick the five things that you most want to change right now. This is where you will focus. As you start to improve those areas, you will likely find you are suffering less in other areas as well.

1. _____

2. _____

3. _____

4. _____

5. _____

You can find a blank change plan template in the appendix of this book. Make copies as needed to define your goals and plan for recovery.

Activity: Pinocchio

Sometimes it is helpful to relate your experiences to something else, in order to more clearly understand it. The movie, "Pinocchio," can be used as a metaphor for addiction, Jiminy Cricket as their "sober selves" or conscience, and becoming a real boy without "strings" as ultimate recovery. I strongly suggest at least looking up the lyrics to the songs from Pinocchio. The can provide great thinking material. Here is one link that is active as of this writing: http://www.fpx.de/fp/Disney/Lyrics/Pinocchio.html. You can usually find the movie Pinocchio at your local library, or on line from services like NetFlix, Hulu or Amazon. Watch the movie. Afterward, discuss the different characters and themes as the relate to recovery.

Geppetto is a lonely wood carver who loves his cat Figaro and his fish Cleo, but very much wants another human to love. He crafts Pinocchio, a marionette to look like a boy. He tends Pinocchio with great care. One night the Blue Fairy came to answer Geppetto's wish because he was such a kind, honest and generous man. With that she made Pinocchio come to life, but he was not yet a real boy. To be real, he had to prove himself honest, courageous and compassionate. He had to learn to choose between right and wrong. To help him, the Blue Fairy made Jiminy Cricket his conscience.

In what ways are you like Pinocchio?

_____

_____

_____

How are the Blue Fairy and Jiminy Cricket like Pinocchio's higher power?

_____

_____

_____

The next morning, Geppetto was surprised to find his doll had come to life. Like a good father, he got Pinocchio ready and sent him off to school. On the way to school Pinocchio was stopped by a fox named "Honest John." Now Honest John was anything but honest. He was a con man. Honest John knew that The Great Stromboli would pay top dollar for a talking, walking wooden doll. He tempted Pinocchio with promises of the amazing things and adventures that awaited him in show business. Jiminy Cricket tried to warn Pinocchio, but fame, adventure and fortune won out. Pinocchio ignored Jiminy Cricket and changed direction.

Who or what was your Honest John? _____

Who made you believe your addiction could make you happy? _____

_____

What clues did Pinocchio miss that would have let him know that Honest John was not honest?

_____

_____

_____

What clues did you miss that would have let you know that certain people were not true friends and your addiction was not good for you?

_____

_____

_____

What did Jiminy Cricket do when Pinocchio ignored him? (Leave him or keep trying)

_____

_____

_____

Jiminy Cricket knew that Pinocchio was making a big mistake, but could not stop him. It was up to Pinocchio to do the next right thing. In the next scene, we see Pinocchio on stage singing "I've Got No Strings."

> I've got no strings to hold me down, to make me fret, or make me frown
> I had strings, but now I am free, there are no strings on me.

Ironically, Pinocchio does have strings. In show business, as in addiction, generally the people we interact with do things for us, but only for a price. Pinocchio really is not free to do what he wants. Stromboli doesn't love him, he just wants him to earn money.

Who in your life is a Stromboli? Who has used you for their own personal gain, while making it seem like they were doing you a favor?

_____

_____

_____

What strings are or were attached that kept you from being free?

_____

_____

_____

_____

_____

Pinocchio is locked in a cage in a trailer, but Jiminy Cricket finds him. Pinocchio misses Geppetto so much, and Geppetto continues his search for Pinocchio. "I should have listened to you Jiminy." At one point, the trailer with Pinocchio passes right in front of Geppetto, but Pinocchio cannot hear Geppetto's calls.

Who was your Geppetto, the person who did not give up on you? This person may have also helped you find your sober self again. _____

The Blue Fairy reappears. She asks him what he has been up to. He was supposed to be proving himself honest, brave and loving. Pinocchio lies to her. His nose grows. The more he lies, the more his nose grows. In what ways is Pinocchio's nose like

The emptiness you felt inside during your addiction

_____

_____

_____

Your addiction

_____

_____

_____

The self-hatred that grew inside you

_____

_____

_____

"Lies keep growing until they are as plain as the nose on your face," said the Blue Fairy. Pinocchio promises never to lie again. The Blue Fairy helps him break out of the cage and escape from Stromboli. Meanwhile Honest John is celebrating his ability to con Pinocchio and all of the money he got from Stromboli. His acquaintance, the Coachman is also there. Coachman wants Honest John to gather all of the disobedient boys so he can take them to Pleasure Island. Honest John did just that. He even caught Pinocchio again. You would think that he would resist temptation after the last incident, but, no. Pinocchio joins the other troubled boys and goes to Pleasure Island. Along the way he makes friends with a boy named Lampwick. There is so much noise and so many bright lights and so many fun things to do, that Pinocchio does not even notice Jiminy Cricket is not there. Once the place is torn apart, everyone has vanished, except Lampwick and Pinocchio, who are smoking and drinking while playing pool. Jiminy finds Pinocchio and confronts the two. Soon, Jiminy discovers their plan; Pleasure Island has the power to transform bad boys into donkeys(Jack Asses), which the Coachman sells into slavery. Jiminy rushes back to get Pinocchio. Lampwick's transformation is complete, but Pinocchio and Jiminy escape the island. Unfortunately, Pinocchio has grown donkey ears and a tail.

Coachman took advantage of children who were struggling to make the right choices. He tempted them with drugs, gambling, and constant fun. Was there someone in your life who promised to take you away from all of it, and then ended up driving you deeper into your addiction?

_____

_____

_____

What was your Pleasure Island? What did you hope to find in your addiction?

_____

_____

_____

Who was your Lampwick?_____

How can you remind yourself to always run things by your inner Jiminy Cricket before you act?

_____

_____

_____

They go back home only to find that Geppetto, Figaro and Cleo are no longer there. They left on a journey to find Pinocchio and never returned. The Blue Fairy tells them that Geppetto has been swallowed by Monstro the Whale. The pair start searching the ocean for Monstro with very little luck. When they ask sea creatures such as clams and seahorses, they swim and hide in fear at the mention of Monstro's name. Once Monstro was found, Pinocchio was able to reunite with Geppetto, Figaro and Cleo. Geppetto was so glad to see Pinocchio, despite all of the trials they had been through. Pinocchio soon thinks of a plan to escape Monstro by making him sneeze. The enraged animal chases after him and his father. The whale destroys the raft, sending Pinocchio and Geppetto into the unforgiving sea. After witnessing his father almost drowning, Pinocchio grabs him and swims to shore as quick as he can, but it's too late. Even before he gets there, Monstro slams into a rocky wall, creating a forty foot tidal wave. Geppetto, Figaro, Cleo, and Jiminy survive. When Jiminy looks for Pinocchio, he finds him lying face down in a large puddle, in which he has drowned. Geppetto, Figaro, Cleo, and Jiminy return home and grieve over Pinocchio. Then the Blue Fairy revives Pinocchio and transforms him into a real boy because he has now proved himself brave, truthful and unselfish.

When you were lost in your addiction, who grieved for you?

_____

_____

_____

In what ways have you become or are you becoming brave, truthful and unselfish?

_____

_____

_____

Now that you are returning honest, courageous and able to love, who welcomes you?

_____

_____

_____

How does it feel to be real? To not have to lie and manipulate. To be honest with yourself and others?

_____

_____

_____

Getting Ready to Take the First Step

The first few activities were probably quite sobering. In order to do the work required for change, it is necessary to identify why you are doing what you are doing, how it is affecting you and what you could do differently. Doing this is kind of like taking the bandage off an infected wound, in order to figure out what is wrong, exactly how bad it is, and determine a course of action. Up to this point, you have explored your reasons for use, your escape behaviors and how addiction and mental health issues have been impacting you. Now you will begin taking the first steps toward change.

It may seem very overwhelming, but there are a few things to remember…

Your past has made you who you are. You cannot change the past, but you can change how it impacts you in the present. For example, if you had a crappy childhood, nothing can change that. However, you can choose to be bitter, resentful and miserable now, or you can choose to make your present as happy as it can be, despite your past.

Everything you do is because it is more rewarding than the alternative. The catch in recovery is that it may not be as rewarding immediately. In your addiction, when you feel bad, you have a drink and … badda bing…. For a few minutes you don't feel so bad (or anything for that matter) anymore. In recovery, it may initially suck to deal with whatever is causing the misery, but once you address it, then you will feel better (and it won't bite you in the butt when you sober up like it did in your addiction).

Motivation involves not only identifying the reasons you want to change, but also addressing all of the reasons you do not want to (or are afraid to change). For example, maybe you want to stop smoking so you can breathe better and have more energy. That's great. However, a part of you also really does not want to give up the relaxing sensation that you get from smoking. The key is to find something else that accomplishes the same thing as smoking— exercise, meditation, journaling…

Before you can achieve sustained recovery, you need to get honest with yourself about how bad things have gotten because of your addiction(s). That means not justifying, minimizing, blaming other people or selectively forgetting things you do not really want to remember. As you embark on your recovery journey, you may find that, after a few weeks, you have forgotten how bad it was. You may start making excuses and trying to convince yourself that it actually wasn't that bad. This is your addicted mind's way of trying to hold on to the addiction. Review the activities you have done up until this point to remind yourself why it is worth it, how bad it was and what a happy, healthy future could hold.

Activity: Taking the First Step

We admit that we are powerless over our addiction(s) and/or mental health issues and that life has become unmanageable because of these behaviors and feelings.

I admit that I am powerless over _____

_____ *and the presence of these*

things in my life has made my life unmanageable.

Admitted is a hard word. It may make you feel like you are confessing to something, or telling a secret. It is against addicted family rules to talk, trust, feel or tell secrets. Sometimes admitting something to yourself is harder than admitting it to someone else. It takes a lot of courage to admit you are not perfect. You will explore what perfection means to you later, but before you go any further, repeat the following to yourself:

"Nobody is perfect." "Nobody can do everything all of the time."

Ask yourself, "If my child came to me and admitted that he or she had a problem, would I think less of him or her?" No, you would not. You would hurt for him. You would want to make it better, but you would not stop loving him.

Okay, now that is out of the way. What does it mean to admit something?

_____

_____

_____

What does it mean to be powerless?

_____

_____

_____

What are some examples that have let you know you are powerless over these things?

_____

_____

_____

How does admitting powerlessness make you feel? Why?

_____

_____

_____

What does it mean to say that your life has become unmanageable because of this?   (Review the consequences of addiction activity if you need help)

_____

_____

_____

What are some examples that have let you know your life has become unmanageable?

_____

_____

_____

Activity: Power, Powerlessness and Unmanageability

Make a list of all of the things in your life that have become unmanageable (such as relationships, finances, health, etc). Make a decision right now to stop trying to change those things you cannot change. Instead, change how you feel about or react to those things, or change the situation.

Example:
Unmanageable thing: Relationships
What parts I can change: My honesty, willingness to communicate and trust
What parts I cannot change: Other people's behavior---Instead of staying angry over something I cannot change, I can choose whether to keep them in my life

Unmanageable thing: _____

What parts of this do I have the power to change? _____

_____

What parts of this do I have no power to change AND what can I do about them? _____

_____

_____

_____

Unmanageable thing: _____

What parts of this do I have the power to change? _____

_____

What parts of this do I have no power to change AND what can I do about them? _____

_____

_____

_____

Unmanageable thing: _____

What parts of this do I have the power to change? _____

_____

What parts of this do I have no power to change AND what can I do about them? _____

_____

_____

_____

Unmanageable thing: _____

What parts of this do I have the power to change? _____

_____

What parts of this do I have no power to change AND what can I do about them? _____

_____

_____

_____

Unmanageable thing: _____

What parts of this do I have the power to change? _____

_____

What parts of this do I have no power to change AND what can I do about them? _____

_____

_____

_____

Activity: Miracle Question

If you woke up tomorrow and you were happy, what would be different?

_____

_____

_____

_____

_____

_____

_____

_____

If you woke up tomorrow and you were happy, what would be the same?

_____

_____

_____

_____

_____

_____

_____

_____

Getting Ready: Decisional Balance

Now that you have started to identify the problem, have identified some of the consequences of addiction you want to change, and identified those things you are powerless to change, you need to get motivated. Part of getting motivated is to understand the benefits and drawbacks of the old behavior and the new behaviors. Remember you need understand the reasons you want to change, AND the reasons you DON'T want to change, and address all of them.

For example, say one thing you decide to do is start eating better.
The change I want to make is eating better
Benefits: Clearer skin, Lose weight, Feel better/more energy, Stop cravings
Drawbacks: Requires planning and cooking, more expensive, will miss certain foods
Solutions to Drawbacks: Identify places with healthy alternatives; find healthy menus with shopping lists online; maintaining a healthy diet means moderation. Do not forbid anything, just find ways to have it in moderation

If I decide to NOT change my eating habits
Benefits: Keep my favorite foods
Solutions/Alternative ways to meet the same needs: I will plan on having one favorite food (in moderation) each day in a controlled setting.
Drawbacks: Will be less healthy; Sets a bad example for my kids; Increases risk of high blood pressure and obesity

Activity: Decisional Balance

In the next activity you are going to choose something you would like to change (such as your addiction or your depression) and practice identifying:

1. The benefits to change

2. The drawbacks / reasons you do not want to change

3. Solutions to those drawbacks/reasons

4. The benefits of staying the same/Reasons you want to stay the same

5. Alternative ways to meet the needs of your current behaviors

6. Drawbacks to current behavior

MY DECISIONAL BALANCE WORKSHEET

The change I want to make is _____

Benefits: _____

_____

Drawbacks: _____

_____

Solutions to Drawbacks: _____

_____

If I decide to NOT make this change

Benefits: _____

_____

Alternatives to make staying the same less appealing: _____

_____

Drawbacks: _____

_____

For the next week I will _____

_____

Chapter 2: Co-Occurring Disorders

Until now, you have been mainly thinking about your addiction. However, most people with addictions also have mental health issues like depression and/or anxiety. The term co-occurring disorders describes a situation in which someone has both a substance use problem and a mental health problem at some point in their lifetime. Substance use/addiction and mental health problems can lead to symptoms and behaviors that look very similar, so not only you, but also treatment professionals may find it difficult to determine whether your current symptoms are being caused by substance use problem or a mental health problem, or both.

It has been my experience that it does not really matter. Depressed, clean people are not likely to stay clean for very long---especially if they have not developed new coping skills to deal with the depression yet. The toll that most addictions (including things like gambling and sex addiction) take on the brain leads to a brain chemical imbalance and problems in your life cause at least temporary depression and/or anxiety. Many physicians will prescribe a short course of antidepressant medication to help you get through the "gray phase." This is the time that it seems like there is no color in the world. Everything is blah. There are no highs, but there are still frequent lows. You can't get excited about staying clean when everyday feels like drudgery. The awesome thing is that, over time, your brain and body will likely recover.

If you are depressed or anxious or struggling with another mental health issue before the addiction starts, you may have tried to self-medicate with your addiction. If your brain did not make enough of certain chemicals responsible for helping you feel happy, you may have "assisted" it through your addiction. This chemical imbalance may need to be treated indefinitely with medication. Most of these medications cannot be abused in a way that allows you to get high. They are used to help you have a similar amount of "happy chemicals" in your brain as other people do. It is important to make sure you talk with your doctor about any medications, making sure he or she knows that you are also struggling with addictive behaviors.

In the next few pages, you will learn about some of the different diagnoses and how they may be impacting you in your addiction and in your sober life. Remember that mental health issues exist along a continuum. Don't get too bogged down in whether or not you are "diagnosable." Everyone has days when they are depressed, anxious or cannot concentrate. If you are mindful of your symptoms on a daily basis, you can do a lot to prevent them from getting out of control and causing a relapse.

Attention Deficit/Hyperactivity/Impulsivity

Attention Deficit Hyperactivity Disorder (ADD) is one of the most common diagnoses. The interesting thing is that it has many symptoms that are very similar to anxiety and depression, so ADD can be misdiagnosed as bipolar disorder, anxiety, or depression and vice versa. It is important to be aware of the symptoms of ADD, because the symptoms of ADD need to be treated and the medications for each of these disorders can be very different. The following behaviors and problems may stem directly from ADHD or may be the result of related problems:

- ☐ Chronic lateness and forgetfulness
- ☐ Anxiety
- ☐ Low self-esteem
- ☐ Employment problems
- ☐ Frequently interrupts and has difficult wanting to speak
- ☐ Difficulty controlling anger
- ☐ Impulsiveness
- ☐ Substance abuse or addiction

- ☐ Poor organization skills
- ☐ Procrastination
- ☐ Low frustration tolerance
- ☐ Chronic boredom
- ☐ Difficulty concentrating when reading
- ☐ Mood swings/irritability
- ☐ Relationship problems

Many famous and successful people have ADHD including: Will Smith, Justin Timberlake, Michael Phelps, Jim Carrey, Ty Pennington, Paris Hilton and Terry Bradshaw.

ADD/ADHD can impact your recovery in a lot of different ways. You may have started using to help you deal with the ADD and feel more focused. You may have had difficulty fitting in because of your impulsivity. Or, you may have felt like a failure growing up because you were frequently in trouble in school, and your disorganization caused you to underachieve. If this describes you, then you may need to talk with your doctor about proper medications to help you stay focused on life and your recovery. As with all things, not everyone needs medication to deal with ADD. Just be aware that some relapses may be caused if you have difficulty concentrating and not being impulsive. They do a daily inventory and ensure that there are significant others who can identify when they are being impulsive or inattentive. Each person is different. Only you and your doctor can decide the medication issue.

Activity: Things to Do if You Have ADD/ADHD

There are several things you can do to improve your quality of life with ADD/ADHD. Take medications as directed, and tell your doctor about all supplements you are taking. Missing a dose, taking a dose late or taking two doses at once to catch up on missed doses can have negative consequences. If you are noticing side effects, talk with your doctor. Many side effects can be successfully managed. If you are having difficulty affording your medications, go to the pharmaceutical company's website and look for the link for patient assistance. Usually, it is just a matter of filling out a form and having your doctor fax it in.

Ensure you are getting adequate, quality sleep. When you are tired, everything is harder to manage, including your ADD.

In order to avoid being tired, I will _____

_____

Sleep is important to my recovery because: _____

_____

Train yourself to become more organized. Make lists of daily tasks (be reasonable!) and strive to complete them. Use a daily planner, leave notes for yourself and set your alarm clock to remind you of appointments.

To improve my organization, I will _____

_____

Organization is important to my recovery because: _____

_____

Control impulsive behavior. If you have a tendency to do things you later regret, such as interrupting or getting angry at others, manage the impulse by counting to 10, or repeating your positive mantra (i.e. "I can handle this" or "It's all good").

To control my impulsive behaviors, I can: _____

_____

This is important to my recovery because: _____

_____

Minimize distractions throughout the day. If you find yourself being distracted by loud music or the television, turn it off or use earplugs. Move yourself to a quieter location or ask others to help reduce distractions. For some people distractions can be visual as well. If you find your environment too cluttered or visually stimulating, close blinds, work at a desk facing a blank wall, clear your work surface of all but the most necessary things.

To reduce distractions at work I can: _____

_____

To reduce distractions at home, I can: _____

_____

Reducing distractions and being able to focus is important to my recovery because:

_____

Find constructive outlets for excess energy. People with ADHD sometimes seem to have more nervous energy than others, and this hyperactivity needs to have an outlet of some sort. A hobby or other pastime can be helpful. For example, in the car, in a waiting room or in a meeting if I have to just "sit still" I feel like I am going to crawl out of my skin. I usually bring my tablet or crochet to keep myself occupied.

My excess energy is a problem in these situations: _____

_____

In order to deal with this I can: _____

_____

Effectively managing my hyperactivity is important to my recovery because:

_____

Activity: My Plan for Dealing with My ADHD

For each symptom, identify examples of how this has been a symptom for you, and brainstorm 2 things you could do to fix the problem.

Chronic lateness and forgetfulness

Examples of how this applies to me _____

_____

Two things I can do to address I _____

_____

Anxiety

Examples of how this applies to me _____

_____

Two things I can do to address it _____

_____

Low self-esteem

Examples of how this applies to me _____

_____

Two things I can do to address it _____

_____

Employment problems

Examples of how this applies to me _____

_____

Two things I can do to address it _____

_____

Anger Issues

Examples of how this applies to me _____

_____

Two things I can do to address it _____

_____

Impulsiveness

Examples of how this applies to me _____

_____

Two things I can do to address it _____

_____

Poor organization skills

Examples of how this applies to me _____

_____

Two things I can do to address it _____

_____

Procrastination

Examples of how this applies to me _____

_____

Two things I can do to address it _____

_____

Depression

Most people feel depressed at certain times. Depression is a very normal emotion, and usually does not require any medication or professional intervention. It is your brain's way of telling your body to stop---either because it is exhausted and just cannot do *it* anymore, or because something is hopeless---you are fighting a losing battle. Depression is also a crucial part of the grief process, and signals the realization that a loss has occurred, and you cannot change it.

For the most part, a chemical called serotonin is responsible for your happy feelings. There are a few others, but most people who are depressed take medication to help them with low serotonin levels. If your body does not make enough serotonin, then you have a biologically based depression. This can be a result of genetics or brain injury. It is important to rule out any other problems such as diabetes, hypo-thyroid or polycystic ovarian syndrome. All of these medical conditions (and many more) can produce depressive symptoms, but require very different types of medications. Biologically based depression is usually treated with a combination of medication, nutrition, exercise and, sometimes, talk therapy.

Once you have ruled out biological or "organic" causes, then it is time to look at what you may be doing to either use up the serotonin too fast, or prevent your body from producing enough. Drug use is the primary way of using it up too fast. When you use drugs that produce a euphoric state, your body is releasing a lot of serotonin, in addition to other "feel good" chemicals. While it feels great at the time, this artificially high dump of serotonin means you have less serotonin in your reserves to feel good the rest of the time. Think about alcohol. When you drink your brain releases feel good and relax chemicals. When you start to sober up there is not enough serotonin left, so you may feel depressed, irritable or edgy. It takes your body a while to rebalance itself.

Stress, lack of sleep and poor nutrition also prevent your body from producing enough happy chemicals. Just like you can only do so many things at once, your body also has to balance its energy. If it is busy helping you get a ton of work done, worry about your finances/job/spouse/children, digest food and whatever else you do, then it does not have time to make the happy chemicals until you go to sleep. However, if you are not sleeping well or enough, then it still does not have enough time to devote to helping you feel better. Have you ever forgotten to breathe? Sometimes you may get overwhelmed with emotions or be concentrating on something so hard that you start to feel light-headed. It is only then you realize that you are not breathing---Oops. So really, if your brain can forget something as important as breathing, it can certainly get too busy to make happy chemicals.

Note: Seek immediate help if you have thoughts of suicide or your depression is severe enough that it is negatively affecting one or more areas of your life.

Since you only have so much energy, and so many hours in the day, it is vital to choose how you use that energy wisely. A happy, content person is usually much more productive and effective than one who is angry, anxious or depressed. Ask yourself, "Is this [person, situation] really worth my energy? Is there a better way I could use my energy right now?" We will revisit this concept several more times.

So how do you know if you are depressed? You are experiencing at least five of the following symptoms in the same 2 week period for major depression or 6 month period for minor depression:

Depressed mood: A depressed mood is much different from sadness. In fact, many people with depression say they cannot feel sadness or even cry. Being able to cry again often means the depression is improving.

Being able to feel feelings, even sadness, is important to my recovery because:

_____

_____

Loss of interest or pleasure in most activities, most days: When depression starts, people can still enjoy and be distracted by pleasurable activities. When people are severely depressed, nothing "does it" for them. They just don't care.

Having activities which make me happy is important to my recovery because:

_____

_____

Weight loss or gain: Many people lose weight when depressed, partly because they lose their appetite or don't have the energy to eat. However, some people want to eat all the time, especially comfort foods, causing weight gain.

Having healthy eating habits is important to my recovery because: _____

_____

_____

Sleep problems: Sleep problems are common in depression. Many people have insomnia. They have trouble falling asleep, wake up often during the night, or wake up very early in the morning. They do not find sleep to be restful and may wake up feeling exhausted. Others may find that they sleep too much, especially during the day which, in turn, prevents them from being able to sleep at night.

Getting adequate quality sleep is important to my recovery because: _____

_____

Physical changes: For some people with depression, their movements, speech and/or thinking slows down. Their body may feel very heavy, and moving around is exhausting. Others may become agitated and cannot sit still. They may pace, wring their hands or show their agitation in other ways.

Loss of energy: People with depression find it difficult to complete everyday chores. It takes them much longer to perform tasks at work or home because they lack energy and drive.

Feelings of worthlessness and guilt: When depressed, people may lack self-confidence. They may not assert themselves and may be overwhelmed by feelings of worthlessness. Many people cannot stop thinking about past events. They obsess about having let others down or having said the wrong things, and they feel guilty.

Inability to concentrate or make decisions: People may not be able to do simple tasks or make decisions on simple matters.

Suicidal thoughts: People with depression often think they would be better off dead. There is a high risk that they will act on these thoughts.

Other symptoms may include:

- ☐ Oversensitivity and preoccupation with oneself
- ☐ Negative thinking
- ☐ Feeling a need to control relationships
- ☐ Inability to function in a normal role.
- ☐ Aches and pains all over
- ☐ Gastro-intestinal problems (constipation, diarrhea etc.)

If you are depressed, then getting your brain chemicals back in balance is going to be very important to:

- ✓ Give you the energy to do what is necessary to recover

- ✓ Give you the hope that life without your addiction can be pleasurable

- ✓ Help you find the energy and desire to create a nurture friendships with positive, supportive people

Most people are either anxious/stressed, angry, depressed or some combination of the three when they start using. Since depression slows you down and makes it nearly impossible to care about yourself or anything else, then people usually choose addictions that will excite them, give them energy and help them forget—Examples: Cocaine, amphetamines, K2, or stimulants like Adderall. One of the great exceptions to this rule is alcohol. Since alcohol initially produces a release of serotonin and is a disinhibiter, many people who are depressed like to drink because it makes them feel "buzzed" and the disinhibition gives them an "F-it" attitude. Regarding behavioral addictions, compulsive eating, gambling, shopping and sex help the person distract themselves and may produce a feeling of comfort or contentment. It is important to understand why you use in order to replace the addictive behaviors with alternate, healthy behaviors, and to recognize when you might be at risk of relapse.

Activity: Things to Do If You Are Depressed

Make sure you are getting plenty of sunshine. Long periods of rain, and even shorter days in winter have been associated with increases in depression. If you notice a marked change in your mood on cloudy days or during the winter, talk with your doctor about taking a vitamin D supplement.

I can get more exposure to sunshine by: _____

_____

This is important to my recovery because: _____

_____

Breathe! Did you know that most people yawn because they are not getting enough oxygen, not because they are tired. Although, lack of oxygen does make you sleepy. Practice taking a few deep breaths a few times a day.

In order to remember to do my breathing exercises, I will: _____

_____

This is important to my recovery because: _____

_____

Move. I did not realize how tired you could get by staying in bed all day until I was put on bed rest when I was pregnant with my daughter. The more you sleep, the more you want to sleep. If you can muster the energy to actually exercise, you might feel a lot better.

Each day I commit to getting at least _____ minutes of movement.

I can do this by: _____

_____

This is important to my recovery because: _____

_____

Drink water. Dehydration can also cause you to feel sluggish, foggy-headed and tired.

I will drink more water by: _____

_____

This is important to my recovery because: _____

_____

Eat a balanced diet, but try to avoid "heavy foods" that make you feel sleepy.

One thing I will do to improve my nutrition is: _____

_____

This is important to my recovery because: _____

_____

Laugh. Bill Engvall, Robin Williams or Jeff Foxworthy can usually give me a good belly laugh (which releases endorphins---other feel good chemicals)

In order to laugh more, every day I will: _____

_____

This is important to my recovery because: _____

_____

Laughter is contagious. Try sharing a joke or two at work. "What did one toilet say to the other toilet?" "What's wrong, you look flushed." hahahaha

Other suggestions

✓ Be good to yourself. Since depression may be your body saying it just cannot go anymore, try allowing yourself to have a much needed break for a day or two.

✓ Turn off your cell phone and do what YOU want to do, but after a day or two, you need to get back on the horse.

✓ Talk to someone you can trust, and who won't judge you.

✓ Get out of your PJs. You can feel like you have not accomplished anything if you fail to even get out of your jammies.

✓ Pet an animal. Much research has shown that cats and dogs can significantly improve people's moods. If you don't own a pet, try going to a local pet store.

✓ Talk with your doctor about supplements like 5-HTP, B Vitamins and Vitamin D

Activity: Dealing with Depression

For each symptom, identify examples of how this has been a symptom for you, and 2 things you could do to fix the problem.

Depressed mood most of the day

I have experienced that by: _____

_____

Two things I can do to address this are: _____

_____

Loss of interest or pleasure in most things

I have experienced that by: _____

_____

Two things I can do to address this are: _____

_____

Changes in eating patterns

I have experienced that by: _____

_____

Two things I can do to address this are: _____

_____

Changes in sleeping patterns

I have experienced that by: _____

_____

Two things I can do to address this are: _____

_____

Agitation or feeling of being slowed down

I have experienced that by: _____

_____

Two things I can do to address this are: _____

_____

Feelings of worthlessness/ guilt

I have experienced that by: _____

_____

Two things I can do to address this are: _____

_____

Inability to concentrate

I have experienced that by: _____

_____

Two things I can do to address this are: _____

_____

Bipolar Disorder

Bipolar disorder used to be called manic depression. People with bipolar cycle through periods when they are depressed, periods when they are manic (off the chain), and times when they are "normal." These periods can range from hours to months. How often they occur cannot be predicted. For many people, there are years between each episode, whereas others have episodes more often. Over a lifetime, the average person with bipolar illness experiences about 10 episodes of depression and mania/hypomania or mixed states. As the person ages, the episodes of illness may occur more frequently.

You just learned about major and minor depression. Mania causes people to be emotional and react strongly to situations and is characterized by either:

- ☐ An abnormally or persistently high mood (different from their usual)
- ☐ Extremely irritable, disruptive, impulsive or aggressive behavior.

And they must have at least three of the following symptoms to a significant degree to be diagnosed with mania or hypomania:

- ☐ Exaggerated self-esteem or grandiosity/Feeling 10-Foot Tall and Bullet Proof
- ☐ Reduced need for sleep
- ☐ Increased talkativeness
- ☐ A flood of ideas or racing thoughts
- ☐ Speeding up of activities such as talking & thinking, which may be disorganized
- ☐ Poor judgment
- ☐ Psychotic symptoms such as delusions (false beliefs), or hallucinations

One of the greatest challenges to treating people with bipolar disorder is that, like a person with an addiction misses the high from the addiction, the person with bipolar disorder misses the highs. This is complicated by the fact that some of the medications, called mood stabilizers used to treat this condition actually can cause the person to feel really sleepy and groggy. You must talk openly and honestly with your doctor about how you are feeling and any side-effects, so that you can have a good quality of life. People with bipolar disorder often abuse a range of drugs depending on their current symptoms. Alcohol or marijuana may help them relax, while stimulants may increase their euphoria. Especially in the manic or hypomanic phase, behavioral addictions can be very dangerous. The increased level of impulsiveness can lead them to take very high risks with financial or safety matters.

Activity: Things to Do if You Are Bipolar

Get enough, quality rest.

In order to avoid being tired, I will _____

_____

Sleep is important to my recovery because: _____

_____

Eat a balanced diet, and avoid too many stimulants like caffeine.

One thing I will do to improve my nutrition is: _____

_____

Proper nutrition is important to my recovery because: _____

_____

Journal, or at least rate your mood and your stress level every day, to identify situations which may trigger a manic or depressive episode and any patterns in your episodes. (See the Mood Journal in the Appendix)

Being aware of my moods and identifying triggers and patterns is important to my recovery because _____

_____

To help me remember to chart and/or journal, I will: _____

_____

_____

Talk to someone you can trust who understands bipolar disorder, and can help you identify changes in your moods, or behavior and warning signs of an impending "episode."

The two people who are best at identifying changes in my moods are: _____

_____

They can help me by: _____

_____

Minimize unnecessary stress.

I can do one or more of the following things to minimize stress:

1. _____

2. _____

This is important to my recovery because: _____

_____

Other Suggestions

- ✓ Take your medication as prescribed, and talk with your doctor about how well it is working and any unacceptable side-effects. If you cannot afford your medication talk with your doctor or pharmacist about the patient assistance programs available through most pharmaceutical companies.

- ✓ If you have problems with remembering to pay bills, gambling or spending thousands of dollars in an episode, work with a certified financial advisor to set up a system to protect your money.

- ✓ Consider a therapy animal. Many dogs, especially Labrador retrievers are very sensitive to mood fluctuations, and can help you identify when you are getting stressed or moody.

Activity: Dealing with Mania

For each symptom, identify examples of how this has been a symptom for you (if it has), and brainstorm 2 things you could do to fix the problem.

Inflated self-esteem or grandiosity

I have experienced that by: _____

_____

Two things I can do to address this are: _____

_____

Decreased need for sleep

I have experienced that by: _____

_____

Two things I can do to address this are: _____

_____

More talkative than usual or pressure to keep talking

I have experienced that by: _____

_____

Two things I can do to address this are: _____

_____

Flight of ideas, or feeling like thoughts are racing

I have experienced that by: _____

_____

Two things I can do to address this are: _____

_____

Increased goal directed activity

I have experienced that by: _____

_____

Two things I can do to address this are: _____

_____

Restlessness

I have experienced that by: _____

_____

Two things I can do to address this are: _____

_____

Excessive or impulsive participation in pleasurable activities

I have experienced that by: _____

_____

Two things I can do to address this are: _____

_____

Anxiety

Anxiety disorders are the most common type of mental health disorder, and come in different varieties. While they have different causes and symptoms, one thing people with anxiety disorders share are feelings of deep fear, concern, stress or being overwhelmed that affect their mood, thinking and behavior. If you have an anxiety disorder, your thoughts and feelings may get in the way of taking the actions needed to be healthy and productive. Anxiety disorders can get worse over time if they are not treated. In this section we will talk about generalized anxiety and panic attacks/panic disorder.

Generalized Anxiety Disorder

People who have, for least six months, felt ongoing and excessive anxiety and tension may have generalized anxiety disorder. They usually expect the worst and worry about things, even when there is no sign of problems. They often experience the following symptoms:

- ☐ Always feeling "stressed out"
- ☐ Insomnia
- ☐ Fatigue
- ☐ Shaking/trembling
- ☐ Shortness of breath
- ☐ Muscle tension
- ☐ Headaches
- ☐ Dizziness
- ☐ Irritability
- ☐ High blood pressure
- ☐ Hot flashes

Panic Disorder

Panic disorder is a type of anxiety disorder. Sometimes when people get really anxious, they breathe shallowly or forget to breathe altogether. This can cause them to feel faint. This in turn freaks them out more and voila, panic attack. There are many causes of panic attacks. It is important to figure out what triggers yours. Panic disorder occurs when people have repeated panic attacks, or the sudden onset of intense fear or terror. During these attacks, people may experience physical symptoms such as:

- ☐ Shortness of breath
- ☐ Heart palpitations
- ☐ Chest pain or discomfort
- ☐ Choking or smothering sensations
- ☐ Fear of losing control
- ☐ Fear of going crazy

Many people with panic disorder develop anxieties about places or situations in which they fear another attack, or where they might not be able to get help. Eventually this can develop into agoraphobia, a fear of going into open or public spaces.

Most people are either anxious/stressed, angry, depressed or some combination of the three when they start using. Since anxiety revvs you up and makes it nearly impossible to stop worrying, then people usually choose addictions that will help them relax, not care or forget—Examples: Marijuana, alcohol, Valium, Vicodin. It is important to note that, although alcohol initially produces a sense of relaxation, as it wears off, it causes rebound-anxiety, racing heart and increases in blood pressure. This rebound anxiety can range anywhere from mild anxiety to a panic attack, or even a stroke if your blood pressure gets high enough.

Regarding behavioral addictions, compulsive eating, gambling, shopping and sex help the person distract themselves and may produce a feeling of comfort or contentment. It is important to understand why *you* use in order to replace the addiction with alternate, healthy behaviors, and to recognize when you might be at risk of relapse.

Activity: Things to Do If You Are Anxious

Minimize stimulants such as caffeine and decongestants.

I can do this by: _____

_____

This is important to my recovery because: _____

_____

Breathe!

I can do this by: _____

_____

This is important to my recovery because if I "forget" to breathe or are breathing shallowly, I can get light headed. This triggers a panic attack in some people.

Move.

I can do this by: _____

_____

This is important to my recovery because it is important to get your mind and body in synch. If my mind is worried and my heart is racing, but I am sitting still, there is a disconnect, and I will feel "wonky." This increases the anxiety. If I start moving around and doing things, my mind will be tricked into believing that my heart is beating fast because I am being active, and be distracted from the worry.

Stop Needless Worrying

Worry is energy tied up in the future. It is a natural emotion designed to get you to do something. Okay, so do something. Identify what you are worried about. Decide whether it is something to be worried about. If it is, then take steps to address the situation. If it is not, then let it go. We will discuss this more in the chapter on emotions.

I can do this by: _____

_____

This is important to my recovery because: _____

_____

Drink water.

I can do this by: _____

_____

This is important to my recovery because dehydration can cause your heart to race, and you to feel light headed.

Other: _____

Eat a balanced diet

I can do this by: _____

_____

This is important to my recovery because low blood sugar can make you irritable and light headed which you may misinterpret as anxiety or a panic attack.

Other: _____

Be good to yourself.

Anxiety is the body's equivalent of driving up a 3,000 ft. mountain in 1st gear. Eventually you are going to either overheat the engine or run out of gas.

I can do this by: _____

_____

This is important to my recovery because: _____

_____

Talk to someone you can trust, and who won't judge you.

I can do this by: _____

_____

This is important to my recovery because: _____

_____

Activity: Worry Journal

Anxiety is fear or worry. Keep a list of things that you worry about. Identify which ones are not worth your energy, and which ones are out of your control. Decide how you can find peace with that. Of the ones that are controllable, make a plan, and one by one, start taking care of them

Worry: _____ Is this worth my energy? _____

What parts of this situation can I control, and how will I do that? _____

_____

_____

What parts of this situation are out of my control, and how will I deal with that? _____

_____

_____

Worry: _____ Is this worth my energy? _____

What parts of this situation can I control, and how will I do that? _____

_____

_____

What parts of this situation are out of my control, and how will I deal with that? _____

_____

_____

Remember that worry/anxiety/stress are real emotions and are designed to motivate you to do something. These feelings become an issue when you continue to worry about and try to change things over which you have no control, or are choosing not to do anything about.

Post-Traumatic Stress Disorder

The last issue you will learn about is Post Traumatic Stress Disorder. Many people who develop substance use/addiction and/or mental health problems either have experienced, or are experiencing horrific physical, psychological or emotional trauma. When trying to decide if an event is or was "horrific or life threatening," it is important to remember the age you were when you experienced the trauma. What is extremely traumatizing to a 6 year old, many not have the same impact on a 26 year old. Your brain and ways of thinking about the world are totally different. Hopefully, as a 26-year old you are more mature, have developed some healthy coping skills and can rely on social supports.

In this section, you will learn specifically about Post Traumatic Stress Disorder, or PTSD. For simplicity, there are basically two types of PTSD. Single Episode Onset PTSD happens when you are the victim of, or witness something so horrific or life threatening, that a single exposure is enough to cause debilitating symptoms. Some people, like cops and soldiers may be exposed to these situations repeatedly, but it only takes one situation to cause the damage. Gradual Onset Posttraumatic Stress Disorder, on the other hand, happens when someone is exposed to abuse or neglect, or horrific experiences over a long period of time, and they feel trapped, helpless and hopeless. This type of PTSD is common among children who grow up in households where there is substance abuse and/or domestic violence. Regardless of which type of PTSD it is, people with posttraumatic stress disorder (PTSD) describe a common set of symptoms.

Symptoms include:

☐ Re-experiences the event through flashbacks, nightmares or memories

☐ Increased awareness of the environment (hypervigilence)

☐ Avoidance of anything associated with the traumatic event.

☐ A sense of numbing or depersonalization

☐ Irritability and/or agitation

It is important to note that not everyone exposed to a trauma develops PTSD. Some factors that make a person more vulnerable to developing PTSD include a history of substance abuse or mental health issues, significant stress in the prior six months, lack of social support immediately after the trauma, and experiencing the trauma close to a place they felt safe, such as home or work. Further, young children are at greater risk if their parents are consumed with trying to cope with the trauma themselves.

When the traumatic experience continues for a long time, it may significantly impact how the person sees themselves in relation to the world. This is sometimes referred to as gradual onset PTSD. Experiences that can lead to Gradual Onset PTSD include:

- Long-term domestic violence, physical abuse
- Long-term child neglect or abuse
- Human trafficking
- Extended deployments in war zones

The first criteria for the diagnosis of Gradual Onset PTSD, is that the person experienced a prolonged period in a situation in which he or she felt helpless or trapped. In most cases, there is no single event or episode that can be identified as causing the PTSD, it is the sum of all of the awful events that strips the person of a sense of safety and personal control.

Symptoms include changes in:

- Mood (e.g., persistent depression, explosive anger or inhibited anger)
- Consciousness or awareness (e.g., forgetting traumatic events, reliving traumatic events or having episodes when you feel detached from your body)
- Self-perception (e.g., a sense of helplessness, shame, guilt, stigma and a sense of being completely different than other human beings)
- Relations with others (e.g., isolation, distrust or a repeated search for a rescuer)
- Your sense of meaning in the world (e.g., a loss of sustaining faith or a sense of hopelessness and despair).

Survivors often avoid thinking and talking about trauma-related topics, because it can be overwhelming. Survivors (anywhere from 50 to 90 per cent) may engage in addictive behaviors as a way to avoid and numb feelings and thoughts related to the trauma. Survivors may also engage in self-mutilation and other forms of self-harm. If you are feeling suicidal or homicidal, that must be addressed first; however, the best treatment results are achieved when both PTSD and the other disorder(s) are treated at the same time rather than one after the other. This is especially true for PTSD and alcohol and other substance use. Treating PTSD without treating any addictions or other mental health issues often makes those things get much worse. Likewise, most addictions and mental health issues in people with PTSD are related to the trauma, and cannot be fully eliminated until the PTSD is.

Activity: Things to Do If you Have PTSD

Learn about PTSD and how prevalent it is. You are not alone.

I will learn about PTSD by: _____

_____

This is important to my recovery because: _____

_____

Be good to yourself. Working through a trauma is exhausting. Now is not the time to offer to make Thanksgiving dinner for your whole family!

I can be good to myself by: _____

_____

This is important to my recovery because: _____

_____

Know your triggers----Smells, sounds, places and people can all trigger a flashback. Know what your triggers are so you can be prepared to avoid them when possible, and deal with them when necessary.

The following situations could trigger a flashback _____

_____

This is important to my recovery because: _____

_____

Create a safe zone in your home where you can relax

My safe zone is: _____ It is safe because: _____

_____

The body and mind are amazing. Most reactions are designed to either protect you, just like the fight or flight reaction, or alert you that something you experienced doesn't "fit" with how you have always understood things. For example, when you touch something hot, you remember not to do that again. When you experience a threat, your mind wants to remind you not to do that again. Likewise, if you believe that your neighborhood is a safe place, and you are a victim of a robbery, your mind needs some help fitting those two ideas together. It will continue to remind you of the danger until you integrate that experience into your thought patterns and, when necessary, do something to help yourself feel better. For example, you might start thinking "My neighborhood is safer than most, but no place is immune from crime. I will add an alarm system to better protect my family."

PTSD symptoms are "designed" to remind you that the world can be unsafe and it is important to protect yourself from people or situations that make you vulnerable or could hurt you. Unfortunately, the parts of your brain that are trying to protect you are also some of the most primitive parts, so fears and anxieties may become generalized---For example, someone who is in a very bad traffic accident may experience significant symptoms when they are in the car. They have nightmares about the accident. They are always on edge when they are in the car. They start to see every car trip as if it were the traumatic event. The easiest way to protect yourself from being in a car wreck is to not get into a car, but that is not practical. If the following activity, you will look at how the symptom is either

In the following activities you will start to understand how the symptoms you are experiencing are your body's way of trying to protect you from being in that situation again, and create a plan to help you deal with flashbacks and night terrors

Activity: My PTSD

Identify the events in your life which may have led to PTSD

_____

_____

_____

_____

_____

Identify the symptoms of PTSD you have and describe how you experience them, how each of these symptoms protect you from re-experiencing the trauma in real-life, and how can you more effectively deal with each symptom.

Re-experiencing the event through flashbacks, nightmares or memories

I experience this through: _____

_____

It protects me by: _____

I can deal with it by: _____

_____

Increased awareness of the environment (hypervigilance)

I experience this through: _____

_____

It protects me by: _____

I can deal with it by: _____

_____

Avoidance of anything associated with the traumatic event.

I experience this through: _____

_____

It protects me by: _____

I can deal with it by: _____

_____

_____

A sense of numbing or depersonalization

I experience this through: _____

_____

It protects me by: _____

I can deal with it by: _____

_____

_____

Mood changes (e.g., persistent sadness, suicidal thoughts, explosive anger)

I experience this through: _____

_____

It protects me by: _____

I can deal with it by: _____

_____

_____

Changes in consciousness, awareness, depersonalization (e.g., forgetting traumatic events, numbing or having episodes in which one feels detached physical body)

I experience this through: _____

_____

It protects me by: _____

I can deal with it by: _____

_____

_____

Self-perception changes (e.g., a sense of helplessness, shame, guilt, stigma and a sense of being completely different than other human beings)

I experience this through: _____

_____

It protects me by: _____

I can deal with it by: _____

_____

_____

Problems in relations with others (e.g., distrust or a repeated search for a rescuer)

I experience this through: _____

_____

It protects me by: _____

I can deal with it by: _____

_____

_____

Altered sense of meaning in the world (e.g., a loss of faith or sense of hopelessness).

I experience this through: _____

_____

It protects me by: _____

I can deal with it by: _____

_____

_____

Remember that each symptom had a function. To deal with that symptom, you need to find something else that does the same (or similar) thing. For example, avoidance of reminders is your mind's way of protecting you from the bad memories/flashbacks. You cannot always avoid reminders though. One of my patients developed PTSD after watching someone die in a traffic crash on the interstate. It is not practical to avoid interstates forever. In his case, if he had to get on an interstate and started to feel anxious, he would call his spouse. They would talk and it would keep him in the present moment, preventing (or at least minimizing) flashbacks. Over time he got to the point that the interstate did not bother him anymore. The key is to occupy your brain so it is too busy to think about the trauma.

Chapter: 3 Motivation

In the first chapter you learned about the symptoms and causes of addiction, what your addiction looks like (your escape behaviors) and its consequences. The second chapter helped you identify whether you have a co-occurring mental health disorder, and ways to deal with symptoms of common issues including depression, anxiety, ADD/ADHD and post-traumatic stress disorder. Now that you are armed with knowledge, it is time to start putting it into practice. Some days in recovery will feel amazing, some days….not so much. They key is to stay motivated to do the next right thing, even when it does not feel so good at the moment. Back to my example of the vaccination, my ultimate goal is to be healthy and available for my kids. I hate needles, so getting vaccinated is a daunting task for me. In order to stay motivated to get that shot, I need to remember my ultimate goal---being healthy for my kids.

It is also helpful if you think of recovery as a journey. You have a destination in mind. The safest way to get there is to take the charted route. Off-roading may seem like a lot of fun, but you may get lost or worse. Likewise, if you stop at every tourist attraction along the way, you may never reach your destination. Motivation is your ability to keep your eye on the destination, and choose to do things that move you closer to that end point, instead of detouring you.

What is Motivation

Motivation is a combination of desire, willingness and ability. If you are motivated, you not only want to do something, but are willing to get up and do it. Sometimes you have to make your own motivation because the task (cleaning, taxes) is, in itself, just not that much fun. You motivate yourself all the time.

Have you ever accomplished something you were not motivated to do? What was it?

_____

How did you get yourself motivated?_____

_____

Example: Some days I am not motivated to clean. Without motivation I will not get myself up off the couch. So….I put on my favorite music, brew a strong pot of coffee and don't allow myself to watch television until the cleaning is done.

74

Motivation involves recognizing that something needs to be done, creating a plan and implementing that plan. Motivation is a key, changeable feature in long-term recovery. Some days you are going to be less motivated than others to do the next right thing. By planning for those low motivation days, you can reduce your chances of relapse.

Let's begin by looking at the following assumptions about motivation:

✓ Motivation is a key to change. –You need to be motivated to do something.

✓ Motivation and people are multidimensional – People are motivated by how things make them feel physically and emotionally, and how things impact their lifestyle.

✓ Motivation is dynamic and fluctuating. That is, some days you may feel motivated to do something, and other days, not so much. This might be because other things are requiring your attention, you didn't sleep well, you are fighting off a cold, or maybe you just lost sight of the reasons you want to change.

✓ Motivation is influenced by social interactions. When you tell someone about a goal, you are more likely to complete the task Friends also influence what is important to you.

✓ Motivation can be modified. Even if it is something that you do not initially want to do (like taxes or exercise), you can find ways to motivate yourself.

Motivation is a Key to Change

Change causes crisis, and crisis causes change.

A crisis is anything that causes discomfort. When you are uncomfortable, you look for alternatives. Generally, little crises cause little changes, and big crises cause big changes. Motivation is your desire to move towards pleasure/happiness and away from pain/stress/anger. When something happens that makes it unpleasant to stay the same (a crisis), you try to change. But, if you start to change, and it seems worse, then you will likely abandon your efforts to change, and stay the same. Think about the last time you tried to go on a diet, start exercising or quit smoking. You had your reasons for wanting to change and making that resolution. You were motivated. When the going got tough, you asked yourself, is all of this struggle really worth it? If you said no, it is not worth it, then guess what, you probably went back to your old ways. If it was worth the effort, you reminded yourself of all the reasons the struggle was worth the effort and tried to continue.

Activity: Creating Crisis

In this activity, you will explore previous times when you have wanted to change.

Example:

       What I wanted to change: Lose weight

       Why I wanted to change it: Clothes did not fit well. Low Energy. Habit eating.

       What was uncomfortable about the change: Having to reduce intake

       Why the crises (changing and dealing with the discomfort) were worth it:
       Longer term happiness was more important than relieving short term discomfort

What you wanted to change   _____

Why you wanted to change it (the crisis)   _____

_____

What was uncomfortable about the change (the other crisis) _____

_____

Why the crises (changing and dealing with the discomfort) were worth it. _____

_____

What you wanted to change   _____

Why you wanted to change it (the crisis)   _____

_____

What was uncomfortable about the change (the other crisis) _____

_____

Why the crises (changing and dealing with the discomfort) were worth it. _____

_____

When talking about motivation you must accept that humans do not do things without benefit. Even things that do not *seem* to have a benefit, actually do. Have you heard the old adage "Why do you keep banging your head into the wall? Because it feels so good when I stop!" Even things that seem unpleasant at the time, are done for a benefit. Using this reasoning, there were some benefits to the old behavior. Identifying what those benefits are, and alternate ways to achieve them is vital. It is also important not to romanticize your addiction---that is, focus on only the really good parts of it.

Something that is romanticized takes on much more motivational power. Think of your first love. You probably romanticized him or her to be perfect and thought you couldn't live without him/her. In that same way you may have a love affair with your addiction. It is there for you. You can count on it. It makes the pain go away. It helps you forget. Its benefits are unconditional. The challenge for Sally, was replacing her best friend (the addiction which always numbed the pain and never judged her) with sober social supports and healthy behaviors. This is not easy. One of the main reasons people fail to change is that they only consider the reasons they want to change. They forget to look at all the reasons they DON'T want to change, and the benefits of those behaviors.

Activity: Addressing the Don'ts of Changing Your Addiction

Reason I don't want to change: _____

Alternate activities to meet the same needs: _____

_____

Reason I don't want to change: _____

Alternate activities to meet the same needs: _____

_____

Reason I don't want to change: _____

Alternate activities to meet the same needs: _____

_____

Motivation and People are Multidimensional

You are more than just the sum of your parts. Every person has emotional, mental, physical, social, spiritual and vocational aspects of themselves that exist within given environment. What does that mean? Well, you only have a certain amount of energy. That energy is divided up to meet the demands you have in all areas of your life. The key to wellness and recovery is to ensure that the energy demand does not exceed the energy supply.

When you need more energy than you have available, you must take it from other (sometimes more necessary) areas such as your immune system. Think about the last time you felt exceptionally "stressed" about getting a project done at work. In order to get the "must dos" accomplished what things did you sacrifice?? Probably things like relaxation, eating good meals, sleep and recreation with family and friends. This is an example of how energy is "diverted" from one area to another. What were some of the consequences of having to divert energy? Sickness? Tiredness? Irritability?

Earlier you learned how addiction and mental health issues interact. For example, drinking worsens depression, and when you are depressed you may want to drink. Now you will take that a step further, and look at how your addiction and mood issues are impacting other areas of your life.

Activity: Dimensions of Motivation

How is your addiction impacting:

Your relationships? _____

_____

Your ability to think and concentrate? _____

_____

Your mood? _____

_____

Your physical health (including sleep and nutrition) _____

_____

Your environment reflects how you feel inside. What is it telling you? _____

_____

Your work (including your work product, desire to go to work and sick days)? _____

_____

How is your mood or mental health issue impacting :

Your relationships? _____

_____

Your ability to think and concentrate? _____

_____

Your mood? _____

_____

Your physical health (including sleep and nutrition) _____

_____

Your environment reflects how you feel inside. What is it telling you? _____

_____

Your work (including your work product, desire to go to work and sick days)? _____

_____

To regain optimal wellness (recover), you must balance your energy expenditure among all areas. You may not be motivated to work on all aspects of yourself right now. That is okay, because positive changes in any one area are going to automatically produce positive changes in the other areas. To recover, nurture each area. Do things that make you happy. Get rest and good nutrition. Try to look at the bright side of the situation. Surround yourself with supportive, positive people. The endorphins and other "good" chemicals the body produces when you are happy will help you recover more quickly.

Activity: Taking Care of Myself/Balancing My Energy

You have identified some of the ways that addiction is impacting your life. Each of these negative impacts is likely the result of energy shortages. In the following activity will identify how you can nurture and/or reduce stress in each area.

Emotional/Happiness

Ways to improve: _____

Ways to reduce stress: _____

_____

Mental/Creativity/Concentration/Time Management

Ways to improve: _____

Ways to reduce stress: _____

_____

Physical/Pain/Sleep/Nutrition

Ways to improve: _____

Ways to reduce stress: _____

_____

Social/Relationships/Hobbies

Ways to improve: _____

Ways to reduce stress: _____

_____

Environmental/Comfort/Organization/Appearance

Ways to improve: _____

Ways to reduce stress: _____

_____

Like people, motivation also has multiple, interactive dimensions. It encompasses your internal urges and desires, external pressures and goals, perceptions about risks, benefits of behaviors and cognitive appraisals of the situation. Examples of the multiple types of motivational dimensions are listed below.

Activity: Identifying and Maintaining Motivations in Each Dimension

Physical Motivators: Pain, illness, discomfort, fear of contracting a disease

My Motivations to Change _____

_____

Ways to Maintain My Motivation _____

_____

_____

Emotional Motivators: Depression, anxiety, panic, PTSD

My Motivations to Change _____

_____

Ways to Maintain My Motivation _____

_____

_____

Cognitive Motivators: Wanting to get out of the fog, believing you can do it

My Motivations to Change _____

_____

Ways to Maintain My Motivation _____

_____

Social Motivators: What friends and family want, what you need to do to be accepted, availability of friends, wanting to set a good example for kids

My Motivations to Change _____

_____

Ways to Maintain My Motivation _____

_____

Occupational Motivators: Fear of losing a job, desire for a promotion, frustration at own poor work performance.

My Motivations to Change _____

_____

Ways to Maintain My Motivation _____

_____

Legal Motivators: Desire to stay out of jail

My Motivations to Change _____

_____

Ways to Maintain My Motivation _____

_____

Once you realize you are responsible for the change process, and have identified your motivators, you will probably feel empowered and more invested in it. A motivational approach allows you to be active rather than passive, by forcing you to choose your treatment goals and take responsibility for changing.

In my first job, drug offenders were referred to me for "treatment." They did not want it, but it was mandatory. I did however, have some control over their situation. They had two choices. One, they would accept that this was part of their probation and we would work together to find something they would like to change (cut down on smoking, improve their relationship...I let them brainstorm), or two, they could work against me. To increase their motivation, for every two groups they attended and were clean, on time and actively participated, I would knock off one group at the end. Ultimately, if they worked hard for eight sessions, they were done. This worked to motivate most of them. They saw it is a controllable and achievable challenge.

Activity: My Commitment, Control and Challenge

Commitment: Why are you committed to your recovery?

I want to make this change for the following reasons: _____

_____

_____

Control: In what ways do you have control over your recovery?

The following are positive choices I can make with regard to:

(People)_____

(Places)_____

(Things) _____

(Thoughts/Feelings) _____

(Actions)_____

Challenge: Remember challenges are events or situations that push you to grow.

In what way do you see recovery as a manageable and exciting challenge?

_____

_____

_____

Now that you are committed to this change, take control by looking at prior relapses to figure out what went wrong, and prior recovery periods to figure out what you need to do again.

Activity: Good Orderly Direction

Because of your control and trust issues, you may have difficulty believing that you can count on anyone or anything to consistently be there for you. You may have difficulty believing that it is better to ask for help than to do it yourself. Carrying the weight of the world on your shoulders is exhausting. It can also take you on multiple detours throughout your recovery journey.

In 12-step programs they say "We came to believe that a power greater than ourselves could restore us to sanity". The phrase "a power greater than ourselves" trips up a lot of people. For some this refers to their higher power. For others, this refers to having a larger plan and long term goals, instead of always doing what feels good at the moment. Additionally, the definition of insanity is repeatedly doing the same thing and expecting different results. So, sanity means doing something different to get different results.

Stated differently: We came to believe that knowing what we want and having a plan can reduce wasted time, stress, and help us live happier, more fulfilled lives.

My Good Orderly Direction (My Destination) is: _____

_____

_____

_____

_____

To get there, I need to follow the following directions (Example: 1) Prepare for the trip by getting well rested. 2) Bring someone along to keep me company and help me avoid detours. 3) Obey the laws and rules of recovery. 4) Stop along the way to look around and appreciate how far I have come.

1. _____

2. _____

3. _____

4. _____

5. _____

This is one way to start developing your change plan.

Activity: Mantras

Mantras are sayings or phrases that you can use when you are struggling, frustrated, or overwhelmed to help you get through, refocus on the positive or give you the courage you need. Share what each of the sayings below means to you and how it can help you stay happy, healthy and sober. Then pick a mantra you can use to help you get refocused over the next week.

First Things First

It means: _____

It will help me stay sober and happy by: _____

_____

Live and Let Live

It means: _____

It will help me stay sober and happy by: _____

_____

GOD = Good Orderly Direction

    It means: _____

    It will help me stay sober and happy by: _____

_____

Let go and let God

    It means: _____

    It will help me stay sober and happy by: _____

_____

HALT = don't get to Hungry, Angry, Lonely, Tired
    It means: _____

    It will help me stay sober and happy by: _____

_____

My worth does not depend on another persons' opinion

    It means: _____

    It will help me stay sober and happy by: _____

_____

Progress, not perfection

    It means: _____

    It will help me stay sober and happy by: _____

_____

Recovery is a journey ...not a destination

It means: _____

It will help me stay sober and happy by: _____

_____

To thine own self be true

It means: _____

It will help me stay sober and happy by: _____

_____

When all else fails, follow directions
It means: _____

It will help me stay sober and happy by: _____

_____

Change is a process, not an event

It means: _____

It will help me stay sober and happy by: _____

_____

Take what you can use and leave the rest

It means: _____

It will help me stay sober and happy by: _____

_____

Easy does it, but do it

    It means: _____

    It will help me stay sober and happy by: _____

    _____

You only get out of it what you put into it

    It means: _____

    It will help me stay sober and happy by: _____

    _____

I cannot be grateful and hateful at the same time

    It means: _____

    It will help me stay sober and happy by: _____

    _____

Feelings are not facts

    It means: _____

    It will help me stay sober and happy by: _____

    _____

I chose the following mantra for this week , _____

because: _____

_____

Motivation is Dynamic and Fluctuating

Motivation changes over time and in relation to different situations. For example, Sam may be ready to address his depression, but not his drinking. Sally may be willing to look at her relationship with her husband, but not her relationship with her father. It is important that you work with your counselor, coach or sponsor to identify what you are motivated to work on at that point in time. If you are in a treatment program, you may have to work with your counselor to develop mutually agreeable goals. You may have as your primary goal to stay out of jail. Your counselor's goal is for you to stay clean. These are not mutually exclusive. Why? Because one of the things you are going to have to do to stay out of jail is….stay clean.

My clients often thought I was insane when I would start their first session with the movie "Star Trek: First Contact." For those of you non-Trekkies out there, this movie introduces the concept of something unstoppable, the Borg, against which "resistance is futile." This is similar to the criminal justice system. In order to stay out of jail, you have to do what you are told to do. Just like the Borg would control the thoughts of everyone in the society, your addictive self is currently controlling your thoughts. Like Captain Picard freed himself from the Borg, you too can free yourself from your addictive self. Try watching the movie and see what other similarities you can find between your life and that of either the Borg or Captain Picard.

Motivation also varies in intensity. You may have come in to treatment very ready to change, but once you are clean and start feeling emotions and remembering, you may quickly be overwhelmed. The pain of recovery becomes worse than the pain of addiction. It is slow going at first. The addiction took the pain away quickly. In sobriety, you have to learn to tolerate some discomfort and focus on the big picture instead of the quick fix. Additionally, if you have co-occurring or multiple disorders, it is important to focus on addressing the mental health and substance abuse issues at the same time. Increases in anxiety or depression will likely make substance use worse and vice versa.

Activity: Maintaining My Motivation/Relapse Prevention

The three things that could take my focus off of my recovery are:

1. _____

2. _____

3. _____

I can deal with them by:

    1. _____

    2. _____

    3. _____

In the past, when I have tried to stop using, these three things have derailed my recovery

    1. _____

    2. _____

    3. _____

I can deal with them by:

    1. _____

    2. _____

    3. _____

The thing I am most afraid of about recovery is _____

_____

I can deal with it by: _____

_____

The part of recovery I dread the most is _____

_____

I can deal with it by: _____

_____

Motivation is Influenced by Multiple Dimensions

You learned in an earlier section that there are multiple types of motivators. Likewise there are multiple things that can influence your motivation. Follow me on this one. Tiredness/lethargy, sleep problems, changes in eating patterns, difficulty concentrating and problem solving, and loss of pleasure in most things are some major symptoms of depression. When you are over-tired, you probably tend to eat poorly, have difficulty concentrating and problem solving, have difficulty finding pleasure in much (except going back to sleep) and feel sluggish/lethargic. When you eat poorly (especially lots of sugars and comfort foods) and/or try to compensate for tiredness with caffeine, you end up feeling more sluggish, having increased difficulty sleeping restfully and still have difficulty concentrating. What is the point? Your nutrition, sleep, emotional, and cognitive issues all can either work in a negative spiral or support your recovery. Can physical interventions relieve depression completely? No. Can they help you start getting rest so your body can recover? Yes. Similarly, changing how you think can help with depression, but if you are still failing to get adequate rest and drinking caffeine into the wee hours, you are not going to reap the same benefits.

Staying with the motivation theory, instead of trying to work on a goal that you may not be that motivated to accomplish, identify what areas you are wanting to work on and start there. It is like unraveling a blanket. It does not matter what string you pull first. They all start unraveling the blanket. By listening to yourself, you will probably find the process to be a lot easier.

Activity: Defining the End

Recovering from your addiction is a noble goal, but it may be a means to an end. Why do you want to recover? That is your end. Recovery is a necessary means to that end.

I want to recover because _____

_____

In order to achieve these things, I need to _____

_____

_____

Example: I want to recover because I want to be happy again and set a good example for my kids. In order to achieve this, I need to figure out how to be happy (supportive friends, less stressful job, maybe medication) and start taking care of myself (eating well, exercising, getting enough rest and improving communication and coping skills).

Motivation Can be Modified

Motivation can be modified or enhanced at many points in the change process. You may not have to "hit bottom" to become aware of the need, and increase your desire for change. You can enhance your motivation for change. Likewise, it is important to remember that your motivation levels will fluctuate. On the days when your motivation is low, modify it!

Activity: Modifying Motivation

Distress levels can increase the motivation to change. For example, many clients are prompted to change and seek help during or following severe anxiety or depression. Identify ways in which your behavior has caused you excessive distress.

_____

_____

Critical life events often stimulate the motivation to change. Identify upcoming life events which may help keep you motivated.

_____

_____

Recognize negative consequences and the harm or hurt you have inflicted on others or yourself. Identify how your addiction or mental health issues negatively impacted you.

_____

_____

Positive and negative external incentives also can influence motivation. Supportive and empathic friends, rewards or coercion of various types may stimulate motivation for change. Make a list of all of the possible rewards for getting and staying sober. Review these rewards periodically to remind yourself of the rewards of staying sober.

_____

_____

Understanding Readiness for Change

Being motivated is only part of the equation. You have probably heard the old saying---Ready, willing and able. Well, readiness is a combination of motivation willingness and ability. When getting ready to change, you will go through a sequence of stages as you think about, initiate and maintain new behaviors (Prochaska and DiClemente, 1984). You will likely move back and forth between the stages and cycle through the stages at different rates. I usually warn people when they first start treatment that, no matter how motivated you are right now, no matter how sick and tired of being sick and tired you are, when you start addressing your "issues" you may start to minimize the problem. When the going gets tough, you will want to get going. That is very normal. Recovery is uncomfortable, and sometimes emotionally painful. It is, however, during these times that you need to talk to your counselor, coach and/or sponsor and review the reasons you want to change in order to stay motivated. We usually talk about taking it one day at a time, but you may find times when you need to take it one hour at a time.

The following pages will help you understand the phases of change. Please remember that, in their own dysfunctional way, the early stages of readiness for change protect you. It is kind of like getting into a cold pool. At first you do not want to get in. You know it is cold and would rather deal with the heat (Precontemplation). Then you think…gee, I am really hot, maybe I'll just put my feet in (Contemplation). If someone splashes you, you might decide you do not want to sit on the edge. Otherwise, you might realize that you are really hot, and just cooling your feet isn't getting the job done. You determine you need to get into the pool to cool off, but spend quite a bit of time thinking about it, then slowly walk down the stairs (Preparation). Finally you take the plunge (Action). If it is too cold, you will jump back out (Back to contemplation again). If you can convince yourself to stay in the water, after a little bit, it becomes less uncomfortable.

Precontemplation

During the precontemplation stage, you are not considering change and do not intend to change. If you are in this stage you usually have not experienced (or are denying) any adverse consequences or crises because of your substance use or mental health issues, and are not convinced that your pattern of use is problematic or even risky. You may be unwilling or too discouraged to change your behavior, because you have had periods of recovery only to relapse. It is important to remember that recovery is possible. If you have relapsed, then you (and/or your therapists) have overlooked something that needs to be addressed to help you stay sober and happy. Look, learn, move on.

If you are reading this book, and are in the precontemplation stage, then you are likely being forced into, or forced to stay in, treatment. Let's take a look at why you might be unwilling or unmotivated to change.

94

Activity: Examining Three Types of Precontemplators

Reluctant precontemplators do not have sufficient knowledge or awareness about the problem, or the personal impact it is having, to think change is necessary.

How is your addiction and/or mental health issue impacting you and your family?

_____

_____

_____

_____

_____

Rebellious precontemplators are afraid of losing control over their lives. "Don't tell me what to do!" Your challenge is to shift this energy into making choices that are more positive for yourself rather than rebelling against what you perceive as coercion. That is…accept the fact that you have to complete this book and stay away from your addiction for a certain period of time, so you might as well try to get something useful out of it. Maybe you can learn how to better help a friend who is addicted?

What things are making me feel forced into recovery? _____

_____

How can I reframe those things, so I feel less angry/annoyed _____

_____

_____

What can I do to make the best of this situation? _____

_____

_____

Resigned precontemplators feel hopeless about change and overwhelmed by all of the energy required. You may have tried repeatedly to quit to no avail. You must regain hope and optimism about your capacity for change.

Identify all the times you have tried to stop using or address your mental health issues and been successful, even if only for a day. This will give you clues about what tools and motivations can work for you.

_____

_____

_____

_____

_____

Remember that most people cannot successfully recover on their own. It is very easy to overlook critical parts of the problem (blind spots). This book is designed to walk you through the steps of change, and make sure you do not miss the important parts, BUT, you will still need someone to help you see when your addiction or mental health issues are trying to take back over.

My support people during my recovery will be: _____

_____

_____

Interventions

✓ Get to know (and trust) yourself.

✓ Find three people who you can count on to provide honest, constructive feedback.

✓ Explore the pros and cons of the problem.

✓ Compare your perception and others' perceptions of the problem.

Contemplation

As you become aware that a problem exists, you will begin to understand that there may be cause for concern and reasons to change. You may be ambivalent, seeing both the reasons to change and not to change. You may not be sure if you can do it, or you may remember how you felt the last time you relapsed. You may still be struggling or using, but you are considering the possibility of making a change in the near future.

Interventions

✓ Accept that it is normal to be ambivalent

✓ "Tip the decisional balance scales" toward change by eliciting and weighing the pros and cons of substance use and change.

Activity: Visualizing Change

Make a poster board collage of the positive aspects of recovery (the big picture). This not only gives you a visual image of what recovery holds for you, but it forces you to answer the miracle question. "What would life be like if you woke up tomorrow and were recovered/sober/happy?" If you also do a poster of the negatives of addiction and mental health problems, make sure you do not use pictures that could serve as triggers such as needles, pills or alcohol.

Activity: Finding Exceptions

Your mental health issues or addiction are not present 24 hours per day 365 days per year. Times you are not significantly distressed or using are called exceptions. List 3 exceptions to using your addiction, what you were doing when you did not want to use, or when you were not being dominated by your mental health problems.

1. _____

2. _____

3. _____

List 3 exceptions to your depression or anxiety (What you were doing 5 times when you were happy)

1. _____

2. _____

3. _____

Preparation

Once you have decided to change, it is time to make more specific plans for change, such as making choices about whether treatment is needed and, if so, what kind. During this stage, you will also examine your perceived ability--or self-efficacy--for change.

Interventions

- ✓ Clarify your goals and strategies for change.

- ✓ Create a menu of options for change or treatment. That is, have a plan B and C, because plan A does not always work.

- ✓ Connect with others in recovery who can offer expertise and advice. You can go to 12-Step meetings, Rational Recovery Meetings, read books or even go to recovery websites online. IntheRooms.com is a good place to start. You can also find recovery meetings by searching online for "AA or NA where and When."

- ✓ Identify and deal with barriers to change.

- ✓ Get a commitment from those close to you to participate in the process by not using alcohol or drugs or gambling in front of you.

- ✓ Review your list of what has worked in the past for you, or for people you know.

- ✓ Remember to plan for handling finances, childcare, work, transportation or other potential commitments.

- ✓ Publicly announce plans to change in order to help yourself become accountable as well as aware of any inner resistance. This other person can be a spouse, friend, family member, coworker, recovery coach or sponsor.

✓ Envision a different life after making changes. This can be a powerful motivator and an effective means of strengthening commitment. In addition, stories about how others have successfully achieved their goals can be excellent motivators. An exercise for envisioning change is to picture yourself after a year has passed, during which time you have made positive changes.

Activity: Howdy from the Future

Write a letter to yourself with a future date and describe what life is like at that point. The letter can have the tone of a vacation postcard, wishing you were here.

_____

_____

_____

_____

_____

_____

_____

_____

_____

_____

_____

_____

Action

Individuals in the action stage choose a strategy for change and begin to pursue it. Now, you are actively modifying your habits and environment. This is hard work, and there are days that you will wonder if it is worth it. It is.

Activity: Creating a Can-Do Attitude

Even if you know you have a serious problem, you are not likely to make a positive change unless you have some hope of success. Self-efficacy is the belief that you can act in a certain way or perform a particular task and get a hoped for result—confidence. For example, a student with self-efficacy would believe that if he studied for a test it would have a positive impact on his grade.

You are most likely to make statements about self-efficacy when you are negotiating goals or developing a change plan. When you hear yourself saying can't, won't or yes, but… statements, you are running into barriers. Those barriers may or may not really be there, but if you believe you can't., then you won't. Remember that you may have high self-efficacy in some situations, and low self-efficacy in others. Most relapses occur during one or more of the following situations. For each, identify examples of how each of those situations could cause a relapse, and what you can do to deal with them. Remember that you can relapse with both your mental health or addiction issues.

Negative emotional states such as anger, depression or frustration.

Could cause a relapse by: _____

_____

I can deal with this by: _____

_____

Social pressures such as seeing others drinking

Could cause a relapse by: _____

_____

I can deal with this by: _____

_____

100

Habit: Using when wanting to relax, watching football, playing cards, etc.

Could cause a relapse by: _____

_____

I can deal with this by: _____

_____

Physical and other concerns such as having a headache, chronic pain, feeling tired or being worried about someone.

Could cause a relapse by: _____

_____

I can deal with this by: _____

_____

Withdrawal symptoms and urges such as craving or wanting to test your willpower.

Could cause a relapse by: _____

_____

I can deal with this by: _____

_____

Points to Remember

- ✓ Remember that change is a gradual process. Your behaviors helped you survive until you were able to start getting other tools.

- ✓ Focus on your strengths rather than your weaknesses.

- ✓ Develop two or three sober, sane social supports.

- ✓ Before you criticize yourself, ask yourself if you would be as critical of your best friend. You are likely much more critical of yourself than anyone else

- ✓ Recognize that you are a probably addicted to many things, and when deprived of your addiction of choice, may seek out other behaviors to help you escape.

- ✓ Recognize that you may have other coexisting disorders that require attention

- ✓ Anticipate possible family, health, system, and other problems.

- ✓ Identify high-risk situations and develop appropriate strategies to overcome these.

Chapter 4: Goal Setting and Behavior Modification

Now that you are getting motivated, in order to set achievable goals, you need to know what your end goals are, what has and has not worked for you in the past, and why. Many people set goals that are too broad, poorly defined or, not what they really need or want. However, even if you set the best goals, if you go about achieving them in a way that does not match your individual needs, you will also likely fail. (I'm just a ray of freaking sunshine aren't I?) You can easily learn how to set good, individualized goals.

Expectations

Let's start by taking a look at your expectations. Expectations imply that if you do something, you expect something else to happen in response. For example, I expect that if I exercise, I will lose weight. In theory, that may be true, but there are a lot of other factors to consider, such as… What else am I doing that is causing weight gain? Do I need to also change my eating habits? What is my motivation for losing weight? If it is to fit into a pair of jeans, then great. Weight loss is a good goal. If it is because I think it will make someone else like me, then weight loss may not be the correct goal.

Activity: Expectation Identification

In working toward a decision about whether recovery is worth the effort or not, you need to understand what change and recovery mean or look like to you, and what your expectations of treatment are.

If I stop using my addiction or recover from my mental health issues, I expect that…

_____

_____

In order to stop using my addiction, or recover from my mental health issues I need to change the following people, places, things and attitudes. _____

_____

One change I am willing to make this week is _____

_____

Learning from the Past

Good goals build on what has worked in the past, and avoids repeating things that have failed. You are the expert on you. You know what has (and has not worked for you). You also probably have a lot of tools in your toolbox which you have been overlooking. A strengths-based perspective encourages you to stop trying to re-invent the wheel and focus on improving the effectiveness of the things that have worked for you in the past.

Activity: More Exceptions

You will remember from the last chapter that it is impossible to be something or do something all the time. In the following chart, identify the behaviors you want to change, and what is different when you are not doing those things or feeling that way. These can give you ideas about the goals and new behaviors you want to choose.

When I am not using my addiction (alcohol, drugs, sex…)

What is different? _____

_____

I can make this happen now by: _____

_____

Another thing that is different is: _____

_____

I can make this happen now by: _____

_____

_____

When I am not feeling anxious

What is different? _____

_____

I can make this happen now by: _____

_____

Another thing that is different is: _____

_____

I can make this happen now by: _____

_____

_____

When I am not feeling depressed

What is different? _____

_____

I can make this happen now by: _____

_____

Another thing that is different is: _____

_____

I can make this happen now by: _____

_____

_____

When I am not feeling angry or irritable

What is different? _____

_____

I can make this happen now by: _____

_____

Another thing that is different is: _____

_____

I can make this happen now by: _____

_____

_____

When I am not _____

What is different? _____

_____

I can make this happen now by: _____

_____

Another thing that is different is: _____

_____

I can make this happen now by: _____

_____

_____

Activity: Pitfalls

List all of the ways you have tried to stop using

Attempt 1: _____

Stayed clean for _____

What was helpful: _____

_____

What did not work: _____

_____

For whom or what reasons were you getting clean? _____

_____

What obstacles kept you from staying clean? _____

_____

What were the first signs of your impending relapse? _____

_____

What addictive or extreme behaviors did you engage in? _____

_____

In what ways did relationships help or hurt your recovery process? _____

_____

What could you have done differently? _____

_____

_____

_____

Attempt 2: _____

Stayed clean for _____

What was helpful: _____

_____

What did not work: _____

_____

For whom or what reasons were you getting clean? _____

_____

What obstacles kept you from staying clean? _____

_____

What were the first signs of your impending relapse? _____

_____

What addictive or extreme behaviors did you engage in? _____

_____

In what ways did relationships help or hurt your recovery process? _____

_____

What could you have done differently? _____

_____

_____

Rome was not built in a day, and neither was your addiction or mental health problem. Recovery is like building a house. Sure, you can throw up something really fast, but the foundation may be unstable, and it will probably not withstand many storms. You do not have to change everything overnight--an overwhelming prospect. As a matter of fact, you are more likely to succeed if you choose one small thing to change every week or two and slowly build on your successes. What have you learned to this point that you can use to help you on your recovery journey?

Activity: What Has and Has Not Worked

The following things were helpful in the past

1. _____

2. _____

3. _____

4. _____

5. _____

I have tried the following things and they did not work (Be specific)

1. _____

   Didn't work because: _____

2. _____

   Didn't work because: _____

3. _____

   Didn't work because: _____

4. _____

   Didn't work because: _____

5. _____

   Didn't work because: _____

As you go through the next few chapters, you might find ways to modify these tools to make them more effective for you.

Behavior Modification

Setting goals is awesome, but following through with those goals requires behavior change. To this point you have learned about yourself, your addiction and any other issues you may have. You have also identified what recovery looks like for you….your end point so to speak. Now you will begin learning the hows of changing behaviors. All behaviors serve a purpose, usually reward, protection, or avoiding pain or punishment. You do what you do, because it was more rewarding than the alternative. *To successfully eliminate a behavior, you must replace it with another behavior that serves the same purpose to the same degree.* If you go on a diet, you may decide to stop eating chocolate. That is fine, but you do not want to replace it with celery (unless you love celery). Both satisfy the urge to munch, but celery does not have the same effect for most people. Maybe you could replace chocolate with an apple, at least both are sweet. You could also choose something like a Fiber One Brownie or a chocolate protein bar. All of these have fewer calories and fat, but tend to be more satisfying than celery. Of course, you can choose other behaviors entirely, but first you need to figure out why you are craving chocolate: Hunger, comfort? Then, find alternate behaviors that serve the same purpose.

You have the ability to make better choices about: What you do; how you choose to react; and who you keep company with.

Behavior Modification Basics

Behavior modification is a wonderful tool that can be used to increase positive behaviors, or to eliminate unwanted behaviors. Behavior modification grew out of the work of John B. Watson, B.F. Skinner and Ivan Pavlov. Essentially, behaviorists believe that behavior is a series of responses to punishing or reinforcing stimuli in the environment. Regardless of your stance on behavioral theory, behavior modification can be helpful as a tool. Here are some basic terms to know when using behavior modification.

- ✓ Behavior: An event that is observable, and measurable. A behavior can be drug use, food eaten, gambling, exercise, viewing pornography etc.

- ✓ Baseline: The frequency, intensity and/or duration of the behavior before you start trying to change it. You will collect baseline data on the behavior you want to change by keeping a daily journal of how often you do it, how much you do it and how much time you spent doing it. This information can be used to identify things that "trigger" the behavior, things that discourage the behavior and reasons for the behavior. For example, if you notice that you binge eat the most in the evening on Thursdays. You might ask "What is different about Thursdays?"

✓ Duration: Means how long a behavior lasts. Example: Gambling for 12 hours or being clean for 30 days.

✓ Frequency: How often a behavior occurs in a given period of time Example: Watched porn on the internet 6 times per day, or went to 90 meetings in 90 days.

✓ Intensity: How loud/bright/strong etc. a behavior occurs. Examples: Blew $1000 in one night on my addiction. I was so mad, I wanted to put my hand through the wall.

Activity: Frequency, Intensity and Duration

For the following behaviors, identify how to measure their frequency, intensity, duration

Substance use

      Frequency (How often): _____

      Intensity (How much): _____

      Duration (How long): _____

Binge eating

      Frequency (How often): _____

      Intensity (How much): _____

      Duration (How long): _____

Watching Porn

      Frequency (How often): _____

      Intensity (How much): _____

      Duration (How long): _____

Temper Tantrums/ Anger Outbursts

      Frequency (How often): _____

      Intensity (How much): _____

      Duration (How long): _____

Activity: Baseline and Logging

Each behavior occurs at a baseline or typical rate. Keep a journal of how often or how intensely a behavior occurs every day for a week. For example, write down each time you have a panic attack, or how much you drink, or how bad (on a scale from 1-4) your depression was. Review the log and answer the following questions…

What caused or triggered the behavior _____

_____

What made the behavior worse _____

_____

What helped eliminate the behavior _____

_____

What purpose does this behavior serve _____

_____

What are some alternative behaviors could I choose _____

_____

_____

_____

Another principle is 3:1: Always add three behaviors for one you eliminate.

The change I want to make is: _____

In order to do that, I need to stop _____

I will do one of the following instead: _____

_____

✓ Behavior interruption: Placing some obstacle in the way of beginning that behavior.

Spending too much time on the internet can be interrupted by setting an alarm and placing it across the room. Your internet focus is broken when you have to physically move to turn off the alarm.

I will do _____ to interrupt

_____ behavior.

✓ Competing responses: Introducing an alternate behavior which prohibits the targeted behavior.

Example: Chewing gum prevents mindless snacking.

Instead of _____ , I will _____

✓ Reinforcement: Eliminating something unpleasant (like a fine, chores, eating your vegetables) or adding something pleasant (like a bonus, a hug or …).

Example: You don't have to eat your vegetables if you clean your room. Your charges will be dropped if you stay clean for 6 months. You will have enough money to go on vacation in 3 months if you don't spend it gambling.

Give an example: _____

Give an example: _____

Give an example: _____

✓ Punishment: A consequence which reduces the likelihood of the behavior recurring

Example: You will have to go to residential treatment if you do not stay clean

Give an example: _____

Punishing a behavior simply removes that behavior without replacing it with a reasonable alternative. You do behaviors for a reason. You must give yourself something to do instead of the behavior you are trying to eliminate. For example, if you drink, smoke or eat when you are stressed out and you punish/eliminate all of those behaviors, what will you be left to do instead? When possible, introduce a positive alternative BEFORE you start eliminating the negative behavior.

Activity: Identifying Reinforcement and Punishment

Identify the potential reinforcers (What makes the behavior rewarding, and likely to happen again) in the following scenarios

Speeding _____

Eating _____

Breaking rules _____

Creating chaos _____

Being impulsive _____

Identify the possible punishments

Speeding _____

Eating _____

Breaking rules _____

Creating chaos _____

Being impulsive _____

Activity: Applying Reinforcement

List 3 reinforcers/rewards for the following behaviors

A child doing his homework

    1. _____

    2. _____

    3. _____

Spouse helping with household chores

1. _____

2. _____

3. _____

✓ Premack Principle: This principle involves linking a positive behavior with one you do not like so much.

Example: You get to see your friends when you go to meetings

Give an example of something you need to do that you do not like so much, and what you could pair it with to make it more tolerable:

_____

_____

✓ Stimuli/Triggers: Things in the environment that trigger a behavior.

Example: The smell of brownies makes you hungry.

Give 3 examples of things that trigger the behavior you want to change:

1. _____

2. _____

3. _____

Give 3 examples of things that trigger the alternate behaviors

1. _____

2. _____

3. _____

Changing Behavior

As humans, we often prefer to stay with what we know. People will tend to resist change until it becomes sufficiently uncomfortable to remain the same. Change causes crisis and crisis causes change. Think about the last few times you tried to change something in your behavior--i.e. lose weight, stop smoking, study more, keep a cleaner house. . . Unless there was a very powerful motivator, you probably returned to your old behaviors in less than a month. The keys are to:

✓ Identify the purpose or function of the old behavior. (Why did you do it?)
✓ Identify and start doing alternate behaviors that do the same thing.
✓ Make it sufficiently uncomfortable to stay the same. Why do you need to change?

For example, maybe when you get mad, you yell at your spouse, but you do not want to do that anymore. First, figure out why you yell. It is probably because you do not feel heard or respected. Now that you know that, what other ways can you get your spouse to hear and respect you? Maybe you can write whatever it is down. Or, maybe you could take a walk and then come back and try to talk to him or her when you have calmed down. Finally, you need to figure out why (do that decisional balance exercise) you want to change your behavior. If you do not believe changing your behavior is worth the effort, you are not going to do it.

Activity: Identifying Stimuli (Triggers)
Identify 3 of your "habits" and the stimuli for those habits

Habit 1 _____

Emotional triggers: _____

Thought triggers: _____

Anger/Resentment triggers: _____

Physical triggers: _____

Social triggers: _____

Environmental triggers: _____

Habit 2 _____

Emotional triggers: _____

Thought triggers: _____

Anger/Resentment triggers: _____

Physical triggers: _____

Social triggers: _____

Environmental triggers: _____

Habit 3 _____

Emotional triggers: _____

Thought triggers: _____

Anger/Resentment triggers: _____

Physical triggers: _____

Social triggers: _____

Environmental triggers: _____

Identify alternative behaviors for each of your habits.

Habit 1

    1. _____

    2. _____

    3. _____

    4. _____

    5. _____

Habit 2

1. _____

2. _____

3. _____

4. _____

5. _____

Habit 3

1. _____

2. _____

3. _____

4. _____

5. _____

Recovery from addiction or mental health issues requires understanding what causes the behaviors (the triggers), what the benefits or reinforcement is for that behavior and identifying alternate behaviors to deal with those triggers.

Activity: Understanding the Functions of Your Behaviors

In the following activity, identify those behaviors that you use in your addiction. Then identify the purpose or why you do it. (There is a reason…If you cannot identify it, ask your counselor or sponsor). Finally, identify three alternate behaviors that serve the same purpose.

Using drugs

Function: Escape from stress/anxiety _____

Three Alternative Behaviors: _____

_____

_____

Manipulation

Function: Get what I wanted to make me happy _____

Three Alternative Behaviors: _____

_____

_____

Lying

Function: Hide my addiction. Keep others off my back. Be what others want me to be.

_____

Three Alternative Behaviors: _____

_____

_____

Being defensive

Function: _____

_____

Three Alternative Behaviors: _____

_____

_____

Stealing

Function: _____

_____

Three Alternative Behaviors: _____

_____

_____

Only caring about me/being self-centered

Function: _____

_____

Three Alternative Behaviors: _____

_____

_____

Impatience

Function: _____

_____

Three Alternative Behaviors: _____

_____

_____

Resentful

Function: _____

_____

Three Alternative Behaviors: _____

_____

_____

After you have thoroughly explored the benefits of use, it is important to identify the drawbacks to change. They seem like the same thing, but there can be things you will identify as drawbacks that did not come up earlier. For example, Tom says a benefit to using is that it gives him something to do, because he cannot afford to do anything else. When we looked at how much he was spending on drugs and alcohol, it became clear that he could actually afford to do a lot if he were not using. We made a list of things he wanted to do and made plans on his calendar. The drawback was that his girlfriend used as well, and he was afraid she would not go along with the plan. We discussed ways to bring up the subject with her and how he would deal with it if she left him when he quit supplying her. There was obviously much more to it than this, but you get the idea.

Another example: John made plenty of money selling drugs to keep a roof over his head, and he was on food stamps. In recovery, John makes $10.50 per hour, which is too much to qualify for food stamps anymore, and his child support is automatically deducted from his paycheck. In recovery, he has to work harder to have the basics: food and shelter. It is important to help John find ways to have food and shelter and a reasonably content life before he gets exasperated and gives up.

As a final example, I had client who had adult ADD. He worked on a construction site and could not focus unless he was using marijuana. Well, of course I could not support continued use, so we had to explore the reasons he could not focus and alternate ways to handle them. This was a pretty easy fix. Once he was diagnosed with adult ADD and got on the right medication he no longer "had" to use. Don't get me wrong, he still wanted to, so we explored other benefits to his use. One of the main ones was camaraderie. Most of his friends on the job would smoke pot during breaks. Here he had to make a decision about whether he cared more about hanging out with his friends on the job, or staying out of jail so he could be with his little girl. We practiced refusal skills, and he agreed to take breaks with people he knew were not smoking pot.

In order to figure out the benefits of the old behavior and the drawbacks to change, brainstorm the emotional, mental, physical, social and possibly environmental (housing, safety, etc) benefits of the old behavior and alternative ways to get those same benefits. This process can seem somewhat tedious, but it is necessary in order to develop a solid recovery and relapse prevention plan. If you feel like you are deprived or missing out, you will be much more likely to romanticize the old behavior and return to it. You will use this information to develop your recovery plan.

Goal Setting

Now that you know the whats and whys of your behavior and the hows of behavior change, you can start to learn about goals setting. Goal setting is nothing more than a recipe or instruction manual to reach a goal. Unfortunately, many people set goals that are not observable, or not realistic. You will start by stating an observable, measurable problem and a description of an observable and measurable goal (What it will look like when the problem is eliminated). Problems and goals can be observed and measured in many ways. For instance, depression can be measured in terms of number of days the patient was able to get out of bed, your self-rating of depression on a scale from 1-5, the frequency and intensity of your suicidal thoughts etc. To determine how to measure it, take the following steps.

1. Ask yourself "If you woke up tomorrow and you were happy, what would be different? What will be the same?" OR "How will you know when you are happy? What will be different? What will be the same?"

2. Aside from the main goal of treatment i.e. you would not be depressed, anxious, using etc, what do you list as being different? This gives you clues into what else needs to change.

3. Follow each "difference" up with "If that were to happen, then what would be different?"

For example, Sally is depressed and using alcohol. She writes: If I woke up tomorrow and were not depressed, I would have more energy to spend time with my kids. I would be more patient. I would not be so tired all of the time. I would get more done at work, and not be irritated by every little thing people do. I might even start trying to get back into some of those things I used to love to do like exercising and knitting.

Good goals are functional (they serve a purpose), observable (you can tell when they have been accomplished, measurable (can be measured and evaluated for progress), time limited (no more than 6 months in the future), and achievable (do not set yourself up for failure.)

Once you have identified the problem and the ultimate goal, you can start asking "What do I need to achieve this goal?" At the most basic level, you have to have the knowledge of how to solve the problem before you can move forward. This can be academic knowledge such as pharmacology, what depression is, communication skills etc., or it can be personal knowledge such as what are your triggers for use, depression, anxiety or what makes you happy, or helps you relax .

The second step is to develop the skills necessary to achieve the goal. You can know everything about addiction or depression, but if you cannot translate the knowledge into some usable skills to deal with the problem, you are still stuck. An electrician has to know about circuits and lot of other stuff (You can tell I am not an electrician) before he can wire a house. He does not just read a textbook and go out and start wiring houses though. He goes through a training period. This is where he learns to translate what he read to skills and use those skills to create a larger product. You are the same way. First you have to have the knowledge about what makes you tick. Then you start taking that knowledge and figuring out how it all fits together in your grand plan.

For example: You want to be able to better deal with your depression. So you LEARN about depression, what causes it and the available treatment. Then you LEARN about what triggers your depression and how your behavior changes when you are depressed that keeps you depressed. Then you start working in workbooks or with a therapist to develop the skills necessary to prevent and/or moderate your depression.

Activity: Defining Goals

The change I want to make is_____

_____

Be specific. Include goals that are positive (wanting to increase, improve, do more of something), and not just negative goals (stop, avoid, or decrease a behavior).

My main reasons for making this change are _____

_____

_____

_____

What are the likely consequences of action or inaction? _____

_____

_____

Which motivations for change are most compelling? _____

_____

_____

The first steps I plan to take in changing are

1. _____

2. _____

3. _____

When, where, and how will the steps be taken?

1. _____

2. _____

3. _____

Triggers and ways to avoid, eliminate or cope with them: _____

_____

_____

_____

Some things that could interfere with my plan are _____

_____

_____

_____

How will I stick with the plan despite these particular problems or setbacks? _____

_____

_____

Alternative, healthy behaviors to deal with distress and discomfort. _____

_____

_____

Other people could help me in changing in these ways: _____

_____

_____

Rewards to keep me motivated _____

_____

_____

I will know that my plan is working if _____

_____

_____

A blank copy of this form is located in Appendix 1—Treatment Plan

Chapter 5: Stop Swimming Up Stream!

Now that you have learned about your "issues" and have started to develop an action plan, let's help you learn more about yourself as an individual, so you can make your plan even more successful. I called this chapter "Stop Swimming Up Stream" because in order to live mindfully and purposefully, you need to consider how much doing things that go against your personal preferences increases your stress, and wastes your energy. For example, I learn by reading and doing. I hate sitting through a lecture or seminar, and don't get me started on podcasts. Unless I am taking notes in a lecture, I can almost guarantee I will not retain anything.   When I was in college, I knew people who could record their notes and listen to them at the gym. I tried that once and it was a complete waste of time. You may learn best by reading, or you may prefer to watch a video or have someone walk you through it. The point is that, if you know how you learn best, you can make learning more enjoyable, more efficient and easier.

The same thing is true for temperament. Temperament describes the range of preferences for how you live your life. I am a very structured person (a "J" as you will learn later). I hate surprises, flying by the seat of my pants or just "going with the flow." I like to make a plan for my day in the morning and stick to it. Spontaneity is something I find extremely stressful. That is not to say that I absolutely cannot handle a sudden change, but I know it will take a lot more out of me, and I will need to give myself more recovery time.

In the following chapter, you will focus on understanding some of the characteristics you were born with, such as how you learn and your temperament. Yes, those things are present from the moment you come into this world. Understanding these concepts not only will help you help yourself, but will also allow you to be more effective in your relationships with other people who learn differently and prefer different things than you do.   By communicating with people in their preferred learning format, you will greatly improve your effectiveness and reduce wasted time.   For example, my son is a very visual person. He can read something once and remember it. I know that it will make it a lot easier for him (and me) if I write down instructions instead of telling him how to do something.

Learning Style

The first step in developing a realistic recovery plan is to learn about your personal tendencies. What works for you? What adds extra dis-stress? What is the most efficient way to approach things based upon how you learn and your personality. Your learning style is how you learn or adapt to your environment. You are probably a combination of more than one learning style, but one style is usually dominant. Learning style is the way you prefer to learn. It does not have anything to do with how intelligent you are or what skills you have. There is no such thing as having a "good" learning style or a "bad" learning style per se. The key is to be aware of how your brain learns best so you can maximize your learning.

There are three parts to the learning process cognition, conceptualization and affective (how much you care about it). Said differently, how you receive the information, make sense of it and whether you care enough to remember it.

Cognition deals with how you get the information into your brain. This is done through a combination of seeing, hearing and/or doing. In recovery you do a lot of learning. You learn about yourself, your conditions, treatment options etc., so it is important for all that information to be presented in a way that is meaningful to you. For example, if you learn by hearing, then you will probably enjoy groups, support meetings like AA, SMART Recovery or Recovery & Resilience (R&R), lectures, or talking about your issues. You will probably not enjoy (as much) reading the Big Book. If the Big Book is an important part of your recovery process, then you need to figure out how to make it "listenable." The two easiest solutions are to either get the Big Book on tape, or to read small parts of it and participate in a study group where you can discuss it.

Once you have the information in your brain, you need to make sense of it. For example, I can listen to my computer guy tell me about slack space, defragmenting and lots of other stuff. Until I have something to relate it to, or he shows me, it is like he is talking to a puppy. "Blah, blah, blah, blah, Rover, blah blah, blah." I hear the words, but none of it makes any sense to me. Conceptualization refers to how you make sense of and process information. Some people focus on a general idea, or abstract concept---"This is a plant." Others like more specific information and details. "This is an edible plant called broccoli." Think about how you have your filing system or your computer folders set up. Do you have a folder for "bills" or do you have separate folders for the electric bill, water bill, house payment, etc.

Once you make sense of the information you need to store it. If you like specifics, and you get vague concepts, it will be hard to do anything with it. You will have difficulty finding the right file or memory pathway. This means that when you learn things you need to know what your mental filing system looks like so you know what questions to ask. Think about the last time you did a puzzle. Did you need to look at the box and do the frame first?

Before you go to a movie, do you need to know what it is about, or can you go and just let it unfold?

Now you have the information. You know where you can file it. The last question is whether it is something you need to keep. This is the affective dimension. It refers to your motivation and emotional preferences (how much does this information matter). In the case of my undergraduate courses like "Architecture of Ancient Civilizations," I read the material and watched the slides, but had little or no motivation to permanently give that information space in my head. Therefore, once I passed the test…it could go away. If I had wanted to remember it for a long time, I would have related it to current architecture, or things I already knew, and probably talked about it with other people.

As you learn information in recovery, some of it will strike a chord. That is, it will seem relevant in some way or you will be able to relate to it. This is the information that you care about, and are more likely to remember. Some of the information you get may seem irrelevant. If that is the case, ask your counselor, coach, sponsor, or yourself why might this information be important to you? How does it sound like you? What other information might you need to make this useful to you in your recovery journey? Asking questions, relating it to other things, and understanding why it matters to you makes it infinitely more likely that you will remember it and be able to use it later.

Learning styles specifically refer how you take in information. It can be conceptualized as auditory/hearing, visual/seeing, or kinesthetic/doing. . .Some environments cater more to one learning style than another. When this happens, you must know how to modify the situation to work best for you. Consider the last time you tried to learn a new computer program. Which method(s) work best for you: A) Reading the manual. B) Using the tutorial or just getting in and playing with it. C) Having someone tell you how to do it. If you chose A, you are a visual learner. Option B would appeal more to kinesthetic learners, option C would be best for auditory learners.

Another common example is getting directions. Do you find your way easiest by: A) Reading a map or written directions. B) Driving it, to know how to get there, or C) Having someone give you directions verbally (such as at a gas station). If you select "A" or "C" you have a pretty good ability to visualize things in your head once you get the information. Their primary difference is the way the information is input. If you chose option A, you get the information through your eyes (visual learner). If you chose option C, you get the information through your ears (auditory learner). If you selected "B" you are strong kinesthetic learners and benefit from actually doing things.

Tips for kinesthetic learners (Do-ers)

✓ Paraphrase and write down important points as you read/talk/listen. For example, you could summarize and write down what you just learned about learning styles.

✓ Manipulate the material through teaching or doing it whenever possible. You never know how much you don't know until you try to teach it.

✓ Use skits, scenarios or acronyms to remember important ideas.

✓ Volunteer to make posters or handouts or manuals.

✓ Manipulate the information by making multiple choice tests for yourself, or applying it in different situations

✓ Try to relate it to something you already know how to do

Tips for auditory learners (Listeners)

✓ Read your material out loud whenever possible.

✓ Tape record your notes and listen to them while you drive, workout etc.

✓ Try to partner with a visual learner if you need to borrow notes.

✓ Listen attentively to lectures.

✓ Try to block out extra auditory (verbal) interruptions.

✓ Record the class so you do not have to worry about taking notes.

✓ Discuss any material you are learning with a friend.

Tips for visual learners (See-ers)

✓ When you read material, visualize it in your mind, then recite it from memory.

✓ Pay close attention to charts, graphs or diagrams and make your own.

✓ You may find you remember things better if people write you letters or memos.

✓ Rewrite your notes in a format which is easy to visualize such as: outlining, color coding, underlining...

✓ Take mental "pictures" of things that must be remembered.

✓ Use flashcards to learn and test yourself. There are a lot of flashcard generators online, so you can even have your flashcards on your mobile device.

Now that you know how you take in information, you need to understand how it goes from your short term memory to being something you actually learn. I can honestly tell you that when I was in undergraduate, I would take in a lot of information, but I learned very little. That is, I would cram the information into my head long enough to pass the test then…POOF. Why did that happen? Let's find out.

The affective dimension is where you need to start. You will probably only remember information that matters to you. To help you care about the information, it is important to learn it in a way that is meaningful to you. If you are an emotion-focused person, how can you use this information "feel" better. If you tend to be more logical, identify all of the reasons the information is important/beneficial to learn. If you know that you have a poor memory, make sure you keep notes and prompts in your mobile devices (i.e. your sponsor or coach's phone number; relapse prevention plan etc.)

Other things that may help you develop your new skills include knowing your energy patterns, how you are comfortable learning, and any particular learning needs you may have. Energy patterns are important, because you will learn better if you are awake and focused. I tend to do better between 8am and 2pm. Once I hit 8pm, my brain turns to jelly, I tend to be more impulsive and unfocused. Some of my friends don't even start waking up until 2pm. I also know that I do not "switch gears" well. If I am working on something I have to turn off my phone, Facebook and any other alerts, or pop-ups. However, I also prefer to be around people, so I often read/study at the library, coffee shop, or lounge at the office. Some people find those settings to be too distracting. You need to figure out when and where it is best for you to learn.

In the case of recovery or personal growth, some people will take in information better by reading, some by watching videos and some by completing workbooks, participating in interactive groups or going discussing the information in individual therapy. You can read the Big Book and other self-help and recovery oriented books (visual learners). You can participate in forum discussions and chatrooms online (visual/kinesthetic learners). You can go to large meetings, small meetings and/or step studies and you can work with a sponsor or a coach (auditory/kinesthetic). It is important in recovery to make sure your sponsor, counselor or coach understands your learning style, and presents information in a way that is meaningful to you. Note: Regardless of your learning style, it is important to work with a sponsor, coach or counselor. The addict in your head is very crafty. Having an impartial person outside of yourself will be vital to helping you see your blind spots and preventing relapse, especially in early recovery. After all, if you could have done it on your own, you would have done it already.

Activity: Learning Style

How do you learn? Seeing, hearing or doing? _____

What motivates you to learn?_____

How do you adapt the following to fit your learning style?

Instructions for new hobby: _____

Information presented in group or a class: _____

Information you read: _____

Go back over the "Defining Goals" activity above and make sure you are

1.   Learning what you need in a way that is best for you (reading, videos, groups)

2.   You are motivated to learn that information (Why do you care?)

How do the following people in your life learn?

Spouse

      Circle one: Seeing/Hearing/Doing;

      What motivates him or her? Circle one: feelings or logic?

      How can you improve your communication with them?

      _____

      _____

Child

      Circle one: Seeing/Hearing/Doing;

      What motivates him or her? Circle one: feelings or logic?

      How can you improve your communication with them?

      _____

      _____

Boss

    Circle one: Seeing/Hearing/Doing;

    What motivates him or her? Circle one: feelings or logic?

    How can you improve your communication with them?

_____

_____

How can knowing your learning style and preferences help you tailor your recovery plan? For example, I would prefer Big Book Studies to open meetings because I am more of a visual learner. I prefer to lead Sunday school instead of sit in the gallery for the same reason.

_____

_____

_____

_____

What parts of prior recovery attempts have failed because you were trying to use tools that did not work for you?

_____

_____

_____

_____

Temperament

Knowing your temperament is just as important as knowing your learning style. Temperament, sometimes called personality, indicates what types of situations are reinforcing and enjoyable, the preferred types of information to be learned (concrete vs. abstract), and what strengths and weaknesses you may have to consider when creating plans or learning information.

For more information read: Please Understand Me by David Keirsey, and Effective Teaching, Effective Learning by Alice and Lisa Fairhurst (If you are a parent, teacher or supervisor, this is an awesome read.)

Activity: Personality Characteristics Inventory

On the following page, you are presented with four dimensions in two columns. The column on the left can be viewed as one end of a continuum and the column on the right represents the other end. You will probably find statements in both the left and right columns that apply to you. Select the dimension that is most accurate. When there are a relatively equal number of statements in each column that apply, it means you can be flexible in that area depending upon the situation. You can also go to http://keirsey.com and take the Temperament Sorter II for a more accurate picture and more information about the dimensions.

EXTRAVERSION (E)	INTROVERSION (I)
_____ Are expansive and less passionate	_____ Are intense and passionate
_____ Are generally easy to get to know	_____ Are generally difficult to get to know
_____ Like meeting new people, have many close friends	_____ Have to exert effort to meet new people
_____ Figure things as they talk	_____ Have only a few close friends
_____ Enjoy background noise like TV	_____ Figure things out before they talk
_____ Know what is going on around them rather than inside them	_____ Prefer peace and quiet
_____ Often do not mind interruptions	_____ Know what is going on inside them than what is going on around them
_____ Think introverts are standoffish	_____ Dislike being interrupted
_____ Are often considered good talkers	_____ Think extraverted people are shallow
	_____ Are often good listeners

SENSING (S)

_____ Are practical and realistic

_____ Prefer facts and live in the real world

_____ Content in general

_____ Would rather do than think

_____ Focus on practical, concrete problems

_____ See the details, may ignore the big picture

_____ Want specifics and tend to be very literal

_____ May think that those preferring intuition are impractical

_____ Believe "if it isn't broken, don't fix it"

INTUITIVE (N)

_____ Are imaginative dreamers

_____ Prefer abstraction, inspiration

_____ Restless in general

_____ Live in the world of possibilities

_____ Would rather think then do

_____ Focus on abstract problems

_____ See the big picture, may ignore the details

_____ Think those who are practical lack vision

_____ Believe anything can be improved

_____ Focus on the future and possibilities

THINKING (T)

_____ Like words such as principles, policy, firmness, justice, standards or analysis

_____ Respond to people's thoughts

_____ Want to apply objective principles

_____ Value objectivity above sentiment

_____ Can assess logical consequences

_____ Assess reality through a true/false lens

_____ Think that those who are sentimental take things too personally

_____ May argue both sides of an issue for mental stimulation

FEELING (F)

_____ Like words such as care, compassion, mercy, intimacy, harmony, devotion

_____ Respond to people's values

_____ Value sentiment above objectivity

_____ Are people oriented

_____ Can assess the human impact

_____ Assess reality through good/bad lens

_____ Think that those preferring objectivity are insensitive

_____ Prefer to agree with those around them

JUDGING (J)

_____ Plan ahead

_____ Are self-disciplined and purposeful

_____ Like things finished and settled

_____ Thrive on order

_____ Get things done early. Plan ahead

_____ Define and work within limits

_____ Maybe hasty in making decisions

_____ Time and deadline oriented

_____ Dislike surprises

_____ Thinks those preferring spontaneity are to unpredictable

_____ Usually make effective choices but may not appreciate or make use of things which are not planned or expected

PERCEVING (P)

_____ Adapt as they go

_____ Are flexible and tolerant

_____ Prefer multiple options

_____ Thrive on spontaneity

_____ Get things done at the last minute

_____ Want more information

_____ May fail to make decisions

_____ Always think there's plenty of time

_____ Love surprises

_____ May think that those who are not spontaneous are too rigid

_____ Adept at handling unplanned events, but may not make affective choices among the possibilities

Review your selections above, and mark the letters that best correspond to your personality dimensions:

- o Are you more of an E or an I
- o Are you more of an S or an N
- o Are you more of a T or an F
- o Are you more of a J or a P

Now let's consider how temperament relates to your recovery and your overall stress level. The first dimension, Extrovert vs. Introvert relates to how you prefer to interact with people and the world. Extroverts get energized by being around people and will feel very isolated and listless if they are in a job and/or living arrangement in which they are not regularly interacting with people. In recovery it is important to develop a social support network of both people who are in recovery, and with people who are not battling addiction or mental health issues, but are willing and able to have fun, clean and sober. Going to meetings and working with a coach or sponsor are also excellent for the extrovert, because it allows you to solve your problems while you talk with someone, and get social interaction at the same time.

The biggest stumbling block for extroverts in recovery is being more in tune with what is going on around you, instead of what is going on inside you. It is vital for you to spend a few minutes each day to mindfully assess how you feel physically, emotionally, and spiritually; to evaluate what your current wants and needs are, and to make sure you are thinking and acting in your "sober self." That is, making sure you are choosing thoughts, actions and reactions that move you closer to where you want to be, instead of just being a quick fix. (That mindfulness and purposeful action thing again…)

Introverts, on the other hand, need down time each day. If you are an introvert, you may be well aware of what is going on inside you, but can get overwhelmed easily. Introverts are very intense. When you make up your mind to do something, you do it 130%. Unfortunately, this may lead you to either get frustrated because you cannot get "it" perfect, get bored after 3 or 6 months, because you feel like you have been there, done that, or get overwhelmed because you lose balance. You focus so intently on one or two areas of recovery, you lose sight of everything else. So, downtime for reflection and re-energizing and balance are crucial for the introvert.

Introverts usually do better journaling or keeping a diary than doing a lot of talking about what is going on. You may not like large meetings, and prefer instead small groups and step studies or workshops. You need to schedule down time throughout the day, so you do not get overwhelmed. Additionally, you need to have a plan for handling interruptions and situations in which you may have to interact with many people. Both of those situations can be very draining for the introvert.

The second dimension, Sensing vs. Intuitive can help you understand how you approach tasks and make plans. Sensing people, or those who are high on the "S" dimension love details and facts. You are good at living in the moment, but may miss the big picture. In recovery, that may mean focusing on not using, going to work, going to meetings, but missing the point….recovery is supposed to help you be happier, healthier, and have a higher quality of life. When you just go through the motions, you do not stay sober very long, because it is hard and lacks any rewards. If you are a sensing person, you need to make sure you keep the end in mind. In my practice, we talk about the concept of Good Orderly Direction. That is, envisioning recovery as a place on a map and every decision as an opportunity to take a detour (and get lost). No matter how tough the drive, if the destination is worth the effort, most people will push on through.

The opposite end of the Sensing-Intuitive spectrum is, obviously, Intuitive. Intuitive people, those high on the "I" dimension, are dreamers. You can see the big picture, but can get caught up in your own fantasies in the future. You can forget to focus on the present and may miss details such as---how you are going to maintain a balanced lifestyle including recovery activities. I am intuitive in many ways. I love writing grants---after all, a grant is basically proposing how you are going to spend someone else's money! I am great at envisioning new programs and, generally, how they will operate. I even like doing budgets. However, I often overlook details such as what forms might need to be created in order to bill for the services….details, details. If you have a lot of qualities of the intuitive dimension, it is suggested that you have someone else (someone detail oriented) review your work, in this case your relapse prevention plan and recovery activities, and point out any missing details.

The third dimension describes how people assign meaning to things. It is important to understand that Thinkers and Feelers both have very intense reactions to things, they are simply conceptualized in a bit of a different way. In recovery, Thinkers can over-intellectualize a problem in order to avoid dealing with their emotional reactions. On the other hand, feelers may get so revved up by their emotions they cannot think straight. In dialectical behavior therapy, Marsha Linehan talks about the wise mind (thinkers) and the emotional mind (feelers). In order to fully experience life, you need to have both minds. The ultimate goal is to stay in touch with feelings without letting them dictate your actions.

If you are a Thinker, take time to identify your reaction before you jump to problem solving. Many thinkers want to immediately "fix it." Once you stop to evaluate the situation, you may realize that whatever the issue is really does not deserve their energy, or it is something that someone else needs to fix. Feelers, on the other hand, need to learn how to feel their feelings without being controlled or overwhelmed by them. In recovery, both types of people need to focus on experiencing their reactions or feelings, identifying why they are reacting that way, and then making a mindful choice about what to do next.

The final dimension is Judging vs. Perceiving. This is basically how you organize your life. Judgers like structure and planning. Perceivers find day planners and too much structure boring. In recovery if you are a Judger, you can keep your to-do lists and day planners; however, you also need to plan for how to handle the unexpected. Children get sick. Cars break down. Things happen. Being a very strong Judger (some might say a bit rigid), I always try to have a plan B. This way, I have planned for the unexpected and it does not throw me for a loop. Even if your plan B is just to call your sponsor, coach or significant other, at least it is somewhere to start. At work, Judgers like to generally do the same thing each day. Teachers, counselors, bank tellers and sales clerks all have jobs in which they can generally predict what they will be doing at any given time. Any situation that is not structured enough for you may cause additional stress. For example, during the Spring, there is always an influx of abandoned animals (and new puppies and kittens) that need rescue. I never know when I am going to get the call. To make it less stressful for me, I keep a foster quarantine area set up with all the supplies I could need. That way, when I get the call, I do not have to run around crazy getting ready. I also set parameters on what I can handle. An un-housebroken puppy is not on the list! There are other people who can handle them. (Although I do have a space set up in one of the garages for the rare emergency). Animals rescue is very unpredictable, which goes against my very nature, but the rewards are totally worth a little additional stress.

Perceivers are so spontaneous that they often feel like there is not enough time in the day to get everything done. They do not like being over-scheduled. There are things that must be done though. If you are a perceiver, try having a combination of daily and weekly to-do list. The only things that go on the daily to-do lists are things that *must* be done each day, such as calling your sponsor or coach, picking up kids from school or taking medicine. In early recovery, I encourage you to also schedule in eating and sleeping, because it is easy to forget the basics. Likewise, it is easy to eat for comfort, or stay up too late when there is less of a schedule. At work, you may get very bored if you are doing a job that is repetitive. You prefer jobs that are rarely the same two days in a row, or that allow you to choose what you want to do. Law enforcement, carpentry and photography are three very different occupations that may appeal to Perceivers.

For the past twenty years, people have been using their knowledge of personality types for career counseling, mental health counseling, organizational psychology, sales and marketing, leadership training and relationship counseling. By knowing your personality type it is easier to select jobs, activities and partners that will fully meet your needs. You will also be able to figure out ways to reduce stress in situations which might not fit with your temperament. Finally, being able to identify others' temperaments helps you create situations that are enjoyable for them, communicate more effectively and reduce everyone's stress.

138

Activity: Exploring Temperament

What is your temperament (Circle the dimension that is more like you):

Extravert/Introvert   Sensing/Intuitive   Thinking/Feeling   Judging/Perceiving

For each statement, circle the characteristic that best represents you and discuss how each aspect of your temperament impact the different areas of your life.

Example: Relationships

Being an Extravert affects me in this area by increasing my need to have multiple friends. I also know that I will be happier and more energized around other people, and while I don't mind interruptions, Introverts do.

Being Intuitive affects me in this area by making me more aware of the big picture….which can mean that, if I am not careful, I miss details (like birthdays and anniversaries).

Being more of a Feeler affects me in this area by helping me experience compassion, but it can also be exhausting because I am frequently thinking about ethical questions.

Being more Judging/Perceiving affects me in this area by helping me plan, but can also make me seem like a stick in the mud because I do not like to change plans at the last minute.

Relationships

Being an Extravert/Introvert affects me in this area by: _____

_____

Being Sensing/Intuitive affects me in this area by: _____

_____

Being more of a Thinker/Feeler affects me in this area by: _____

_____

Being more Judging/Perceiving affects me in this area by: _____

_____

_____

Work

Being an Extravert/Introvert affects me in this area by: _____

_____

Being Sensing/Intuitive affects me in this area by: _____

_____

Being more of a Thinker/Feeler affects me in this area by: _____

_____

Being more Judging/Perceiving affects me in this area by: _____

_____

_____

Addiction Recovery

Being an Extravert/Introvert affects me in this area by: _____

_____

Being Sensing/Intuitive affects me in this area by: _____

_____

Being more of a Thinker/Feeler affects me in this area by: _____

_____

Being more Judging/Perceiving affects me in this area by: _____

_____

_____

Mental Health Recovery

Being an Extravert/Introvert affects me in this area by: _____

_____

Being Sensing/Intuitive affects me in this area by: _____

_____

Being more of a Thinker/Feeler affects me in this area by: _____

_____

Being more Judging/Perceiving affects me in this area by: _____

_____

_____

What can you do in each of these areas to prevent and/or reduce stress now that you know your temperament?

Relationships_____

_____

Work_____

_____

Addition Recovery_____

_____

Mental Health Recovery_____

_____

_____

How can this information help you increase your motivation?

_____

_____

Now that you know about temperament, does it help explain why some relationships and activities are easier than others? Yes   No

If yes, explain: _____

_____

_____

_____

_____

Example: My son is very much an introvert. He hates interruptions, needs quiet/down time each day and finds crowds stressful. This helps me understand why he gets irritable when I interrupt him, gets stressed out when we go on family vacations and he has no quiet time and is exposed to large crowds.

Chapter 6: Mindfulness

In this chapter, you will switch gears a bit and start actually doing some things to help you change. The first task is to start learning how to "be" in the present moment. Mindfulness helps you to stop and be aware of what is going on inside and around you and what you need before you act. Once you are actually present in the present, you can choose the next right action. As you embark upon your recovery journey, it will greatly benefit you if you practice being mindful.

Six Foundations of Life (and Recovery)

Part of being mindful is developing some core characteristics: Honesty, Hope, Faith, Courage, Discipline, and Love. Each of these can be an end goal in and of itself, but they also build on each other. For example, in order to be truly happy, you need to be able to be honest with yourself and others, and have faith that they will be honest with you. You need to have hope that better things are possible and faith that, if you do the next right thing, good things will follow. Not surprisingly, the spiritual principles that underlie the 12-steps promote these concepts, but even if you are not a 12-Stepper, would any of these things be bad to have in your toolbox?

Step 1: Honesty

Step 2: Hope for the future, that things can get better

Step 3: Faith in yourself, other people and karma/the universe/Higher Power

Step 4: Courage to do the next right thing

Step 5: Discipline and Integrity to do what is right, not just what feels best

Step 6: Willingness to learn, consider other points of view

Step 7: Humility and Gratitude

Step 8: Forgiveness, Compassion and Brotherly Love

Step 9: Justice

Step10: Perseverance

Step 11: Spiritual Awakening

Step 12: Service

Honesty

Honesty is a tricky concept. You have likely been lying to yourself and others for so long, that now it is hard to tell when you are lying, bending the truth, minimizing or denying things. You have lied about your behaviors, your intentions, your feelings, and probably much more. You have spent so much time trying to please others that you may not know what you want, need or like anymore. You may ignore everything from your bodily cues to what you think would be fun---all in the name of trying to get someone else's approval. That stops now! I hate to break it to you, but not everyone is going to like you---and it is virtually impossible to make them like you. Ultimately, the only person you can make like you is you. That's a hard concept to accept. We have been raised in a society that bombards us with messages like "People will like you more if you (buy/wear/say/believe)_____" When you stop to think about it, they probably do not like you more, they just like an image. If that is a false image (a lie), then they still do not like, you, just who you are pretending to be.

There are lies of omission and lies of commission. Lies of omission mean you only tell part of the truth or just fail to say anything at all. A lie of commission means that you flat told a story. Complete the activities from this chapter with an eye toward complete honesty---the Truth, the Whole Truth and Nothing but the Truth. One of the easiest tests of honesty is the head-heart-gut test. If it makes logical sense then it may have head honesty. If it makes you feel proud or happy, then it has heart honesty. If your stomach does not get all tied up in knots, then you have gut honesty. I often tell people to listen to their "Spidey Senses." Many addicts can rationalize anything, but if you have to drink, use or otherwise distract yourself from your feelings---then it may be a lie. Honesty is not always easy, but lying is a LOT harder in the end.

Activity: Honesty

List 5 lies of commission that you made to deny your addiction (Stories you told)

1. _____

2. _____

3. _____

4. _____

5. _____

List 5 lies of omission you made to deny your addiction (Things you chose not to say)

1. _____

2. _____

3. _____

4. _____

5. _____

Identify 5 lies you often tell yourself. (i.e. I don't need anybody; I don't care if…, I feel fine (when you don't)…)

1. _____

2. _____

3. _____

4. _____

5. _____

Hope

Hope is defined as the expectation and desire for a certain thing to happen. Hope is the belief that things can get better. It is the light at the end of the tunnel, the anticipation of the destination after the (sometimes challenging) journey. Hope helps you identify your goals, but that is only the first step. Hope and faith without putting the work into making something happen will simply leave you disappointed. Whenever I think about hope, I remember Yoda's quote "Do or do not, there is no try." Some things you hope for (like a cool, sunny day) are out of your control. Other things, like getting to work on time, are well within your control.

Activity: Hope

What do you hope for and why? One of the biggest challenges in setting good goals, is setting the correct goals. If you say you hope to lose weight, for example, is it because you would be healthier and have more energy? Or is it because you think that would make you feel better or make someone else feel differently toward you? These are very different end-goals. In this activity, you will identify what you hope for, and why you are hoping/wanting it.

This week I hope that _____ because

_____

By next month, I hope that _____ because

_____

In three months, I hope that _____ because

_____

Within a year I hope that _____ because

_____

Faith

Faith is the belief that change is possible, that people will do the next right thing and that if you do good, good will come to you. Sometimes that good is not exactly what you expected, or wanted. You can have faith in a lot of different things: Yourself, other people, humanity, your higher power…

Activity: Faith

I have faith that I can _____

_____

_____

I have faith in the following people to be supportive and dependable _____

_____

_____

I have faith that _ _____

_____

_____

Courage

With faith and hope also comes challenge and, sometimes, disappointment. It takes courage to face challenges. It also takes courage to get back in the saddle when you have been knocked down, and do things that are hard (and sometimes unpleasant).

Activity: Courage

Complete the next few statements in order to prepare yourself for the challenges in your recovery process.

The things that scare me the most about recovery are _____

_____

_____

I can deal with them by _____

_____

_____

When I feel tempted, I will have the courage to _____

_____

_____

When I feel afraid, I will have the courage to _____

_____

_____

When I make a mistake or fail at something I will _____

_____

_____

Discipline

Faith is the belief that you can achieve your hopes, dreams and goals, but discipline is required to actually use your courage and do the work to face the challenges.

Activity: Discipline

Part of addiction is wanting what you want, when you want it. The other part is avoiding feeling feelings. It takes great discipline to feel your feelings, without acting on them, until you can decide what the best course of action is. For example, when you are stressed you may want a drink. Discipline helps you be honest with yourself about what you are feeling instead of running from it. Discipline helps you remember the things (long term goals) you are hoping for and have faith that you can achieve them. Discipline gives you the courage to feel your feelings (stress, anger etc.) and to choose not to drink so that you can achieve your hopes, dreams and goals. We will discuss these concepts more in future chapters. For now, think of discipline in terms of purposeful action. You have identified what your hopes are, developed a plan to deal with the bumps in the road now you need to tie it all up with one simple question…

Will this __(behavior/choice)_____ help me achieve my goals or set me back?

_____

_____

Love

Without love, there is no purpose for the rest of it. As corny as you may think it sounds, you must love yourself enough to believe you deserve to be happy, then identify those things in life that you love---that make you happy---that give your life meaning. Love gives you the motivation to be disciplined and face challenges, the hope that things can get better and the faith that by doing the next right thing you can achieve those things you hope for. When you love something (or someone) you will do almost anything for it, so why would you not do the same for yourself?

NOTE: When completing this activity, focus on your sober self—who you are when you are not obsessed with your addiction or paralyzed by your depression or anxiety. That is who "you" are. You are not your addiction or your addicted behaviors.

Activity: Love

I deserve love because, when I am sober and happy I am:

_____

_____

_____

_____

_____

The things in my life that I love (are important to me) are:

_____

_____

_____

_____

_____

_____

Mindfulness, Serenity and Purposeful Action

Up to this point you have learned about addiction and mental health issues, learned about *your* addiction, explored any mental health issues that you may currently have, started increasing your motivation for change, and begun practicing concepts such as mindfulness and purposeful action. You have also started developing a change plan.

In the following chapters, you will learn more about yourself and what makes you tick. You are encouraged to identify things that will help you and integrate them into your plan. For example, when I first started my recovery journey, I did not understand how much sleep (or lack of sleep) impacted my productivity, my mood and my tendency to use addictive behaviors to escape from that unpleasantness. Not every suggestion works for every person. That is where mindfulness comes in. Ask yourself, what parts of this might apply to me. When I do this, how do I feel?

Staying with the mindfulness theme, if you have an addiction, anxiety, depression or PTSD, you may have regularly tried to control things that were out of your control. When you could not control it, you may have spiraled into a tornado of self-pity and feeling helpless, depressed and anxious. One of the hardest parts of recovery is staying focused and learning how to deal with life on life's terms, and feeling feelings without having to act on them. Mindfulness encourages you to stop and think before acting.

You will check in with yourself to assess how you are doing. Mindfulness encourages you to check in with yourself. It takes you off autopilot. What is it that you need? What is it that you want? The following activity should be done every morning and every evening for the first six months of recovery.

Activity: Mindfulness

Physically

> How do you feel right now _____
>
> _____
>
> What could help you feel better _____
>
> _____

Emotionally

    How do you feel right now   _____

    _____

    What could help you feel better _____

    _____

Mentally

    How do you feel right now   _____

    _____

    What could help you feel better _____

    _____

Spiritually

    How do you feel right now   _____

    _____

    What could help you feel better _____

    _____

Interpersonally/Relationships

    How do you feel right now   _____

    _____

    What could help you feel better _____

    _____

What am I excited/happy about? _____

_____

What am I grateful for? _____

_____

Mindfulness helps you hone in on what you really need and want, so you can use your energy wisely. Too often when you don't feel well you reach for the first thing that you think might make you feel better, like chocolate. In reality, this is simply a distraction. Mindfulness encourages you to look deeper. What are you *really* wanting? Once you figure that out, the next step is to choose things that will get you closer to what you need. This is called purposeful action (Because you are acting with a purpose---to achieve a goal). You have already done some mindfulness work by identifying what you want your life in recovery to be like. However, it is also important to practice mindfulness in the present. Relapses happen when you are on autopilot for too long and are not paying attention to "stuff." It is important to have future goals, and to recognize that your past has impacted you and will continue to impact you. However, you have the ability to choose how your past impacts you in the present. It is also important to remain keenly aware of what you need right now to stay safe, happy and sober.

The Serenity Prayer may serve as a reminder of what steps you need to take to live a happier life. While the term "prayer" may turn some people off, I encourage you to think about it more as a plan. The first part talks about staying focused on your end goal. The second part talks about learning how to accept that some things are out of your control. The third part reminds you that there are some things you can change, but change requires effort and hard work. Finally, the fourth part points out that in order to effectively make choices, you have to be mindful and wisely choose your actions.

Serenity Prayer (Plan)

Written by Reinhold Niebuhr (1892-1971)…modified to be more secular…

Good Orderly Direction/ God will give me
The serenity to accept the things I cannot change,
The courage to change the things I can, and
The wisdom to know the difference.
Living one day at a time;
Enjoying one moment at a time;
Accepting hardship as the pathway to peace.

Activity: Good Orderly Direction

Recovery is a journey. Good Orderly Direction is your roadmap. It helps keep you from getting lost. It helps you resist taking uncharted detours or "shortcuts." Some people call it direction or long-term goals. Some call it God. Some call it conscience. Whatever it is for you, it helps you stay the course.

Example: In one year, I will be clean, have a full-time job, be able to move into my own place, will own a car, have a license and will get my kids back.

In one year I will...

_____

_____

_____

_____

_____

_____

_____

Now that you know the destination, how do you get there? Google maps cannot tell you—I tried. There is a Rock Bottom (incidentally it is a brewery) in Arlington, VA. There is also a place called Recovery Place in Ambler, PA. Have you ever noticed on Google Maps that it charts the fastest route based on general information? If you drag the route line, it will replot the course, but it usually takes a lot longer. And if you do not give it an end point, it randomly picks one, usually across the world. The same is true for recovery. You need to know the starting point, your destination and get some guidance on, in general, the best way to get there. If you start monkeying with the route, it will take you a lot longer to reach your destination. In early recovery there are usually four major causes for detours. 1) Trying to change things you cannot change, 2) Thinking you know a "short cut" 3) Making major (unnecessary) changes along the way, or 4) Plain and simply acting impulsively. (Squirrel!)

Activity: Serenity to Accept the Things I Cannot Change.

Serenity is a state of calm and acceptance, including acceptance of the fact that you do not have control over everything all of the time. To continue the metaphor, serenity is the ability to deal with traffic jams along your route. If you have felt victimized, used, rejected or simply hopeless and helpless, you may have developed an overwhelming desire to be in control---all the time. Serenity is when you can accept that something "is" and that you do not have any control over it. What you *do* have control over is your reaction to it and how much energy you choose to invest in a losing battle. Does revving your engine when traffic is at a complete stop get you anywhere? No, it just burns up your gas. Same is true for trying to change things you have no control over. (This includes other people)

Feelings are natural. They serve a purpose. However, when you feel overwhelmed by negative emotions, you may be trying to change something over which you have no control. When you find yourself in this situation, try telling yourself something like:

It stinks that _____. However, there is nothing I can do about it.

Instead of wasting my energy by continuing to feel _____ and trying

to _____ I choose to _____

Examples:

It stinks that I am stuck in a traffic jam with no exit for miles. There is nothing I can do about it. Instead of staying angry, I will use this time to call a few friends I have not talked with in a while.

Activity: Serenity

List 4 things that you have no control over that cause you to feel stressed

    1. _____

    2. _____

    3. _____

    4. _____

List 5 things that you can change which cause you stress

    1. _____

    2. _____

    3. _____

    4. _____

    5. _____

Activity: Courage to Change the Things I Can.

While it is true addicts like control, they also do not like discomfort. Sometimes the right thing is not the easiest or most comfortable thing. It takes a lot of courage to admit when you are wrong, take responsibility for your actions (instead of blaming someone else), or make other changes.

What are two things you can change today that will help you in your journey?

    1. _____

    2. _____

What does courage mean to you?

_____

_____

_____

_____

_____

Activity: Changing the Things You Can

Have you ever met one of those people that sees every glass as half-full? You may find it irritating, because they do not share your point of view or because they have something you do not---contentment. Identify 4 things that irritate you or cause you stress, and write a positive reframe of for each of them.

Example

Irritant: My boss is an unreasonable jerk

> Positive Reframe: At least I have a job for now, and I am looking for another one

Irritant: Long lines and slow cashiers

> Positive Reframe: At least I can read the tabloids while I wait. This may be the best he/she can do.

Irritant: _____

Positive Reframe: _____

_____

Irritant: _____

Positive Reframe: _____

_____

Irritant: _____

Positive Reframe: _____

_____

Irritant: _____

Positive Reframe: _____

_____

Activity: Wisdom to Know the Difference

You are back to that whole control thing. Most of the time, you probably know what you can and cannot control, but you choose to fight a losing battle anyway. (If you are feeling irritated that I said that, then your addicted, control-freak mind is rearing its head.) Think of your emotions like a tornado. Right now, when you feel an emotion (especially a negative one), the emotion takes over, like being sucked into the tornado. In order to make wise choices, you need to learn how to feel feelings without having to immediately act on them. Just because you are angry doesn't mean you have to hit a wall, drink or throw a hissy fit. Actually none of those behaviors is probably effective. Wisdom is one part impulse control (thinking before you act), and one part knowledge.

- ✓ Start by asking yourself "Why do I feel _____ "
- ✓ Follow up with "Is this something I can control, and is it worth my energy?"
- ✓ If not, then let it go. Move on. If it is, then the fourth and fifth questions are "What do I want to be different, and how can I make that happen?"

Too often people stop at "What do I want to be different?" It's as if they think they can wish for it, and magically it will happen. This is just not the case. When something is wrong, you need to either change it or accept it. For example, I had plans to go hiking today. However, the forecasters completely missed the HUGE storm that was coming this way. I could get mad about it, but if I stop and think (impulse control), I will realize it is not worth the energy of getting angry, because I cannot change the weather.

How can you help yourself stop and think before you act or react? _____

_____

_____

How do you know the difference between which things to accept and things to change?

_____

_____

Activity: Living One Day at a Time, Enjoying One Moment at a Time

People get "stressed out" and "anxious" because they are so busy worrying about and trying to plan for the future or dwelling in regrets and resentments from the past. Don't get me wrong, a little Good Orderly Direction is wonderful, but living in the future or the past sets you up to miss today. One of my clients once said to me: If you live with one foot in the past and one foot in the future, all you can do is crap on the present. What is it that is awesome about right now?

Yesterday is history. Tomorrow is a mystery. Today is a present.

In what ways do you get yourself caught up living in the future? _____

_____

_____

In what ways do you get yourself caught up living in the past? _____

_____

_____

How can you help yourself stay grounded (and grateful) in the present? (Examples: Journaling, gratitude list, daily meditation…) _____

_____

What are some things you are grateful for right now?

1. _____

2. _____

3. _____

4. _____

5. _____

Activity: Accepting Hardship as the Pathway to Peace.

There will always be challenges. Peace comes from accepting these challenges and dealing with life on life's terms. It requires just as much strength to accept those things you cannot change, as it does to change the things you can. Sometimes hardship can make you realize how grateful you are for what you have and how strong you really are. There are a lot of songs that speak to this. Lori Morgan's "I Didn't Know My Own Strength," Britney Spears' "Stronger," Kelly Clarkson's "What Doesn't Kill You, " and Christina Aguilera's "Fighter."

What hardships have you already dealt with?

Hardship: _____

How I dealt with it: _____

Hardship: _____

How I dealt with it: _____

Hardship: _____

How I dealt with it: _____

What else needs to happen so you can be at peace with these things? _____

_____

_____

_____

How can mindfulness and purposeful action benefit your recovery process? _____

_____

_____

What can you do to start learning to be more mindful of your wants, needs and feelings? (Remember to consider learning style such as journaling if you are a visual person, or checking in with a sponsor or coach if you are an listener or do-er; and temperament--- it is important to be mindful of both your preferences, but also those things you tend to overlook.)

_____

_____

_____

_____

_____

What have you learned about yourself and recovery so far that you can use to improve your quality of life?

_____

_____

_____

_____

_____

_____

_____

_____

_____

Chapter 7: Physical/Biological Needs

Up until now you have been learning about addiction and mental health issues, how to set goals and what some of your personal preferences are. In recovery, you need to consider the whole person. If you are sick, tired, in pain or malnourished, it is going to be hard to really be motivated to stay clean and sober. Remember in the chapter on mindfulness you learned that it is important to pay attention to your thoughts, feelings, needs and wants. According to Abraham Maslow we all have needs that are based on a pyramid. The foundation of the pyramid is your physical needs. This includes physical fitness, food/nutrition, shelter, general health, pain management and rest.

Just above that are your safety needs. Safety needs include (obviously) being in a safe place physically, but also being emotionally safe not only from what other people are currently saying, but what you are saying to yourself. (Example: I am a loser. I can't do anything right…) Even if nobody is threatening your person, what you hear can be very harmful. You have probably internalized a lot of those negative messages. It is these critical "tapes" that you play over and over in your head that can sabotage your recovery and happiness.

Once you are rested, fed, have a roof over your head and are safe from others as well as that internal critic, then it is time to start really developing your supportive relationships. You are probably already making friends and getting to know people, but until you know and accept yourself, you are not going to be able to fully know, accept and, dare I say it….even trust another person.

Finally it is time to put some final touches on your self-esteem. Throughout the process you have discovered who you are, what you believe in and why you are worthy of respect and love. (Corny I know, but I had to say it.) In this final step, you will really start taking stock not only of who you are, but of how much you have accomplished, your strengths and your courage.

We will start by looking at your foundation---your physical needs. Think for a minute about how it affects you when you are sick, in pain all the time, overweight or eating poorly. Emotionally it is hard to be happy if you are puking your guts out, in agony or sluggish and tired because you are not treating your body well. Most people are lax in more than one area of physical health, so choose where you are going to start and make a SMALL change. Do not start training for a marathon tomorrow or become a vegan overnight.

Neurochemicals

Emotions are produced when the brain produces certain chemicals in response to stimuli (an event, something you see etc.). These chemicals are called neurotransmitters. Some of the neurotransmitters that help you feel happy or calm include serotonin, norepinephrine, GABA and Dopamine. It is not really important that you know the names of these chemicals, unless you want to research them more. The important part is to understand that emotions/feelings/reactions are normal, and are produced in a very primitive part of the brain. But, as humans, we have a unique ability to use our rational mind to assess the situation and change our emotional response. Take, for example, a dog who has a fear of thunder. No amount of rationalizing with Fido will get him to believe it is okay. You, on the other hand often may feel an initial startle when there is a loud clap of thunder, but then your rational mind kicks in, tells you that you are safe and your brain sends out the all-clear.

Exactly how the neurotransmitters work is more than you probably care about. What is important is that each time you have an emotion or reaction, you are using up some of the neurotransmitters. If you use them up faster than they can be made, you will feel depressed, have difficulty concentrating or just not care about anything. In order to make sure you have enough neurotransmitters there are a few points to remember…

✓ Each time you feel an emotion or have a reaction, you are using up some of the neurotransmitters

✓ The amount of neurotransmitter used up increases with the intensity of the emotion or reaction.

✓ Just like you need to rest and eat well when you are sick so your immune system can fight off the bugga buggas, you need to give your proper nutrition and rest so it can make more neurotransmitters.

Activity: Nutrition and Mood

Think back to a day you ate a lot of junk. How did you feel?

_____

_____

_____

_____

What about a day you ate pretty well? _____

_____

_____

In the table below, day rank how you feel each day on a scale from 1 to 10 (10 being great). Keep track of how you feel for one week when you eat whatever you want.

Then, for one week, eat a balanced diet with only moderate amounts of caffeine, sugar, fat and refined carbohydrates, and eating a small meal every 3-4 hours. Each day rank how you feel again

	Monday	Tuesday	Wednesday	Thursday	Friday	Saturday	Sunday
Week 1 Eating Normally							
Week 2 Eating Healthfully							

Remember that it takes time for your brain to make these chemicals. It will likely take several weeks to feel the full benefit of eating well and getting rest. The same holds true for most medications you may take to help you feel better. In addition to eating well, getting enough sunlight, oxygen, exercise and sleep will greatly help you maintain healthy neurotransmitter levels.

What will you start doing, today, to help your body recover? _____

_____

_____

_____

Intro to Psychopharmacology

Sometimes, no matter how healthfully you are living, your body needs a little help to balance those brain chemicals. This could be a short term thing to help you recover after years of cocaine or alcohol use, or it could be a long term thing because your brain never did make enough of some chemicals.

There are a variety of medications that can help you. Although, a pill will not make the problem go away. (You probably found that out in your addiction.) However, some people, either due to an organic chemical imbalance, or due to the effects of long-term substance use, may need some help leveling the playing field. For example, if you have "low" levels of serotonin (happy chemical), you may find it nearly impossible to concentrate, remember anything, get out of bed or find any pleasure in being clean. One of my patients once told me that the first 18 months for him was "gray." There were no colors. Everything was muted and sort of ran together. He identified this as a major reason for several or his relapses. His quality of life was awful. Once he started taking antidepressants, he found that he could experience a wider range of emotions, could tolerate stress without becoming completely incapacitated, could concentrate, and was able to more effectively apply what he was learning in treatment.

In early recovery you may have to deal with some depression or anxiety in addition to your addiction. It is important to address all of these things, because, once you have started doing what you need to do to be happier and healthier, and your brain has started to recover from the effects of the addiction you may not need medication. You may, however, figure out that you always had a problem and were self-medicating with your addiction.

In the following pages, you will learn about many different kinds of medications and their side effects. For a more in-depth look, go to http://Drugs.com. All medications have the possibility of side effects. It is important to understand:

    1) How you will feel when you start taking the medication

    2) What side effects are temporary and which ones will not go away

    3) How long until the medication takes effect

    4) What the medication is supposed to help with.

With this information, you can tell your doctor whether the medication is working as it should, and if you are experiencing "unacceptable" side effects. That is, if being on the medication is making your quality of life worse than without it. Additionally, you can prepare yourself so the medication does not end up triggering a relapse.

Medications for Depression

Antidepressants (SSRIs/Selective Serotonin Reuptake Inhibiters or SNRIs/Selective Norepinepherine Reuptake Inhibitors) are used to treat depression and anxiety. There are many different antidepressants, and each one works in a slightly different way. This means that you may have very different effects with different antidepressants. If the first one does not work for you, all is not lost. There are lots of others that can be tried. By educating yourself about some of the more common medications, you can work with your doctor to make the best choice for you.

The following is a list of some of the more common antidepressants, and information I have read or gotten from my patients about the effects and side effects. Please note: This is information is anecdotal and not intended to replace medical advice.

1. Prozac (fluoxetine) is often stimulating. This drug is helpful for people who are so depressed they cannot think straight, are in a "fog" all of the time and do not have the energy to get out of bed. Some of my patients have reported it makes their anxiety worse though.

2. Paxil (paroxetine) is typically "sedating." I have found that patients with anxiety and/or insomnia do well on this medication, however, many have to take it at night because it makes them feel too sleepy.

3. Zoloft (sertraline) is usually neither sedating or activating.

4. Celexa (citalopram) is usually neither sedating or activating.

5. Luvox (fluvoxamine) can be very sedating in children.

6. Remeron (mirtazapine) can be used as sleep aid at lower doses. Most frequent complaint is weight gain.

7. Wellbutrin/Zyban (Buproprion) is also used for ADHD and smoking cessation, and can be used with other antidepressants to increase their effectiveness.

8. Effexor (Venlafaxine) is a drug some believe may be helpful in ADHD and depression. Like Prozac, it is considered activating. At higher doses there is also a risk of elevated blood pressure.

9. Tricyclic acid antidepressants (TCA) including Tofranil (imipramine), Pamelor(nortriptyline), Anafranil (clomipramine), Elavil (amytriptyline) are older generation antidepressants and have more side effects than the newer medications. TCA's are also used for headache prevention and pain syndromes.

10. Desyrel (trazadone) is an older antidepressant that is known to make people sleepy, so it is often used to help with insomnia.

Medications for Bipolar Disorders

Mood stabilizers are another type of medication that is used to treat people with bipolar disorder (manic-depression), aggression and impulsivity. These medications often make people feel sleepy and lethargic.

1. Depakote (Valproic Acid) is often used for bipolar disorder although the side-effects are numerous and include sedation, dizziness, weight gain and hair loss.

2. Tegretol (Carbamazepine) is also used for bipolar and pain conditions, and is a very popular as a medication for aggression and rage in children and some adults.

3. Eskalith (Lithium) is thought to be the drug of choice for the treatment of mania especially in "classic" bipolar patients and severe depression that has not been helped by other medications. As with most mood-stabilizers, it needs frequent blood monitoring for levels and indicators of toxicity.

Medications for Anxiety Disorders

Anxiety/stress/anger/irritability are huge triggers for relapse. It is important for you to identify your stressors and develop an adequate plan to deal with negative feelings when they arise. Benzodiazepines (antianxiety medications Xanax, Valium etc) are often prescribed for rapid relief of intense anxiety. However, benzodiazepines are easily abused, and should be avoided when possible. They get into your system and "make you feel better" really quickly, but, like other drugs, the anxiety and problems are still there when the drug wears off. Other medications for anxiety include antidepressants and buspirone.

Buspirone is in a class all its own. It has a very low likelihood of abuse, because it takes a while to build up in your system. It used most frequently to treat mild-moderate anxiety. One of my patients described it as helping her to not make mountains out of mole hills. Another said it did not make the anxiety go away, it just helped to keep her from going from 0 to 120 in 2.1 seconds.

Neurontin (gabapentin) may be effective in treating some anxiety disorders and is also prescribed for chronic pain. Like most other types of drugs, Neurontin is not without its side effects. (http://www.drugs.com/neurontin.html)

166

Medications for Psychotic Disorders (Schizophrenia)

A psychotic disorder is one in which you have hallucinations (seeing or hearing things that are not really there) or delusions (believing things that are highly unlikely to be true). Schizophrenia is the most common psychotic disorder. However, it is possible to have hallucinations or delusions when you are severely depressed as well. Antipsychotics are used to treat these symptoms as well as impulse control difficulties.

Atypical antipsychotics tend to have fewer side effects than the older antipsychotics. (http://www.drugs.com/drug-class/atypical-antipsychotics.html)

1. Risperdal (risperdone) has side-effects include agitation, anxiety, and headache.

2. Zyprexa (olanzapine) is most likely to cause significant weight gain.

3. Seroquel (quetiapine) is known to be very sedating, but has fewer side-effects.

4. Geodon is the newest antipsychotic on the market since about August, 2000.

5. Clozaril (Clozapine), like most of the others is very sedating, but thought to have very little risk for causing serious side effects.

Other antipsychotic medications such as Haldol (haloperidol) or Thorazine (chlorpromazine), Haldol and Prolixin (fluphenazine) are also available by injection. Some of them have long acting forms that allow psychiatrists to dose on a weekly, bi-weekly or monthly basis.

Medications for Attention Deficit Disorder

Stimulants are often used to help treat Attention Deficit Hyperactivity Disorder, and narcolepsy. Because they work on the dopamine and norepinephrine systems, these medications can produce a feeling of euphoria when improperly used, and are therefore often abused. Side-effects of stimulants include loss of appetite, dizziness, anxiety, irritability and occasionally headache. "Rebound" syndrome includes fatigue, excessive sleepiness, increased appetite and depression.

1.   Ritalin, Ritalin SR, Concerta (methylphenidate)

2.   Adderall, Dexedrine (dextroamphetamines)

3.   Focalin (Dexmethylphenidate)

4.   Cylert (pemoline)-Not usually a first choice due to documented liver toxicity.

Activity: Medication Log

I am taking the following medications…

Medication_____ Reason: _____

Dose: _____ Date started taking it _____ Date stopped taking it _____

Prescribing Doctor _____ Is it Effective? Yes   No

If it isn't effective, why not? _____

Side effects _____

Medication_____ Reason: _____

Dose: _____ Date started taking it _____ Date stopped taking it _____

Prescribing Doctor _____ Is it Effective? Yes   No

If it isn't effective, why not? _____

Side effects _____

Medication_____ Reason: _____

Dose: _____ Date started taking it _____ Date stopped taking it _____

Prescribing Doctor _____ Is it Effective? Yes   No

If it isn't effective, why not? _____

Side effects _____

It is crucial to your recovery that you understand what medications you are taking, the reason for them, their side effects and how they may interact with each other. Do not feel intimidated by doctors or pharmacists who may use a lot of technical words. It is your right and need to know what you are taking and why. It is also your right to advocate for yourself if a medication is not working or if you want the doctor to consider adding a medication. Remember that medications will not fix everything. The goal of these medications is to help you sleep, concentrate, think and have the energy to do what needs to be done to change your situation.

General Health

Your mind and body are connected. When you have a stressful day, you may feel "drained." This is because the body diverted a lot of its energy to support the fight or flight response. You were "revved up" all day. Additionally, if you are not taking care of your body by getting enough sleep, drinking enough water and eating somewhat healthfully, you will find your body cannot make the happy chemicals, or even the adrenaline to keep you going. When you are physically well, it is easier to get things done because you are clear-headed, can concentrate, it is easier to remember things and you have the energy to be motivated to get things done. (Remember you learned that motivation means being willing AND able. Without the energy, you may be willing, but not able to do what needs to be done.) This is not an overnight change. Start slowly by doing something positive. Some suggestions are listed below.

Emotional: Dealing effectively with your emotions will help reduce stress on the body and illness. People who tend to be healthier possess a sense of commitment, a view of problems as challenges and a sense of personal control. Try finding the silver lining in everything for a day (or more). When something bad happens, immediately ask yourself, what is the upside to this?

Mental: Meditation and positive self talk can help people deal with pain or feeling ill. Prioritize what must be done and leave the rest for when you feel better. Keep a notepad handy so you can jot down things you need to remember. This is especially important at night, so you don't stay awake trying not to forget things that have to be done tomorrow.

Physical: When you are well enough, start an exercise program. Exercise improves sleep, helps eliminate general aches and pains, improves your mood and may help your self-esteem. Start slowly with walking and/or stretching. Good nutrition provides the building blocks for neurotransmitters and physical health. No matter how well you eat or how much you exercise, the body needs a break. Relaxation and adequate sleep are also essential.

Social: Exercise with a buddy. Have friends pitch in to get things done when you are sick or too tired. If you are an extrovert, you need to be around people to get recharged. Social supports are also one of the greatest stress buffers. Let your friends help you deal with stress.

Environmental: Get some sunshine. This not only just makes people feel better, but it also helps reset the body's clock improving sleep.

Activity: General Health Improvement

List 5 ways you can improve your physical health---start easy like drinking more water, making sleep a priority, eating more fruits and veggies or walking.

1. _____

2. _____

3. _____

4. _____

5. _____

As you have already learned, there are a lot of physical issues including high blood pressure, diabetes, thyroid problems, Chron's disease, and low testosterone which can make you feel bad---sluggish, tired, confused/foggy, irritable, anxious/shaky, achy all over, migraines… Get yourself evaluated by a physician. This will not only help you rule out physical causes, but it will also ensure you are healthy enough to start making physical changes. Share with your physician what you are doing and ask for any input he or she may have.

The next step is to take a thorough inventory of how you are taking care of yourself. Then start working on one or two things, and do not make drastic changes. Trying to do too much or make big of a change sets you up for failure. For example, don't go from drinking a pot of coffee a day to no caffeine at all, or eating junk to a vegetarian diet. Drastic changes will cause more discomfort and will be harder to maintain.

Activity: Physical Health Inventory

	Yes or No	How motivated are you to work on this 1= Not much to 4= Let's do this
Sleep		
Are you sleeping at least 7 hours per night		
Are you sleeping through the night		
Do you have difficulty falling asleep		
When you awaken, do you feel refreshed		
Do you avoid taking long naps during the day		
Nutrition		
Do you drink at least 8 glasses of water a day		
At each meal do you have at least 3 different colored foods on your plate		
Do you drink too much caffeine		
Do you cut back on your caffeine after 2pm		
Do you have a serving of protein at each meal		
Do you eat at least 3 small to medium sized meals each day		
Exercise		
Do you exercise at least 3 days per week		
Do you stretch		
Are you significantly overweight		
Do you take breaks to move around at work instead of sitting on one place all day?		
Do you take time to relax each day		
Do you get enough sunlight (both for vitamin D and to help your body know it is daytime)		

Exercise and Fitness

Exercise is simply moving your body…or even just tensing and relaxing your muscles. Gardening, housework, playing golf, and walking the dog are all forms of exercise. It is important to exercise, but it is just as important to find physical activities you like to do. Remember that temperament thing… If you like structure and schedules, then make an appointment with yourself for your exercise. If you are more spontaneous, go when the mood strikes, but make sure you do it each day. If you are an extrovert or extremely competitive, you will probably do better exercising where there are other people (gym, park, walking around your neighborhood). If you are an introvert, you may feel more comfortable exercising at home. The key is finding something comfortable for you.

Benefits of Exercise and Fitness (Mark the ones that you want to achieve)

- ☐ Improved energy
- ☐ Improved sleep
- ☐ Reduced muscle tension
- ☐ Normalized weight
- ☐ Reduced blood pressure
- ☐ Socialization
- ☐ Increased awareness of your physical self
- ☐ Improved self-image
- ☐ Stronger bones
- ☐ A way to burn up extra nervous energy/irritability at the end of the day

Activity: How can exercise help with recovery

Do some research on the internet, or brainstorm at least 5 ways exercise helps with recovery. (Ex. Aches and pains, improved sleep, dissipating the fight or flight response)

1. _____

2. _____

3. _____

4. _____

5. _____

Exercise Basics

Physical fitness can be considered "tune up and maintenance of our body, the machine." Take a minute to consider the similarities between your body and a machine. They both require fuel/energy to run, regular maintenance to run smoothly. In machines when belts and gaskets are over used they break. In humans when muscles and tendons are over used they also break. Belts must be tightened for optimum performance, and muscles must be strengthened for the same reason. When something goes wrong in one part of a machine or the body, the whole thing begins operating below optimal standards.

There are 5 components to fitness: cardiovascular, strength, flexibility, endurance and body composition. Below you will find definitions of each as well as prompts to help you improve each area. Start slowly. If you push too hard, you will be sore and likely will stop doing it.

Activity: Exercise Options

Cardiovascular

- ✓ The #1 killer in America is poor heart and circulation system efficiency

- ✓ Aerobic exercise means exercise which uses oxygen, such as low to moderate intensity exercise and activities of daily living

- ✓ Aerobic activity, such as walking will help release endorphins, loosen tight muscles and use up excess nervous energy. It also encourages you to breathe more deeply which increases energy, alertness and improves concentration.

- ✓ Identify 5 things you could do for aerobic exercise (hint: If it makes you breathe even a little harder, it's aerobic exercise)

1. _____

2. _____

3. _____

4. _____

5. _____

Strength

✓ Many people experience pain due to muscle imbalances. One set of muscles, like your back muscles, are stronger than the opposing set, like your abdominals. This throws your posture out of alignment and can cause pain. Strength training does not mean becoming Arnold. It simply means working each muscle so it is in balance.

✓ A repetition is one instance of the exercise, such as one sit up

✓ A set is several instances of an exercise without a rest in between.

✓ Identify 3 things you could do for building strength (Think of things you do on a daily basis like carry babies or bags of dog food)

1. _____

2. _____

3. _____

Flexibility

✓ Lack of flexibility can cause: strains, sprains, back pain, and poor posture.

✓ The most common muscle lacking flexibility is the hamstrings, leading to strains of the hamstring, and low back and knee pain. *Back pain can also be caused by weak abdominals.

✓ A proper stretch can be executed only after the muscle has been warmed up and it must be held for a minimum of 30 seconds without bouncing.

✓ When you stretch, you will feel a tightness in your muscles, which is *slightly* uncomfortable but feels better after 15 or 20 seconds. Hold the stretch without bouncing.

✓ Identify 3 times/places where you can stretch

1. _____

2. _____

3. _____

Activity: Exercise Profile

Have you exercised within the last two months? _____

Have you had a physical within the past year? _____

If you have not exercised in the last two months or have not had a physical within the last year, or if you have any limiting physical condition such as high blood pressure, diabetes or asthma you should get medical clearance before beginning to exercise.

The American Heart Association recommends that working in your target heart rate range for at least 30 minutes three times a week. Nevertheless, most Americans do not work out at all; therefore, any exercise is a step in the right direction.

What is your resting heart rate? (Take your pulse for 6 seconds in the morning before you get out of bed and multiply by 10) _____ Average is between 60 and 80 beats per minute.

Your maximum heart rate is approximately 220 – your age. So if you are 40, your maximum heart rate is 180 beats per minute. What is your maximum heart rate?

_____

What is your target heart rate range?

What is your maximum heart rate multiplied by 0.6? _____

What is your maximum heart rate multiplied by 0.8? _____

If you have not been exercising at all, start slow. Do not even try to get in your target heart rate range for a while. Choose exercises that you enjoy at a proper intensity in duration so you don't get frustrated and quit. That is, do not go from doing nothing to trying to run 5 miles. You will be in agony. Start with 10 minutes, or a slow stroll down the street. Add 5 minutes every day or two until you are exercising for 30 minutes. Workout with a friend, or at a gym. You will be more likely to keep going to see the new friends you are making and to cave to peer pressure---

What do you like about exercise? Circle any that apply.

Stress Relief   Weight Loss   Opportunity to Socialize   Renewed Energy

Meeting People With Similar Interest   Sense Of Accomplishment   Better Sleep

Muscle Definition   Reduced Appetite   Increased Fitness Level

What do you dislike about exercise?

Pain   Sweat   Time Commitment   Don't Know How   Feel Out Of Place

Get Bored Easily   Other: _____

*Brainstorm ways to eliminate these negatives. _____

_____

What are your fitness goals?

Weight Loss   Increased Cardiovascular Fitness   Toning   Increased Strength

Stress Relief   Blood Pressure Reduction   Diabetes Control   Other:

What activities do you enjoy?

Walking   Hiking   Jogging   Weight LiftingCycling   Stair Climbing

Team Sports   Roller Blading   Tennis   Swimming   House Cleaning

Dancing   Instructor-Led Classes   Cardio Machines   Lifting Free Weights

Walking the Dog   Stretching   Zumba   Yoga   Pilates   Playing Tag

Exercise Videos   Gardening   Other:

What motivates you? _____

_____

_____

Set a fitness goal for yourself

I_____ will (Name the exercise) _____ at least

_____ times per week for a period of not less than _____ minutes on any exercise day.

General Fitness Principles

The average person aims for 30-40 minutes of aerobic activity three times per week at 60-85 percent of their target heart rate range, and strength training three times a week with exercises for every body part at a rate of 1-3 sets of 8-10 repetitions. Incorporate both cardiovascular and strength training exercises

Frequency

Strength training exercises should never be done on consecutive days. Your body needs at least 48 hours of recovery before you can use the same muscles to strength train again. Cardiovascular exercise can be done up to seven days a week, but if you are working in your target heart rate zone you should give yourself at least one day of rest per week.

Duration

Begin your fitness program by increasing the amount of activity you do by 5 minutes each work out day until you reach 30-40 minutes three times per week.

Intensity

Begin your strength training workouts with one set of 8-10 repetitions for 3-6 different exercises. For example: squats, abdominal crunches, bicep curls, tricep extensions, and chest press. You can find excellent tutorial videos for different exercises at http://Bodybuilding.com

The intensity of your aerobic workout should gradually increase until you are spending at least 30 minutes in your target heart rate range.

Activity: Muscle Memory

Your body can roughly be divided into front and back and right and left side. For every muscle group on the front, there is a corresponding muscle group on the back. If the front muscle is working, the back muscle is relaxing. Likewise, on the left and right side, you have a mirror image of the muscles. When there is muscle imbalance, or a muscle is tight or strained, you will feel pain. If you "store" your stress in your back, you know what I am talking about. One of the best ways to work out knots in your muscles is to work out the muscle. Always warm up first without using any sort of weights or resistance. Not too hard, just enough to coax the muscle to tense and relax a bit. It is kind of like warming up frozen taffy. If you pull too soon, the taffy breaks…so don't push it.

Stretching and gentle movements are especially helpful at working out knots and kinks.

Additionally, there are a lot of muscles and different exercises if you are interested in strength training or toning. If you go to websites such as Muscle and Strength http://www.muscleandstrength.com/ you can see videos of different exercises and how to do them. You do not necessarily have to lift weights though. As you learned earlier, any movement is better than no movement. Do what you enjoy.

Nutrition

Good nutrition is vital to helping your body repair itself and produce the chemicals that help you feel happy and calm. Food provides you the energy you need to get things done. When your blood sugar is low, you probably do not concentrate very well. This is partly because the brain is one of the greatest users of blood glucose. When you have been eating crappy for a week your energy level and mood may go down and cravings may increase. This is because, if you are not getting enough protein, the body will break down its own muscle to get what it needs. Likewise, if you are not getting the correct vitamins, it will be harder for your body to make the energy you need.

Your body also needs these building blocks to make the brain chemicals that help you feel motivated, happy, and, yes, even stressed. It gets these building blocks from good healthy food. (As a side note, taking vitamins is not a replacement for a healthy diet.) Nutritional causes of depression can be linked to imbalances in or lack of: L-tryptophan, vitamin B6, magnesium, serotonin, melatonin, acetylcholine, and 5-HTP. As you will learn, a balanced nutritional program that includes foods like walnuts, bananas, cottage cheese, spinach, kale, chicken, turkey and brown rice will provide all of those building blocks.

American culture is especially bad about equating love, comfort and self-soothing with food. We celebrate with food. We grieve with food. We drown our sorrows in a pint of ice cream… Some companies have even gone as far as saying to eat one of their brownies when you need a hug. Aside from the cultural influences, there are biological reasons you may crave "comfort foods." The main reason is that the sugar rush when you eat them can temporarily distract you from feeling bad. Unfortunately, if you are dealing with stress by eating, all you have done is substituted addictions. You aren't dealing with the problem. You are "stuffing it."

Activity: Emotional Eating

In the following activity, you will try to identify which emotions you avoid dealing with by eating. You will also figure out if there are particular binge foods (brownies, ice cream, pizza) that you tend to crave. Those are the foods you do not want to keep in the house. Most dieticians will tell you that you should not make any food "forbidden," because that just sets you up to crave it more. However, limit your access to binge foods to times when you are less likely to binge (i.e. out with friends, at work etc.)

Emotion/Feeling/ Situation	Craving
Anger/Frustration	
Anxiety/Worry	
Exhaustion	
Resentment	
Guilt	
Grief	
Disappointment	
Embarrassment	
Loneliness	
Sadness/Depression	
Dehydration	
Low Blood Sugar	
Anemia/Need Iron	

Part of recovery and mindfulness is staying in tune with what your body is telling you. If you take care of it, it will take care of you.

180

Nutrition Basics

Since most people have no idea what good nutrition means, the following section will give you a very brief introduction. According to The U.S. Department of Agriculture and U.S. Department of Health And Human Services, the average American needs:

Grains	6 -- 11 servings	serving size: 1 slice bread, 1/2 c. prepared or 1 cup cold cereal or 1/2 roll or muffin
Vegetables	3 -- 5 servings	serving size: 1/2 cup cooked, 1cup raw
Fruits	2 -- 4 servings	serving size: 1/2 cup or one medium fruit
Dairy	2 -- 3 servings	serving size: 1 cup milk, yogurt or 1 ounce cheese
Protein	2 -- 3 servings	serving size: 4 ounces raw, or three ounces cooked meat; 1/2 cup cooked beans, or 2 eggs

BEWARE The "Serving Size" on the nutrition label is NOT equal to a serving from the food pyramid. The "Serving Size" on the package represents how much the average person eats. For instance, 2oz of dry pasta is 2 food pyramid servings of grain, but listed as one serving on the side of the box.

- ✓ To improve nutrition without getting bogged down in details:
- ✓ Use a 24 oz. glass at meals, and drink water
- ✓ Use a salad plate instead of a dinner plate. This will make you feel like you are eating more
- ✓ Have at least 3 colors on your plate at each meal. The different colors trick your brain into thinking that you are eating more.

Grains

✓ These consist of bread, rice, cereal, and pasta.

✓ The average number of calories per serving is 80-100.

✓ Grains provide B-vitamins necessary for good health and serotonin production.

✓ Grains are a wonderful "filler" to most meals. Consider adding a whole wheat roll, brown rice, or whole grain pasta to your afternoon or evening meals.

✓ Grains--especially bread crumbs, corn flakes or oatmeal make great meat-extenders when using ground beef, turkey or sausage.

✓ What are your 5 favorite grains? _____

_____

_____

Vegetables

✓ Servings in this group consist of various types of green, yellow, orange, red and sometimes purple vegetables.

✓ Select vegetables with multiple colors each day the different colors represent different vitamins. For instance, iron and calcium are high in green, leafy vegetables. Whereas vitamin A is high in orange and yellow vegetables. Tomatoes are extremely high in potassium and vitamin C.

✓ When cooking vegetables it is best to leave them slightly crisp, because the more you cook them the more vitamins you lose.

✓ When you cook vegetables, try to steam them above the water instead of boiling

✓ Likewise when selecting vegetables from the market, the darker the color of the vegetable, the higher in vitamins it is said to be.

✓ Frozen vegetables preserve their vitamins for up to 3 months in the freezer.

✓ What are your 5 favorite vegetables? _____

_____

_____

Fruits

✓ Use the same guidelines as stated in vegetables for selecting your fruits each day.

✓ Canned fruits are packaged either in juice or syrup. The juice provides extra vitamins if you choose to use it, and does not add many extra calories. The syrup adds significant non-nutritive calories from sugar.

✓ Apples and citrus fruits provide excellent sources of fiber.

✓ Fruit juices provide less fiber, but one glass of orange juice contains 20 times more potassium than most sport drinks

✓ Try using juices, pureed bananas or applesauce instead of oil when you bake cakes, fruit muffins or spice breads.

✓ What are your 5 favorite fruits? _____

_____

_____

Dairy

✓ Milk, yogurt, and cheese are your most common dairy sources

✓ Yogurt provides beneficial bacteria to your intestines. This is especially useful when you are on antibiotics or recovering from an illness.

✓ Be very aware of "hidden" fat and sugars in these foods. For instance, regular yogurt with fruit adds up to four tablespoons of sugar (that's 1/4 cup). And regular cheddar cheese (like the kind found at most salad bars) can have up to 12 grams of fat in a 2 ounce serving. Whole milk, in a one cup serving, can have up to 8 grams of fat; whereas, skim milk has less than one gram of fat.

✓ Cottage cheese is an excellent source of protein.

✓ What are your 5 favorite dairy products? _____

_____

_____

Proteins

✓ Meats, eggs, poultry, fish, beans and nuts are extremely high in hidden fats. The more expensive a piece of beef is, generally the more fat is in it, because fat adds "flavor." Try to get meats which are labeled "extra lean" or "97% fat free." Salmon, even though it is a fish, is also extremely high in fat

✓ Nuts are high in protein, but also high in fats; although, the fat found in nuts is the "good fat"

✓ Vegetable proteins are incomplete proteins. This means you must combine foods in order to create a protein that your body can assimilate. For example:

✓ Grains should be combined with legumes or vegetables note: combining grains and nuts forms a very weak protein

✓ Nuts should be combined with vegetables or legumes

✓ Vegetables should be combined with grains, legumes or nuts/seeds

✓ Legumes should be combined and with grains, nuts/seeds or vegetables

✓ Grains, nuts, vegetables or legumes can be combined with dairy or other protein sources to form complete proteins.

✓ Fish provides Omega-3 fatty acids which are essential for health

✓ Beans are also an excellent source of fiber. Consider adding beans to vegetables stew, chili or mashing a can of kidney beans (drained and rinsed) to your spaghetti sauce in order to thicken it and increase nutrient value.

✓ What are your 5 favorite proteins? _____

_____

_____

Activity: Ways to (Painlessly) Improve Nutrition

1. Use applesauce, pureed bananas or sweet juices, instead of oil, when baking

2. Limit meals eaten out to 1 per week and/or order lower-fat options

3. Eat meats which are low in fat

4. Eat at least once every three to four hours

5. Before snacking, ask yourself if you are hungry, or just bored, stressed, sleepy etcetera. This is one of the biggest traps of students and shift workers, because the cues for stress and hunger are so similar, often their body is too tired to accurately differentiate.

6. Be aware that fat-free substitutions often have just as many calories as their whole-fat counterparts, the calories just come from carbohydrates

7. Rinse and blot the fat from meats before adding to recipes and cut excess fat off of meat before cooking

8. Combine meat with cooked lentils in a ratio of 3 parts meat to 1 part lentils

9. Use oatmeal, potato flakes, cornmeal for fillers in ground meat

10. Use 1% buttermilk instead of heavy cream in recipes

11. Use butter substitute or extract in vegetable dishes instead of real butter

12. Keep fresh fruit in the house

13. Keep chocolate, cookies etc. out of the house or in a locked cabinet

14. Do not use food to reward good behavior or comfort yourself

15. Do not add butter or fats to your food

16. Use cooking spray instead of oil to sauté your food

17. Keep water extra cold and try to drink from a larger cup or bottle

18. Mix 1/4 c. Soy flour with regular flour

19. Make casseroles and Italian dishes with vegetables in them

20. Constantly have a water bottle with you

21. Limit fried food to only one meal per week

22. Find out exactly what your meals are made from (1/4 c. Oil is used to coat the pan for every small pizza + oil in the dough) EEEW!

23. Eat at least one balanced meal each day with every food group represented

24. Don't get in a rut eating the same thing every day

25. Get a dinner group together. One person cooks a healthy meal for everyone each night and everyone takes a turn.

26. Learn about a new food and three recipes for it, lentils for instance.

27. Challenge yourself to eat as many different colors each day as you can (yellow, orange, brown, white, green, blue, red, purple)

28. Don't buy in bulk if you tend to eat the whole package of whatever it is.

29. Drink a 32 oz. glass of water with lunch and dinner, more if you tend to consume caffeine or alcohol

30. If you want to eat junk-food, split it with a friend

31. Keep fresh vegetable salads in the refrigerator: cucumbers, carrots, mushrooms, sliced bell peppers in fat free dressing or red wine vinegar

32. List your favorite foods and find healthier alternatives: Either reduced in fat or sugar

33. Dress-up vegetables with melted low-fat cheese, lemon juice or 2 tablespoons of a "sauce" made from fat free cream soups

34. Use plain yogurt instead of sour cream

35. When cooking meat, rinse the fat off of it half-way through the cooking process

36. Read the labels to find out how much sugar and fat is in your food

37. Vegetables that are limp and dull in color have lost most of their vitamins.

38. Red sauces are much lower in fat than white or cream sauces

39. Avoid breaded, fried or sautéed foods. Opt for boiled, broiled or baked.

40. Caffeine inhibits the absorption of iron. Watch the caffeine if you are anemic.

41. Take a cooking class to improve your culinary skills

42. Take a multi-vitamin

43. Keep a food diary to see exactly what you eat

44. Vitamins and antioxidants in foods work synergistically. They need to be eaten in combination. Don't eat all of your vegetables for the week in one day.

45. Too much simple sugar on one day can leave you feeling sluggish throughout the next day, so try to satisfy that sweet tooth with a piece of fruit. It is higher in fiber so you will feel full and you will not "crash" as hard.

Activity: Food Journal

Keep a journal of what you eat, when, why and how much for the next week.

Date _____

Time: _____ What you ate/drank _____ How much _____

    Why: _____

Time: _____ What you ate/drank _____ How much _____

    Why: _____

Time: _____ What you ate/drank _____ How much _____

    Why: _____

Time: _____ What you ate/drank _____ How much _____

    Why: _____

Time: _____ What you ate/drank _____ How much _____

    Why: _____

Time: _____ What you ate/drank _____ How much _____

    Why: _____

Time: _____ What you ate/drank _____ How much _____

    Why: _____

Time: _____ What you ate/drank _____ How much _____

    Why: _____

Time: _____ What you ate/drank _____ How much _____

    Why: _____

Time: _____ What you ate/drank _____ How much _____

    Why: _____

Did you drink at least 8 glasses of water? _____

Did you eat at least every 6 hours? _____

Did you get a lot of your calories from sugary drinks and junk food? _____

Did you eat at least 2 vegetable servings each day? _____

Which things do you tend to over-do?   Fats   Sugars   Caffeine   Protein/Meat

Activity: Improving your nutrition

Identify 3 changes you will make tomorrow to try and improve your nutrition

1. _____

2. _____

3. _____

Remember that nutrition and exercise can help you improve your health, your mood and even your self-confidence. It is an easy, positive change that will help not only you, but also your family.

Sleep

Sleep (or tiredness) is one of the big four warning signs in relapse prevention --HALT (Hungry Angry Lonely Tired). People who are overtired tend to be overly emotional, more impulsive, and may feel disconnected from themselves. Part of this is because people who are not sleeping well often do not have enough serotonin to help them feel calm and happy. Darkness tells your body to secret serotonin which is converted to melatonin which regulates your sleep cycle. If you do not have enough serotonin, then you can't make enough melatonin and will not sleep well. If you do not sleep well, then your body cannot make enough serotonin and the cycle continues.

Many shift workers report not being able to tell if they are hungry, sleepy or stressed. They are constantly in a state of not feeling "right." Getting enough sleep reduces cravings for "pick-me-ups," helps keep you from making mountains out of molehills, gives you energy to exercise and gives your body time to repair and restore itself.

Activity: Sleep and My Recovery

How does lack of sleep impact your mood? _____

_____

_____

How does lack of sleep affect your judgment and decision making? _____

_____

_____

How does lack of sleep affect your self-awareness? _____

_____

_____

Sleep Basics

Sleep loss comes in many "forms" poor quality sleep, not going to sleep, drug-induced sleep etc. Sleep studies examining the effects of sleep loss have shown problems with memory and attention lapses, poor reaction time, problems with speech fluency, distractibility, and difficulty with complex reasoning and planning. You may not even be aware at how much you are being impacted by your lack of quality rest.

A variety of factors can increase the negative effects of sleep loss. Situational factors such as noise, temperature, physical activity, and drugs can alter the quality of sleep. Subjective and individual factors such as motivation, interest, age, type of sleeper (e.g., long, short, good, poor), personality, and sleep loss experience have been demonstrated to also affect how much a person is impaired by sleep loss. Studies on the recovery from sleep loss have demonstrated that "payback" is not accomplished on an "hour-for-hour" basis. Some studies show initial and sometimes full recovery after one night of recovery sleep, while others show only partial recuperation after two nights of full sleep. Either way, it is thought that you can "recover" from sleep deprivation with a couple of consecutive good night's sleep.

Tips for Improving Sleep

- ✓ Keep work and bills out of the bedroom

- ✓ Do not use your bed for anything but sleep

- ✓ Eliminate as much light as possible

- ✓ Turn on an air purifier for "white noise"

- ✓ Wear comfortable clothing that breathes like 100% cotton

- ✓ Try doing something relaxing before going to bed.

- ✓ Keep a pad and pen by your bed in case you think of something--you can write it down so you do not worry about forgetting it.

- ✓ Do not exercise or eat a heavy meal within 3 hours of going to bed

- ✓ Try to go to bed at the same time each night

- ✓ Eliminate naps in the late afternoon. If you must nap, limit them to 40 minutes

- ✓ If it takes less than 7 minutes to fall asleep, you are sleep deprived. If it takes more than 15 minutes to get to sleep, get up and do something for 30 minutes then try again.

Activity: Improving your sleep

Did you ever wonder why it is important to put your children on a bedtime routine? The same reason it is important for you to be on a bedtime routine. Your wind-down activities cue your body to start releasing melatonin and getting ready for sleep. Unfortunately it takes about a month for your body to figure all of this out, but once it does, then not only will it be easier to get to sleep, but also to wake up.

Create a sleep routine. Plan on eating dinner, winding down and going to bed around the same time every night for 2 weeks.

What is your wind-down routine?

_____

_____

_____

_____

_____

_____

_____

_____

Sunlight

Sunlight helps the body absorb vitamin D. It also helps set your circadian rhythms so your body knows when it is supposed to be awake and when it is supposed to be asleep. Exposure to sunlight has also been associated with improved mood. Think about the last time it was rainy for several days. How did you feel? Could you figure out what time it was without looking at a clock? Did your body know when to eat and when to sleep? Probably not.

Sunlight tells your body it is time to wake up and conquer the day. It is also vital for the production of vitamin D. Vitamin D deficiency has been linked to depression. So, one of the first things I suggest for my patients with depression or seasonal affective disorder is to get up at a reasonable time each day (by 9am) and go outside. Sit on the porch to drink your orange juice or read the paper. In the morning it is usually more temperate, so sitting outside or by a sunny window is more relaxing than doing it later.

Part of recovery is getting in touch with yourself, your feelings etc. When your sleep and circadian rhythms are out of whack, that is very difficult. It is easy to feel tired and sluggish all the time.

Activity: Here Comes the Sun

Brainstorm 5 ways to bring some light back into your life (at the right times), so you can reset your circadian rhythms.

1. _____

2. _____

3. _____

4. _____

5. _____

Pain Management

Coping with chronic pain in recovery is important because it affects you in many ways. Physically, you are uncomfortable and may have a hard time sleeping. Emotionally you may feel depressed, hopeless and frustrated. Socially you may feel isolated and more impatient with other people. All of these things can make your mood worse and, lead to a relapse.

The first step in coping with chronic pain is to receive a thorough medical evaluation to determine the cause of the pain. In some situations, such as a herniated disc in the spine, it may be important to pay attention to the level and type of pain so that it can serve as a warning signal of impending damage. In other cases, especially when the pain is chronic and the health condition unchangeable, one goal can be to try and keep the chronic pain from being the entire focus of your life. Regardless of the medical condition, there are a number of effective strategies for coping with chronic pain. These techniques generally include:

Relaxation training: Relaxation involves concentration and slow, deep breathing to release tension from muscles and relieve pain. Learning to relax takes practice, but relaxation training can focus attention away from pain and release tension from all muscles. Relaxation tapes are widely available to help you learn these skills.

Biofeedback: Biofeedback is taught by a professional who uses special machines to help you learn to control bodily functions, such as heart rate and muscle tension. As you learn to release muscle tension, the machine immediately indicates success. Biofeedback can be used to reinforce relaxation training. Once the technique is mastered, it can be practiced without the use of the machine.

Visual imagery and distraction: Imagery involves concentrating on mental pictures of pleasant scenes or events or mentally repeating positive words or phrases to reduce pain. Guided imagery tapes are also available.

Distraction techniques: These techniques focus your attention away from negative or painful images to positive mental thoughts. This may include activities as simple as watching television or a favorite movie, reading a book or listening to a book on tape, listening to music, or talking to a friend.

Hypnosis: Hypnosis can be used in two ways to reduce your perception of pain. Some people are hypnotized by a therapist and given a post-hypnotic suggestion that reduces the pain they feel. Others are taught self-hypnosis and can hypnotize themselves when pain interrupts their ability to function. Self-hypnosis is a form of relaxation training.

Learning to relax takes practice, especially when you are in pain, but it is definitely worth it to be able to release muscle tension and start to remove attention from the pain. Try putting yourself in a relaxed, reclining position in a dark room. Either shut your eyes or focus on a point. Then begin to slow down your breathing. Breathe deeply, through your belly. If you find your mind wandering or you are distracted, then think of a word, such as the word "Relax", and think it in time with your breathing...the syllable "re" as you breathe in and "lax" as you breathe out. Do this for a minute or two. Once you feel yourself slowing down, you can begin to use imagery techniques.

Listed below are several imagery and chronic pain control techniques that have been found to be effective. Experiment with some of them the next time you have pain---chronic pain, or even just a headache or kink in your neck.

Activity: Pain Control Techniques

Go online and research each of the following techniques. There are videos available to guide your through most of them. Then write down which ones work best for you.

1. _____

2. _____

3. _____

Altered focus

Focus your attention on any specific non-painful part of the body (hand, foot, etc.) and alter sensation in that part of the body. For example, imagine your hand warming up. This will take the mind away from focusing on the source of your pain, such as your back pain. This can also be accomplished by having someone give you a massage. You will be so focused on the good feeling, that you will temporarily forget the pain.

Dissociation

As the name implies, you mentally separate the painful body part from the rest of the body, or imagining the body and mind as separate, with the chronic pain distant from your mind. For example, imagine your painful lower back sitting on a chair across the room and tell it to stay sitting there, far away from your mind.

Sensory splitting

This technique involves dividing the sensation (pain, burning, pins and needles) into separate parts. For example, if the leg pain or back pain feels hot to you, focus just on the sensation of the heat and not on the hurting.

Mental anesthesia

This involves imagining an injection of numbing anesthetic (like Novocain) into the painful area, such as imagining a numbing solution being injected into your low back. Similarly, you may then wish to imagine a soothing and cooling ice pack being placed onto the area of pain. Alternatively, you can imagine your brain producing massive amount of endorphins, the natural pain relieving substance of the body, and having them flow to the painful parts of your body. Visualize them going from your brain, down your neck and out to the painful part of your body.

Symbolic imagery

Envision a symbol that represents your chronic pain, such as a loud, irritating noise or a painfully bright light bulb. Gradually reduce the irritating qualities of this symbol, for example dim the light or reduce the volume of the noise, thereby reducing the pain.

Positive imagery

Focus your attention on a pleasant place that you could imagine going - the beach, mountains, etc. - where you feel carefree, safe and relaxed. For upper back tension you may imagine someone rubbing your back and taking the pain away. With practice, you will find that the relaxation and chronic pain control effects become stronger and last longer after you are done.

Massage

Massage therapy can provide pain relief, soothe stiff sore muscles, and reduce inflammation and swelling. As muscle tension is relaxed and circulation is increased, pain is decreased.

TENS Units

TENS (transcutaneous electrical nerve stimulation) utilizes low-voltage electrical stimulation to the nerves to block pain signals to the brain. Electrodes are placed on the skin and emit the electrical charge. This is used primarily for chronic, localized pain. Although it sounds barbaric, it actually feels pretty good. Depending on the intensity of the current (which you control) it can feel like a gentle vibration to a gentle tapping.

Biofeedback

Biofeedback uses a combination of relaxation, visualization, and signals from a monitor to gain control of pain. When you are in pain, your heart rate and blood pressure rise, and your breathing often becomes more rapid and shallow. In biofeedback, you wear a blood pressure monitor and/or heart rate monitor, and learn how to relax and reduce your blood pressure, muscle tension, and heart rate

This specialized type of training allows you to gain control over physiological reactions that are ordinarily unconscious and automatic. Athletes use heart rate monitors to tell them if they are training hard enough. Anger management classes may use heart rate or blood pressure monitors. This is because heart rate, respiration rate and blood pressure are all good indicators of overall stress. Although it's not a sure cure, biofeedback helps many people with chronic pain, tension, anxiety, chronic insomnia, fatigue, depression, and hyperactivity. It requires intensive participation as you learn to control such normally involuntary ("autonomic") functions as heart rate, breathing, and blood pressure.

There are a lot of expensive, fancy machines that can be used, but a heart-rate monitor and attention to breathing can also do wonders. Heart rate monitors help identify when your heart rate and respiration increase as the result of a stressor, and can help you learn to slow your heart rate and breathing thereby relaxing and reducing stress.

Biofeedback is a "mind over matter" form of therapy that has only recently begun to filter into mainstream medicine. Although Eastern Medicine has long been convinced that the mind could influence the body, either causing or curing illness, the concept fell into disrepute as Western medicine began to discover alternative explanations. It was only when modern instrumentation made it possible to measure subtle changes in our unconscious physical reactions that Western medicine once more turned its attention to the mind-body connection.

Note: If you use a pacemaker or have a severe heart disorder, check with your doctor before using a biofeedback device that has any sort of electrical current or magnetic component. Even though no problems have been reported to date, there is a chance that they may affect your pacemaker or damage your heart. And, like always, regardless of known pre-existing conditions, you should always inform your doctor of any alternative (or conventional) treatments you elect to begin. Also, if you are pregnant, some research has indicated high levels of electromagnetic radiation can be harmful to the baby.

Cold

Cold therapy is a preferred treatment for some people as opposed to heat therapy. The cold works to relieve pain by numbing nerve endings in affected areas of the body. It also decreases activity of body cells and slows blood flow, resulting in decreased inflammation. Cold compresses, wrapping a plastic bag filled with ice cubes, or frozen gel packs can be applied locally.

Warm Water Therapy

Warm water therapy can decrease pain and stiffness. Exercising in a pool, spa, or hot tub may be easier because water takes some weight off painful joints. Some also find relief from the heat and movement provided by warm water exercise.

Managing Your Stress

When you are stressed, you tend to tense your muscles, which often makes chronic pain worse. Stress management is an important component of pain management. While this includes relaxation strategies such as those discussed above, a well-rounded recovery program involves more than relaxation. It also involves managing your daily stress by looking at your schedule, planning your day, and setting your priorities. It means scheduling "appointments" with yourself for taking care of you. Getting a good night's sleep is also important for restoring your energy and spirits. Looking carefully at the activities you schedule for yourself and learning to say "no" to some requests for your time is important to do so you do not overload yourself.

Remember to use these techniques on a daily basis to prevent worsening of chronic pain as well.

Relaxation

Unlike pain management, relaxation is not related to any specific source of distress. Relaxation techniques do nothing to change or block feelings about events, they are simply designed to help give your mind and body a time-out. You may get going in so many different directions, you feel like you do not know which way is up. Relaxation techniques help clear your mind and find your "center" or get "grounded." Relaxation techniques can also help you identify and address sources of wasted energy in your life. When you feel like you are going in a million different directions, you are less efficient about making decisions or accomplishing tasks. Further, when you are physically tense, you are using needless energy to maintain that muscle tension we all know so well. Relaxation techniques can be as simple as taking a deep breath, taking a step back and re-approaching a situation with a clear head or from a more objective point of view.

Diaphragmatic Breathing

This is a method of deep breathing designed to maximize oxygen intake and impurity discharge. It forms the foundation for pain management and many other types of relaxation such as meditation, biofeedback and progressive muscular relaxation. First, either sit up straight or lay down. Slouching decreases the effectiveness of this technique. Inhale deeply through the nose, for a count of 4, feeling the stomach then the chest. Then exhale through the mouth for a count of 4, pressing the air out from the bottom of the stomach up through the chest. As you inhale, hear the air coming in through your nose, and notice the tension as your belly expands. With each exhale, try to let your body become progressively limp and relaxed. Repeat this several times then rest for a minute or two, breathing slowly still inhaling through your nose and exhaling through your mouth.

Stretching

People carry a lot of stress in their muscles. That achy, stiff, tired feeling can really drain emotional and physical energy. When stretching for relaxation, make sure your movements are smooth and controlled. The key is to start slowly and gently. As your muscles warm up, you will be able to get a better stretch. Stretching will help relieve muscle imbalances and release the tension from the day. Pay attention to stretching your neck, upper back, lower back, and hamstrings. There are many videos online that can walk you through stretching activities if you would like a guide. As of this writing, there are even free apps for that ☺

Reflexology and Massage

Reflexology is an ancient healing art based upon the premise that, by massaging certain pressure points, you can relieve energy blocks, or deposits and thus reduce distress. However, the current scheme linking various parts of the foot with specific parts of the body got its start in the early 1900's, by Dr. William H. Fitzgerald. In the 1930's, Eunice Ingham, a nurse refined the system, identifying especially sensitive areas she called "reflex points" and creating a map of the body as represented on the feet.

Although reflexologists don't promise to cure the underlying cause, they do believe that their technique can alleviate a wide variety of problems, as well as headache (tension and migraine), premenstrual syndrome, digestive disorders, and chronic pain. While many people report positive effects from reflexology, there have been no major clinical trials to verify its effectiveness. It is recommended as an adjunct to traditional therapy.

Unlike massage, which involves a generalized rubbing motion, reflexology uses gentle to intense pressure to specific points of your foot, ear or hand that correspond to your health problems. You can learn to do reflexology for yourself by having your practitioner demonstrate the techniques appropriate for your problem.

In its early years, reflexology was thought to work in much the same way as traditional Chinese acupuncture. Practitioners maintained that a life force, or vital energy, flows along channels from the feet and hands to all areas of the body, and that any blockage in the flow will eventually lead to dysfunction. Stimulation of reflex points in the foot could, they believed, break up blockages in the flow further along the channel. There is still much speculation to the actual way that reflexology works. Some say that manipulation of the feet reduces the amount of lactic acid in the tissues while releasing tiny calcium deposits accumulated in the nerve endings of the feet that stop the flow of energy to corresponding organs. Others speculate that pressure on the reflex points may trigger the release of endorphins, chemicals in the brain that naturally block pain. Some believe that the therapy's benefits are that it stimulates a relaxation response that opens the blood vessels and improves circulation. Regardless of why it works, if it works for you, then wonderful. I personally have found that reflexology works wonders to help relieve the discomfort of my TMJ.

Note: Reflexology and massage are not a substitute for regular medical care. See your doctor for a reliable diagnosis of the symptoms for which you're seeking treatment.

Cued Progressive Muscular Relaxation (CPMR)

Building upon what you have already learned, cued progressive muscular relaxation starts with diaphragmatic breathing to increase the flow of oxygen to the body and   decrease toxins. The entire process takes from 20 minutes to an hour. Begin by choosing a "cue" which you will continue to repeat to yourself every time you exhale and go into a relaxation phase. Just like you used to get a knot in your stomach when you were in school, and the teacher would say, "Pop Quiz." Your mind automatically responded to the words and initiated a stress reaction. CPMR teaches you to do the same thing in reverse, by training your body to relax.

Prepare for this exercise by creating the most comfortable environment possible, paying attention to smells, lighting, temperature, sounds and general comfort. CPMR will begin at one end of your body and work toward the other end and from the center to your fingertips. Ideally, you will contract and relax every single muscle in your body 4-6 times.

A typical script with the keyword "relax" may look something like:
Now that you are comfortable, concentrate on your breathing. As you breathe in, feel the oxygen flowing to all parts of your body bringing energy. As you exhale, feel all of the tension leave your body and you become more relaxed. Now, tense all of the muscles of your scalp. Feel the tightness. Tighten up your scalp a little more. Hold and feel the sensation. Now, relax. . . Feel the muscles release. Relax. . . feel the blood flow to your scalp and relax. Notice the difference between tense and relaxed as you once again tighten the muscles of your scalp. Tighter. Feel the effort required to tighten those muscles further. Now relax. . . Feel the muscles loose and let the blood warm and nourish them. Now relax them further. Feel your head become heavier as you relax and let it sink into the pillow. . .

You would repeat this script for every single set of muscles from your head to your toes--- envisioning the tension leaving through your fingers and feet.

Meditation

The calming mental exercises of meditation are useful for treating stress, tension, anxiety, and panic, reducing high blood pressure and relieving chronic pain. Many people have also found it helpful for headaches and respiratory problems. Each session typically takes 15 to 20 minutes, once in the morning and again in the evening. Advocates recommend scheduling your sessions for the same times each day, before rather than after eating.

Meditation involves the focused concentration of your mind on an object, idea, image or state of being.   Meditation is a deliberate clearing of the mind in order to create a sense of mental tranquility and physical relaxation. There are many different approaches to meditation, each with its own specialized techniques. As you learned earlier, pain relief is another of meditation's more successful applications. While it can't completely eliminate discomfort, it does help people cope by reducing their tension and anxiety.

Cautions: If you find that meditation is increasing your anxiety or depression, or that it just doesn't feel right, stop.

Creative Visualization

Creative visualization has been used by pain management therapists, counselors and sports psychologists to help people achieve their goals. By introducing an idea into your subconscious, theory says you will consciously be more apt to do things toward that goal and believe in yourself. For instance, a diver may rehearse the perfect dive in her head each day before going to practice, or each night before going to sleep to "prime" her mind to send the right signals to her body. In pain management, you either visualize something taking the pain away, or their body removing the pain from itself.

Another form of creative visualization is called guided imagery. In this technique, you are lead through a scripted scene such as a forest. You incorporate the sense of hearing, touch, sight and smell. Not only do you attend to what is around you, but you also attend to yourself. You may be instructed to "see" the trees, their plentiful leaves that rustle in the cool breeze. Feel the crisp temperature in the air. Smell the crisp breeze. The script is very detailed with the goal of transporting you to a relaxing place.

Activity: Guided Imagery

- ✓ First start by actually noticing your surroundings with all of your senses.
- ✓ What do you hear?
- ✓ What do you see?
- ✓ Look around. What else do you see?
- ✓ What do you smell?
- ✓ What do you feel?

As you get better at noticing the world with all of your senses, then you will be better able to transport yourself back there using guided imagery.

Art therapy

Art therapy has long been used to help people get in touch with and express their subconscious. It also is a way of conveying ideas without using words. Art therapy often appeals to people who are more intuitive in personality and visual or kinesthetic in learning style. Highly structured things like coloring books do not allow for much self-expression (and there is always that doctrine of staying in the lines).

One of the first things people notice when looking at art, is the pieces creativity. Whether it is a picture or a complex equation, people begin drawing conclusions about the creator. Go to the library or bookstore and look at some of the book covers. Do you find yourself trying to identify what the picture is first?

The next thing people may try to figure out is what was trying to be conveyed. Publishers have very real reasons for choosing the book covers that they do. Most books are purchased (compared with others in the same genre) based on the feeling the cover and title convey. This includes the picture, title and colors. Which book would you be more inclined to buy "How to write a book from start to finish" or "Book idea to Bestseller"

The same is true about the way you decorate your office and your home. What messages does it convey? A colleague of mine once told a patient that the way you look on the outside and maintain your personal space reflects how you feel on the inside. It is very true. When I feel stressed and overwhelmed, my environment tends to get a bit—errrr--- messy. I often try to make myself feel more in control by cleaning and organizing.

Color and Texture

Whenever the artist can choose the color, it is a vehicle for further, subtle expression. For instance:

- ✓ Yellow is supposed to energize. It also is thought to make people hungry.
- ✓ Blue is calming and cool
- ✓ Red represents passionate feelings from love to anger
- ✓ Black often represents death, doom, or the unknown
- ✓ White is associated with purity happiness
- ✓ Pastels tend to represent less intense feelings that primary colors.

Which colors make you feel relaxed and content? _____

Much like you, art can have many dimensions. By changing the texture, a color can convey a very different feeling. Even a color as benign as brown---compare the image of a fluffy brown bunny to a brick fireplace or even mud. Collages, paintings, sewing etc. often have various texture possibilities from rough and gritty to soft and silky. Sometimes the textures are merely used to recreate reality, other times there is more meaning. Remember, every event and picture is subject to individual interpretation.

Activity: What Is Your Environment Saying

What colors do you usually choose? _____

_____

Do you prefer sharp or rounded corners/ modern or fluffy furniture? _____

_____

What can you do to make your environment more relaxing and/or cheerful?

_____

_____

_____

_____

_____

_____

_____

_____

_____

_____

_____

Collages

Collages are a fun way of expressing your creativity. You can use just about anything, create it in any format and represent many different themes. You can use pictures, paint and brushes or, my personal favorite--finger paint! Making collages is even easier in the modern age of computers. You can integrate, color, action, sound, scan-in images, add digital pictures, enhance or reduce the size, definition or color of things. Experiment.

Activity: Make a Collage

Possible Themes: Who am I

What do I want

What brings me happiness

What am I grateful for

What does _____ represent.

Music Therapy

Music can have a great effect on your mood due to the beat, the words and any associations you may have to that song. Music, or sounds, can be very soothing. Try going to the library and checking out tapes/cds of spring rain, waterfalls or some other sound that is soothing. (Many crib toys now have babbling brook or spring rain sounds in them).

Activity: Using Music

For each feeling listed, name a song that elicits that feeling in you:

1.   Energized: _____

2.   Happy/content: _____

3.   In love: _____

4.   Bitter/vengeful: _____

5.   Depressed/sad: _____

Many times people "wallow" in their depression by turning out the lights, pulling the covers over their heads and listening to sad music. In the short term, there is absolutely nothing wrong with that; nevertheless, set some time limits (i.e. one afternoon). Other ways to use music are to get in a certain mood, such as before going out, while working out or before a romantic evening. You can also keep relaxing tapes in the car for when traffic starts getting to you.

Aromatherapy

Just like colors, textures and virtually anything else, scents hold special meaning for people based upon their previous association. The following are several examples of different scents and what they are supposed to do. 90% of reality is what we do with our perceptions, so if you believe that scents and fragrances have no effect, then they will probably fail to work on you. Likewise, your previous associations with these smells may alter the effects, for instance, you may have previously associated ginger with negative feelings or exhaustion due to the fact that most people eat ginger-based foods to relieve nausea. Therefore, ginger may not work for you.

Essential oils used in aromatherapy can be added to candles, room sprays, massage oils and lotions, humidifiers or diffusers. Essential oils are very strong, so make sure to do your research, especially when applying essential oils to the body. There are many websites and books that can help you discover combinations and mixing instructions for essential oils based upon the desired outcome.

Purchasing and mixing essential oils is often cost-prohibitive, messy and time consuming. A cheaper, less messy way is to try pre-mixed combinations of the essential oils (such as Healing Garden), or, for the more common fragrances like ginger, cedar and pine find them in their natural form, smell it and see what you think.

Scents

The bolded scents are those which can be found in most spice racks. Add about a tablespoon to 8 oz. of boiling water and inhale the steam and/or wait until the water cools to a tolerable temperature and dampen a towel to apply to your chest or face. Some, like rosemary, become very aromatic when combined with lotion or hair conditioners and used as an exfoliant/circulation stimulant. Again, always consult your physician, and NEVER ingest essential oils.

When dealing with fragrances other than essential oils which are often 400 times more powerful than the natural source, experiment. Place fresh rose petals in a zipped, mesh sack in the dryer with your darks (just in case there is any color bleed). You will dry the flowers and freshen your laundry at the same time. Use pine cones to absorb essential oils and place them in a decorative basket on your counter (Make sure to cover it with lace, or mesh if you have animals or children, because ingesting essential oils can be deadly).

1. Angelica Root: Relieves fatigue, migraines, anxiety,

2. Sweet Basil: Brightens mood, strengthen nervous system, improve mental clarity and memory, relieve headache and sinusitis

3. Bay Leaf: Relieves depression and burnout/exhaustion

4. Bergamot: Balances nervous system, relieves anxiety, improves quality of sleep, relieves hopelessness/helplessness

5. Black Pepper: Increases circulation, relieves stiffness

6. Cardamon: Relieves mental strain and fatigue, aphrodisiac, mood elevator

7. Carrot Seed: Eases anxiety and stress

8. Catnip: Relaxation and (of course) happy kitties

9. Cedar: Calms emotions (try smelling cedar chips in the gardening department).

10. Chamomile: Sedative, relieves anxiety, improves quality of sleep (tea)

11. Clary Sage: Relieves stress and tension, improves quality of sleep, aphrodisiac

12. Clove: Aphrodisiac, relieve tension, worry, guilt and hostility

13. Coriander: Helps improve sleep, removes feelings of self-doubt, and irritability

14. Cypress: Immune stimulant, increases circulation, relieves grief, jealousy

15. Fennel: Deals with mental, creative and emotional blocks, and resistance to change.

16. Fir (Balsam): Relieves anxiety and stress through helping ground one mentally (especially common at Christmas as this is one kind of pine tree)

17. Frankincense: Elevates mind and spirit, helps reconnect with repressed feelings

18. Geranium: Relieves fatigue, nervous tension, discontentment, heartache, fear

19. Ginger: Stimulates appetite, helps relieve confusion and nausea.

20. Helichrysum: Helps people with addictions, grief, panic, burnout and emotional sensitivity. Produces a sense of calm

21. Jasmine: relieves depression, labor pains, and provides a sense of calm when dealing with bitterness, guilt and repressed feelings.

22. Juniper Berry: Improves mental clarity, and improves empathy

23. Lavender: Promotes restful sleep, calming influence

24. Lemon: Uplifting, helps energize and relieve apathy

25. Lemongrass: Helps relieve stress related exhaustion

26. Lime: Uplifting and cheering

27. Marjoram: Promote restful sleep, help ease migraines, calms and helps relieve anger. Use as the moisture on a moist-heat heating pad.

28. Myrrh: Helps relieve lack of spiritual connection and emotional blocks.

29. Neroli: Good for anxiety relief

30. Nutmeg: Invigorates and stimulates the mind and helps regain focus.

31. Sweet Orange: Brightens mood, relieves apathy and burnout

32. Oregano: Energizes mind and body and helps relieve headaches

33. Peppermint: Improves energy, mood and relieves exhaustion (mints)

34. Pine: Increases energy and repels fleas

35. Rosemary: Improves mental clarity and memory, relieves headache

36. Sanadalwood: Relieves apathy and melancholy

37. Spearmint: Eases nausea and headaches; energizes and relieves fatigue (gum)

38. Thyme: Relieves fatigue and may help with bronchitis

39. Ylang-Ylang: Aphrodisiac, mood brightener, promotes restful sleep, relieves anxiety. Very "flowery" sweet smell

Activity: Using Aromatherapy

Circle the different ways you might use aromatherapy.

Atomizer/Diffuser   Massage Oil/Lotion   Body Spray   Candles

On a Cloth Tucked into a Drawer   On Your Pillow   Added to Fabric Softener

In the Return Air Filters   Vacuum Sachets   Other: _____

Journaling

Journaling appeals to some people, especially visual learners. Other people despise it. This is important to know not only for relaxation and coping, but also if you ever want to enter counseling. Many self-help books have fill-in the blank exercises or structured writings such as: "Write a page about how you felt when ..." If even thinking about doing that exercise makes you cringe, journaling is probably not for you. You may prefer to talk it out with someone. If you do not have someone there on a regular basis, you can talk into a recorder. I talk to my dog, but that is a whole different issue!

The following are examples of different journaling styles that may fit better with different personality types. Remember that journaling is a method of releasing pent up feelings, but often does not change the way you feel or change the situation. Journaling can be used to keep track of good times and memories. It is also a way to get in-touch with your true self. You are often so swept up in day-to-day activities that you fail to think about how you feel about things or appreciate precious moments. Journaling gives you an opportunity to reflect.

Hint: When reflecting on and re-reading journals, remember that often what is not written is just as important (if not more important) that what is written.

Journal Examples

Activity: Journal Example 1:

Today I feel good about:

Today I was afraid when/of:

Today I learned:

Right now I am feeling:

Today is different than yesterday because:

Today my sources of support were:

Today I was accepting of:

Activity: Journal Example 2:

This week _____ happened.

My main feeling this week was:

My week was _____ beacause:

I remember the following 5 things with fondness/joy:

The coping skills/wellness strategies I used were:

The coping skills/wellness strategies I wish I had used were:

This week I reflected on:

Journal Example 3:

Try writing a theme entry relating to one of the following:

- ✓ Perceptions: Today it seemed like everyone was in a bad mood. It seemed like nobody was paying attention to anyone but themselves. . .

- ✓ Feelings: List all of the feelings you felt today and all of the reasons you felt that way.

- ✓ Memories: Write about what your life was like as a child, or your favorite holiday traditions etc.

- ✓ Self-awareness / Self-reflection: reflect on what you did today and how that coincided with your values and overall purpose. Also write about how you felt today-- emotionally, mentally, spiritually, physically etc.

- ✓ From different voices or roles: child, parent, student, woman. . .
  For instance, how would a child have seen your day? Write it like a ten year old would talk. (i.e. I had to go to school today. It was stupid, but I had fun when I came home. I watched a really neat program on t.v.)

- ✓ Words and sayings which represent the day: For example: A bird in the hand is better than 2 in the bush was true when I got a job offer from one of the places I interviewed. Hakuna Matata really hit home when I realized that I forgot my workbook for physics lab.

  Sample sayings:

  Let go and let God.   One Day at a Time   Fake It Until You Make It

  It's All Good   Serenity   Hope   Courage   Patience   Compassion

  Other: _____

Letter Writing

As a society, we often are so caught up in our lives, afraid of rejection, or so full of anger and resentment, that we fail to say all that needs to be said. Letter writing is a good way to say everything that needs to be said to those people who are no longer available, if you are too afraid to say it to person's face, or when the moment has passed. Write in the voice of the person who has something to say: You as a child, a parent, etc. These letters are not necessarily grievances. They can be words of appreciation.

Activity: Letter Writing

Write an uncensored letter to yourself and then re-read it and reframe all of the anger and hurt, address all of the fears and try to gain self-acceptance. This can be a useful coping skill because it helps you learn to use cognitive restructuring in order to change the way you feel about a situation.

_____

_____

_____

_____

_____

_____

_____

_____

_____

_____

_____

Humor

Humor is a form of relaxation and creativity. Humor lets you experience joy even when faced with adversity. People who are comedians are also sharing their creative view of the world. This section describes the effects of using humor as a self-care tool to maximize happiness and lessen distress.

Finding humor in a situation and laughing freely with others can be a powerful antidote to distress. Your sense of humor gives you the ability to experience joy, release tension, stimulate the immune system, enhance perceptual flexibility (get outside the box), and renew spiritual energy. Laughter momentarily banishes feelings of anger and fear and provides moments of feeling carefree, lighthearted, hopeful and energetic. When your energy is depleted and you feel like you have nothing left, finding humor in your work and life can lift your spirits and your energy levels.

Stress has been shown to create unhealthy physiological changes such as high blood pressure, muscle tension, immunosuppression. In 1979, believing that negative emotions had a negative impact on people's health, therapists wondered whether the opposite was also true. Could laughter improve health? Several studies indicated that the experience of laughter lowers cortisol levels and increases immunity. So, the short answer is yes. Laughter also triggers the release of neurotransmitters in the brain that can improve overall mood.

Laughter is cathartic. That is, it can provide a release of emotional tension. Laughter, crying, raging, and trembling all help you get rid of negative energy.

Humor empowers you by giving you a different perspective on your problems. As comedian Bill Cosby is fond of saying, "If you can laugh at it, you can survive it." You cannot control events in your external world but you can control how you view these events and the emotional response you choose to have to them.

Frequently people are too immersed in a problem to find any humor in it. It can help to seek out others with that special flair for seeing the funny or ironic side of a situation. Another way to keep laughing is to stay in touch with your "inner child", that playful nature that all people have but perhaps fail to acknowledge due to the seriousness of our work. Spend the day acting like a child. Build a blanket fort and watch cartoons all day.

Humor and laughter can be effective self-care tools to cope with stress. They help you feel happy emotions, be creative, improve your immune system, be more open to others and be more productive when it is time to "get to business." An ability to laugh at situations or problems can give you a feeling of power which can foster a positive and hopeful attitude.

Activity: Laughter

List 3 comedians you find funny? _____

_____

Review humorous sites on the internet such as Philosoraptor, Grumpy Cat and Science Cat

_____

_____

_____

40 Ways to Have Challenge Your Mind and Express Your Creativity

1. Play a board-game: Clue, Scrabble, Trivial Pursuit, Mind Trap, Chess

2. Cook a new meal

3. Creatively frost a cake or bake it in a special cake form (heart, bunny, race car)

4. Go hiking in a new park: find your way in and out

5. Create greeting cards on your computer

6. Create a new web page

7. Get the Book of Questions by Gregory Stock and discuss with friends

8. Plan a party

9. Find a social problem and create a plan on how to improve the situation

10. Write a grant

11. Surf the Internet and learn as much about a single topic as you can

12. Start taking leisure classes

13. Turn one of your hobbies into a business

14. Sewing: cross-stitch, needlepoint, quilting, crochet, knitting, embroidery

15. Decorate something ordinary: bulletin board, photo album,

16. Paint your room (or use wallpaper attached to the wall with thumbtacks)

17. Choreograph an aerobics, dance or exercise routine

18. Listen to a book on tape while you run or walk

19. Each night at dinner, discuss one current event

20. Plan the most romantic date you can think of (then do it)

21. Hang-out at the bookstore and read books which represent your different interests

22. Start a "coffee club" to gather and discuss books, ideas

23. Plan a scavenger hunt for you and your friends

24. Teach your dog a new trick

25. Collages

26. Flower arranging

27. Invent something to solve your most nagging problem

28. Make soaps/lotions/candles with your favorite scent

29. Paint/color/draw

30. Help a civic organization decorate for an event

31. Write poetry, short stories

32. Create a new recipe

33. Join an acting/drama club

34. Join a choir

35. Take pictures of nature, weddings, parties etc.

36. Redecorate a room in your house

37. Gardening, landscaping--make your patio a sight to behold

38. Create a new game and teach your friends/kids how to play

39. Crossword puzzles

40. Be a freelance writer for the local newspaper

My favorite relaxation activities are: _____

_____

_____

_____

_____

Chapter 8: Creating Safety

You thought about this some in the section on relaxation. Now you are going to expand the definition of safety to include not only physical safety, but emotional safety from criticism (including self-criticism). When you are safe, you can more easily explore both the good and the bad (and sometimes even the ugly).

Environmental Safety/Safety from Others

Feeling physically safe is probably what you thought of when you read the chapter title. This one is, in many ways, the easiest to do. What helps you feel safe depends in large part on your experiences up until now. For example, my dogs have always made me feel safe. Unlike a burglar alarm that can lose power, dogs are pretty reliable. On the other hand, if you had a bad experience with a dog, then dogs may not help you to feel safe. The next activity will help you identify what you need to make you feel safe in your environment.

Activity: Physical Safety

Imagine yourself in each of the following places. What do you need in order to feel safe? What things do you need to be there (dogs, cell phone, flashlight…)? What do you need to be able to see? Describe why you feel safe (i.e. Doors are locked. Neighbors are home..)

When I am at home during the day _____

_____

When I am at home after dark_____

_____

When I am sleeping _____

_____

When I am at work _____

_____

_____

Personal Safety/Safety from Yourself

Once you are physically safe, it is time to start thinking about making that space in your head safe too. You are likely your own worst critic and your beat yourself up mercilessly for not only the things that are your fault, but also the things that are not your fault and things that are out of your control. You learned that from somewhere. Someone or someones in your life criticized you and you didn't feel good enough. You are still holding onto that message now. All of that negative, critical or undermining self-talk can make it really hard to start getting honest and recover. Think about it. Which person is more likely to take on a challenge…someone who is repeatedly told they are a failure, stupid and   incompetent, or a person who has been told they are capable, but fallible at the same time?

Nobody is perfect. Part of personal safety is accepting and learning from your mistakes and flaws instead of punishing and holding yourself hostage for them.

Activity: Identifying Negative Self Statements

People have said things to you in the past that have probably "stuck." If they were good things, then great. This activity is designed to help you identify those negative things people have said to you that you continue to replay in your head. (For example—You are stupid. You are lazy. You are a slob. If you would have tried harder….) Write down the negative statement, then write a rebuttal.

Negative Statement _____

Rebuttal _____

Negative Statement _____

Rebuttal _____

Negative Statement _____

Rebuttal _____

Negative Statement _____

Rebuttal _____

To this point, you have learned about

- ✓ Addiction---What it is and why it develops---A last ditch effort to numb the pain you were unable or unwilling to deal with. This pain can be emotional, physical or the result of disrupted brain chemicals from recreational use or poor self-care…

- ✓ How addiction has impacted you emotionally, physically, in your relationships and in your way of thinking and viewing the world.

- ✓ What your needs and wants are now. What makes you happy? What helps you to relax? What do you want to be different 6 months from now.

- ✓ How to start setting goals to achieve those needs and wants

- ✓ How to nurture yourself in order to build up your energy reserves through nutrition, sleep, exercise, understanding yourself and relaxing.

- ✓ What your story is to date…

In the next few sections you are going to explore how thoughts can trigger emotions, and how to deal with them in a healthy, non-destructive manner. Remember, you are a product of your past. You did what you needed to do, with the tools you had at that time to survive. If nobody taught you how to trust yourself, take care of yourself, or cope with the unfairness of life, then you never learned it. Unfortunately, we learn what we live. That was then, and this is now.

The first part of your journey has involved caring enough about yourself to care for yourself, and starting to get honest about what you want and how you feel. As I said before, that probably has been very hard, and may have caused you to feel guilty, regretful, angry, depressed, and/or resentful. All of these are very normal emotions. What matters is what you do with them. If you let them fester and eat away at your heart and mind…well…that's probably not going to be helpful. If instead, you figure out how to deal with it, you can free up that energy to be used for something else.

In the next few sections you will start evaluating some of your assumptions about life and people to decide whether your beliefs about it, them and yourself are accurate.

Perceptions

"Life is 10% reality and 90% what you make of it."

No two people are exactly alike. For that reason, no two people perceive the same situation exactly the same way. From birth, you have taken information and fit it into schemas (internal ideas about the world). You form ideas about people, places and events based on these past experiences. These ideas or schemas shape your reaction to, and interpretation of, the world. They act as filters through which information is processed. When information is new or unexpected, you have to either: 1) do some creative remembering to make the event fit into the current schemas, 2) create a new schema to store the information, or 3) change the schema to accommodate the new information.

Schemas allow you to predict what will happen next. For instance, you have a schema about stop lights. From past experience you have learned that after a stop light turns yellow, it turns red. If there was a glitch in the system and the light went from yellow to green, that would be unexpected. You would have to either assimilate that into your current schema--"I must have daydreamed through the red-cycle" or accommodate your schema to fit the situation--"Sometimes yellow lights will turn green."

Think about a time when you experienced an unexpected event and figured it was just a fluke. This is your mind's way of fitting the experience into the current schema. When your entire set of beliefs and expectations about a person change, you are changing the existing schema. People have "stereotypes" or schemas about almost everything.

Activitiy: Schemas

Identify 3 times when something has happened that did not fit your expectations.

_____

_____

_____

How did you deal with those situations?

_____

_____

_____

Stereotypes are type of schema. In general, based on your past experience, stereotypes help you predict behaviors and events. For example, when you think of a hospital, what do you think of? If you walked into a hospital that was dirty and disorganized, but all of the staff were friendly, would that fit your schema? Probably not. You might think of it as a fluke. You might attribute it to the particular hospital system. How would that affect what you expected the next time you went to a hospital?

List one example in each category of a stereotype you hold:

People _____

Places _____

Things _____

For example, I believe that most people are inherently good and their poor choices are, or have been the most effective way they have found to fill a need that they have, given their current life situation and available coping skills. This schema reduces my stress and helps me help people. If I viewed people I as self-centered, lazy criminals who just want to take the easy way out, I would have a much harder and more stressful time.

Attributions

Let's take the discussion a bit further and look at attributions. Attributions are characteristics assigned to those people, places and events, and have three aspects. They are either: Global or specific; stable or changeable, and internal or external. Global means the characteristic is all-encompassing—it represents the whole person or situation. Specific, on the other hand means that the characteristic does not necessarily mean anything else about the person. For instance, if someone keeps a messy closet, a global attribution would be to say the person is an all-around slob! A specific attribution would be to say that s/he keeps a sloppy closet. The next dimension is stable vs. changeable. Stable attributions are everlasting. They are the same across time and situations. Changeable attributions mean that depending on the time and place, this characteristic may not apply. Going back to the messy closet--- A stable attribution would be that the person always has a messy closet. On the other hand, a changeable attribution would give a little leeway--"The closet is messy right now because s/he just got a new job and has been exhausted." The last type of attribution is internal vs. external. Internal attributions place the blame on the person--s/he is a slob, whereas external attributions are assigned to objects or events--The closet is sloppy.

You make attributions about other people's behavior all of the time. When someone trips as they walk, you may assume that they are very clumsy. That is a global, internal and stable attribution. Global because you assumed that the person is clumsy in generally everything. Internal because you assumed that it was the person and not something in the street that caused them to trip. Stable because you assumed that the person is always this way. Think how quickly you make attributions about people (and they make attributions about you) every day.

One problem with attributions is that you may let them guide your beliefs or interpretations of a situation and create a self-fulfilling prophesy. When you expect a certain type of person to act a certain way, you often: 1) bring out that behavior from that person, and 2) assign meanings to the person's behavior to support what you expect...

Your attributions about yourself play a large part in your self-esteem. Remember, self-esteem is how you feel about your skills and abilities in comparison with what you believe you should be. Unfortunately that is not always very simple. As Shakespeare said, "Every man's an actor and all the world, his stage." As humans with multi-faceted lives you take on many roles. Roles are those "scripts" or personas you take on in your daily life. When you change one area in your life, it affects all other areas.

Consider how many roles you fulfill and how much energy each of those roles requires. Remember that you are not "just a banker" or "just a girlfriend." You are many things to many people. People's schemas change as their roles do. For instance, what is important to a mother is different than what is important to a business-woman. Nevertheless, there are many people who are both mothers and business-women.

Activity: Attributions

Review the roles listed below. State what title you give this role for yourself and describe the schema associated with each of these roles. For instance, for gender, write either male or female and describe the characteristics you associate with that title.

1.   Gender: _____

_____

2.   Race/Ethnicity: _____

_____

3.   Socioeconomic status: _____

_____

4.   Occupation: _____

_____

5.   Religion: _____

_____

Other roles and schemas to consider:

Student   Employee   Employer   Teacher   Friend   Role Model

Parent   Brother/Sister Aunt/Uncle   Grandparent Daughter/Son   Athlete

Sorority/Fraternity Member   Spouse   Other: _____

Do these roles ever conflict? _____

If they do, what do you do to fix the situation? _____

_____

How do your attributions impact your mood and attitude? _____

_____

_____

How could you improve the way your attributions impact your mood and attitude?

_____

_____

What positive global attributions do you have about yourself? (Example: I am nice)

_____

_____

What negative global attributions do you have about yourself? (Example: I am a disappointment)

_____

_____

Do those global, negative attributions reflect how you feel about yourself? Yes No

If yes, how can you change them? _____

_____

_____

_____

Cognitive Restructuring

Literally, changing your thoughts, cognitive restructuring can help change the way you feel about, think about or perceive a situation. For example, when you think that something is dangerous, your body will respond with either fear or anger (fight or flight). Primitive animals like cats and dogs are not able to rationally evaluate a situation. They react to a stimulus. A loud noise, for instance, will usually signal "danger" to an animal, who will then fight or flee. (Have you ever had a dog attack the vacuum cleaner?). As humans, with the ability to rationalize, we may initially startle, but then, based on our prior experiences, we can determine if it is worth getting upset about.

There are several methods of cognitive restructuring, the ABCs and optimism are the most popular. Remember that your personality type strongly affects which techniques are helpful. If you hate to write things down you may not have much success with the ABCs unless you modify it. Suggestions have been included, but as long as the intent of the method is preserved, many variations are possible.

Since dysfunctional behavior, including substance abuse, is caused in large part by faulty thinking, the role of therapy is to teach you how to change the negative or self-defeating automatic thoughts that you have. You can learn to notice these thoughts and change them, but it is difficult at first. Cognitive therapy challenges your understanding of yourself and your situation. Therapists, coaches and sponsors can help you become more objective about your thinking, and recognize thinking errors or faulty logic brought about by automatic thoughts. An automatic thought is one that happens almost without thought. For example, a light turns red, the automatic thought is "stop." You don't have to consciously try to think about that a red light means. Unfortunately, many people have incorrect automatic thoughts such as "Nobody can be trusted." "I am a complete failure." Once a specific faulty thought is identified, you will be challenged to look at alternative ways of seeing the same event.

Cognitive therapy helps you understand why you think and react the way you do to things in your current life. While it does not focus on the past per se, cognitive approaches help you understand why you formed the automatic thoughts, and evaluate whether they are still useful or accurate today. For example, young children internalize concepts like success and failure globally and dichotomously. When they do not make the lead in the school play, they may feel like they are a failure. That is, they are a failure as a person at everything. Children have difficulty interpreting events as isolated incidents. If they are not taught to understand that this does not mean they are a failure as a person, then they will maintain this global belief into adulthood. "I must succeed at everything or I am a failure." This global thinking often causes a lot of distress. The good thing is that with some simple techniques, those thinking patterns can be changed. You can go back and re-evaluate the situation with a different perspective, stronger coping skills and more life experiences.

As you explore different feelings, you will be asked to:

- ✓ Explore the automatic beliefs that cause those feelings

- ✓ Accept or reject those beliefs

- ✓ Examine the consequences of your beliefs and decide whether that is a useful reaction. And if not, change the reaction.

Irrational Beliefs

Carl Rogers said that when you evaluate your past "beliefs" which cause you distress, you will often find that they represent irrational, automatic thoughts. These thoughts can be identified because they contain words like: should, should have, must, cannot, everyone, all the time, or they indicate that an event would be completely unbearable, or the worst thing in the world. These types of statements often cause unnecessary worry or guilt and disempower you from realizing your own ability to make choices.

The following is a list of some of the most common irrational thoughts:

1) You must have love, approval and affection from others almost all the time

2) In order to be worthwhile, you must be competent at everything all of the time

3) People who make you feel bad are evil and should be punished

4) If you do not get my own way, awful things will happen.

5) Unbearable emotional misery comes from external pressures

6) If something is dangerous or fearsome, you can't help but to dwell on it.

7) It is easier to avoid than face life's difficulties.

8) Your past must determine your feelings and actions today.

9) It is awful if you do not find quick solutions.

Another way of thinking about it would be to ask yourself---"Is this something I would say to my kids?" or "If my child said this to me, what would my response be?"

Activity: Irrational Thoughts

Take a hard look at yourself. Place a check by the automatic thoughts that often occur in your mind. Now, write a sentence or two disputing each of the above statements.

✓ You must have love, approval and affection from others almost all the time

_____

In order to be worthwhile, you must be competent at everything all of the time

_____

✓ People who make you feel bad are evil and should be punished

_____

✓ If you do not get my own way, awful things will happen.

_____

✓ Unbearable emotional misery comes from external pressures

_____

✓ If something is dangerous or fearsome, you can't help but to dwell on it.

_____

✓ It is easier to avoid than face life's difficulties./ I cannot handle this.

_____

✓ Your past must determine your feelings and actions today.

_____

✓ It is awful if you do not find quick solutions./ I cannot wait.

_____

Cognitive Distortions

Cognitive distortions refer to ways you may take in information, but often only see part of the picture. Unfortunately, when you are angry, depressed or anxious, the distortions are likely to be negative, which compounds your misery. In the following exercises, you will see how irrational or distorted thinking could be helping to keep you miserable.

Activity: Cognitive Distortions

Give an example of how you have used some of these distortions:

✓ Arbitrary inference: Drawing conclusions without sufficient information. Example: You had money on your dresser. It is missing. You assume that your teenager took it without your permission. How do you know this? What evidence do you have?

_____

_____

✓ Selective abstraction: Only seeing what you want (or do not want) to see. Example: A person you are friends with has several good qualities, but your friends regularly point out all of the ways the relationship is destructive. You make excuses or just don't see it.

_____

_____

✓ Over generalization: Generalizing things about one situation to all similar situations. Example: When Paul has been late coming home in the past it has been because he stopped off at the bar and is getting drunk. Therefore, whenever Paul is late getting home, you assume he is at the bar getting drunk.

_____

_____

✓ Magnification and exaggeration. Example: Your roommate leaves dishes in the living room. You get upset with her for *always* leaving stuff *everywhere*. (in reality she rarely does)

_____

_____

✓ Personalization: Everything is either your fault or a personal attack. Example: If you do not call your friend for a week, she assumes it must be because she did something to make you mad and you hate her.

_____

_____

✓ Polarized thinking: all-or-nothing. Example: If I can't do it right the first time, then I shouldn't even try.

_____

_____

The ABCs

You have learned about cognitive distortions and irrational beliefs. Knowing it is one thing. Applying it is something different. This section will help you start identifying your beliefs and pick out which ones are irrational or distorted. The ABCs are designed to help you identify your automatic (and often irrational) thoughts and ways of reacting to situations. Once they are identified, they can be better dealt with.

The basic structure is as follows:
Fill in "A" activating event and "C" consequence first.

> A= Activating event or the stimulus
> B= Your Beliefs (and often unrealized irrational thoughts) about the situation
> C= The Consequence of those thoughts
> D= Determine if your thoughts and consequences are rational/constructive
> E = Evaluate your reactions to determine if they were productive

Example of the ABCs:
A= You get cut off in traffic
B= The person is a lousy driver, rude and has no respect for anyone else.
C= You get angry
D= To determine the effectiveness of your beliefs and consequences, try to make your "unconscious" thoughts "conscious."
E= Evaluate whether the consequence (your reaction) was a beneficial use of your energy. If not, determine how to handle the situation differently.

For people who do not like to write things down, ask yourself the following:

I am _____ about _____
            state the feeling   state the event

Why do I feel this way? _____
                state the first belief

Is this rational (Circle one)? Yes/No because _____
            State the reason it is or is not rational

Why else do I feel this way? _____
              state the second belief

Is this rational (Circle one)? Yes/No because _____
            state the reason it is or is not rational

Or you can attack the reaction first and be done with it.

I am _____ about _____
            state the feeling   state the event

Is it productive to feel this way? Yes/No because _____

A better use of my energy would be to: _____

Activity: ABC Application

Apply the ABCs to the following situations:

A: You get blamed for something that is not your fault

B: _____

C: _____

D: _____

E: _____

A: You are worried about getting your annual evaluation

B: _____

C: _____

D: _____

E: _____

A: _____

B: _____

C: _____

D: _____

E: _____

A: _____

B: _____

C: _____

D: _____

E: _____

A: _____

B: _____

C: _____

D: _____

E: _____

Activity: Challenging Questions Sheet

Below is a list of questions to be used in helping you challenge your maladaptive or problematic beliefs. Not all questions will be appropriate for the belief you choose to challenge. Answer as many questions as you can for the belief you have chosen to challenge below.

Belief:_____

1. What is the evidence for and against this idea?

      FOR: _____

      AGAINST: _____

2. Is your belief a habit or based on facts? _____

3. Are your interpretations of the situation realistic? _____

4. Are you thinking in all-or-none terms? _____

5. Are you using words or phrases that are extreme or exaggerated? (i.e., always, forever, never, need, should, must, can't and every time) _____

Dispute those: _____

_____

6. Are you taking the situation out of context, or focusing on one aspect of the event? _____

      If so, what other factors do you need to consider? _____

_____

7. Is the source of information reliable? _____

8. Are you confusing a low probability with a high probability? _____

9. Are your judgments based on feelings rather than facts? _____

10. Are you focused on irrelevant factors? _____

If so, what are those factors? _____

_____

Optimism

As you grew up, you learned to interpret the world through the eyes of the significant people around you. If they tended to view things negatively or pessimistically, then that is probably how you learned to interpret the world. This likely contributed to the development of your current problems. If, on the other hand, they taught you to look for the silver lining, then guess what…you are probably an optimist. Optimism is a behavior that can be learned. By viewing the glass as half-full instead of half-empty you can save yourself a lot of needless worry. Optimism is way of changing your perception of a situation. Optimistic people tend to have more energy, report being happier most of the time and have better relationships.

Before you can really start looking at optimism, you need to consider optimism's arch rivals, worry and regret. Worry and regret are two by-products of pessimism that drain people's energy, but serve no functional purpose. Worry is energy tied up in the future, and regret/ guilt is energy tied up in the past. Just taking a more optimistic view may be sufficient. Other times, it also requires a behavior change. For instance, many people are concerned about getting cancer or AIDS. If you spend all your time worried about getting sick, you will drain yourself of energy and decrease your natural immunity. You will probably enjoy life a lot more if you look at situations optimistically: 1) Right now you are healthy, 2) the cures for these diseases may not be that far away, and 3) if you take reasonable precautions, you will lessen your chances of getting sick.

Now, if you have had an oozing lesion on your back for three months, the worry is well founded, but will serve no functional purpose. That energy must be diverted to making an appointment and getting to the doctor. Most of the time when you procrastinate, it's because you are putting off something you either do not like, or something that frightens you. This is where optimism comes in. If you look at a visit to the doctor and see it as ominous, then you are going to have a hard time motivating yourself to go. If, on the other hand, you see the doctor's visit as a means of getting early intervention for something that is treatable, then it becomes a more "do-able" task.

Likewise, regrets are in the past and there is nothing (yet) you can do to change the past. Therefore, you must simply view it as a learning experience and move on. Moving on can mean anything from not dwelling on something that cannot be changed, to actually doing something constructive in the present to alleviate that regret such as making amends.

Activity: Worry and Regret

Write down several situations in your past about which you have worry or regret.

Worry #1: _____

Optimistic restatement: _____

_____

Worry #2: _____

Optimistic restatement: _____

_____

Worry #3: _____

Optimistic restatement: _____

_____

Regret #1: _____

Optimistic restatement: _____

_____

Regret #2: _____

Optimistic restatement: _____

_____

Regret #3: _____

Optimistic restatement: _____

_____

Activity: Daily Journal (Fill out at least 3 per week)

Three things that made me happy: _____

_____

_____

Three positive affirmations: _____

_____

_____

I got upset/angry/frustrated about/by/because: _____

_____

I handled it by: _____

_____

Other ways I could have handled it are:

- Optimistic Restatement/Positive Reframe: _____

- REBT:

   A: _____

   B: _____

   _____

   Cross out the beliefs that are not rational or realistic

   State more rational/realistic beliefs: _____

   _____

   _____

C: You got upset

Was getting upset a reasonable AND helpful reaction? Yes No

If not, what would be more helpful (circle all that apply)?

Let It Go   Cognitive Restructuring/Optimism   Being Assertive
Improved Communication   Time Management
Taking A Positive Action (Explain) _____

Is this something worth getting upset about? _____

If so, why? _____

What can you do to deal with your upset? _____

_____

Does this involve worry, regret or envy? _____

If so, how? _____

What can you do to deal with those feelings? _____

What did you do to treat yourself today? _____

What relaxation technique did you use today? _____

What aspect of spiritual maturity did you work on today (circle)?

Patience, honesty, humility, gratitude, acceptance, awareness, authenticity, discipline, compassion, service integrity, courage, other _____

How did you do this? _____

_____

Powerlessness, Unmanageability and Locus of Control

Your locus of control is where you believe that your life is controlled from. If you believe that you control your own destiny, then you have what we refer to as an internal locus of control. You believe that your thoughts, your actions and your will affect your destiny. In recovery it is helpful to have some sense that you can impact your future.

If you believe you have no control over your life and everything just happens to you, then you have an external locus of control. Everything is out of your control, and there is a predetermined destiny that will inevitably play out. Just like it is important to believe that positive changes will lead to positive changes, it is also important to remember that there are some things which are out of your control. However, if you can see the *majority* of things as being within your control, you are empowered to make choices that will guide your life.

There are a lot of things out of your control, for example, the weather. You can control, however, how you react and/or adapt to the weather. Instead of being angry and upset that the weather is not how you want it to be, look at the bright side. The rain will wash your car for you. You can also replace the word "can't" with the word "won't" or "choose not to" as they are much more accurate. Can't often means "I do not want to" or "I don't know how." For example "I can't live without her" is better stated "I do not want to live without her." "I can't stand that" can be translated into "That irritates me and I am choosing to let it bother me."

Activity: Can'ts

List 4 of your can't statements that keep you from being happy and healthy, then rephrase them in a way that gives you more power.

I can't: _____

Rephrase: _____

I can't: _____

Rephrase: _____

I can't: _____

Rephrase: _____

Activity: What is your locus of control?

Read the following statements. Place a 1 next to every statement with which you agree and a 0 next to every statement with which you disagree.

1		I believe that I control my own destiny
2		I believe that much of what happens to me is beyond my control
3		When I make a mistake, I look at what I could have done differently
4		When I get in trouble, I blame other people for their part in my misfortune
5		When I see someone fall, I assume they are clumsy
6		When a friend of mine does not call when they are supposed to, I assume they got delayed
7		Generally, our environment determines who we are and what we do
8		The environment has an impact, but I can choose how to think and behave
9		Most criminals are good people who are products of bad environments
10		Most criminals are evil and have no regard for anyone else except themselves
11		I believe in a predetermined fate or destiny
12		I believe there are consequences to every action which constantly change my destiny

Results: This was a brief survey designed to evaluate how much you believe you have control over your thoughts, feelings and behaviors. More statements in the "Internal" category means that you believe you have control over what happens to you. A high number of "External" statements mean you have a somewhat helpless sense, and you attribute the cause of most things to environmental causes beyond your control. Ideally, you will have marked some statements in each category.

Internal: 1, 3, 5, 8, 10, 12   External: 2, 4, 6, 7, 9, 11

Review each statement. Discuss why each can both increase and decrease stress.

1. I believe that I control my own destiny

    Increase: This places a lot of responsibility on people for making the right choices and can unnecessarily burden them when factors beyond their control do affect their life.

    Decrease: Empowers people to take control and not feel like they are at the whim of an unseen force.

2. I believe that much of what happens to me is beyond my control

    Increase: _____

    Decrease: _____

3. When I make a mistake, I look at what I could have done differently

    Increase: _____

    Decrease: _____

4. When I get in trouble, I blame other people for their part in my misfortune

    Increase: _____

    Decrease: _____

5. When I see someone fall, I assume they are clumsy

    Increase: _____

    Decrease: _____

6. When a friend does not call when they are supposed to, I assume they got delayed

    Increase: _____

    Decrease: _____

7. Generally, our environment determines who we are and what we do

    Increase: _____

    Decrease: _____

8. The environment has an impact, but I can choose how to think and behave

   Increase: _____

   Decrease: _____

9. Most criminals are good people who are products of bad environments

   Increase: _____

   Decrease: _____

10. Most criminals are evil and have no regard for anyone else except themselves

    Increase: _____

    Decrease: _____

11. I believe in a predetermined fate or destiny

    Increase: _____

    Decrease: _____

12. I believe there are consequences to every action which constantly change my destiny

    Increase: _____

    Decrease: _____

Chapter 9: Feelings, Emotions, Reactions

Part of feeling safe is understanding the function of your feelings, emotions and reactions. In the chapter, Creating Safety, you learned about cognitive restructuring, and started to see the connection between negative thoughts and negative feelings. Now, you will take a more in-depth look at a couple of the more unpleasant emotions: Anger, fear and grief. Don't forget that feelings have a function. Anger and fear protect you by telling you to fight or flee because there is danger. Grief is a bit more complicated, but it involves both anger and depression. There are two major points here. First, make sure your reactions are accurate, that is, you are not creating unnecessary misery for yourself. Secondly, let your feelings and reactions motivate you to take a positive step. Don't just dwell on your misery.

The way you react to any event is dependent on your previous experiences which shape how you view the world. Two people may encounter the same situation, but one person had a previous experience that was negative. The other person had a previous experience that was positive. Each of these people will interpret the situation differently. Take for example cops. Some people have very negative prior experiences with cops, while others, like me, have had very positive ones. When I see a police officer, I feel safe. Other people may not feel that way.

It is also extremely rare to experience a simple, one dimensional emotion. Emotions are complex and composed of levels much like the earth. The crust, or most visible emotion, is often the emotion with which you are most comfortable. The underlying emotions are the ones with which you are increasingly uncomfortable. For instance, if you are uncomfortable expressing fear and/or a need for help, you may instead be outwardly extremely aggressive. Once you realize that anger that is protecting you from feelings of fear and/or helplessness, then these issues can be dealt with. You have not completely dealt with any situation until you have dealt with all emotional facets. Another example is grief. You will learn that anger is part of the grieving process. When there is a death, people are often angry about the loss of their loved one. That part is pretty easy to understand and deal with. Often they are also angry at themselves for things they did or think they should have done or said before that person died. It is the last part that many people hang on to, which keeps them from fully dealing with the loss. You will look at all of these in depth in this chapter.

Dealing with your emotions is important because you probably fail to attribute how much your moods affect you mentally, socially, vocationally, spiritually and physically. When you are relaxed and "happy" you tend to require much less energy in other areas of your life to complete necessary tasks. On the other hand, when you are depressed, afraid, grieving or angry, you often have trouble finding the energy to do simple things like getting dressed, cooking a good meal or even bathing.

Dealing with all of the stuff that makes you feel angry, resentful, guilty or depressed, or that you have been avoiding for all of these years takes a LOT of mental and emotional energy. It is not meant to be done in isolation. If you have read this far, then it is probably safe to assume that you are your own worst enemy. Getting objective feedback from someone who is supportive, sober and healthy is vital. If you can, I recommend taking at least a month to practice living mindfully, paying attention to your physical, mental and emotional cues and recharging yourself. On a scale of 1(sick and tired or being sick and tired) to 10 (the energy and enthusiasm of a 5 year old), aim for beginning each week at a 7 or 8 and never dropping below a 5.

That is going to be hard. Not only do you have to get over the idea that making your happiness a priority is selfish, but you also must really work to be mindful and attentive. You may be thinking that you do not deserve to be happy, or to make yourself a priority. Those are messages you got in your past which are killing you today. If you just cannot get past it, then "fake it 'til you make it." That is, pretend you deserve to be happy.

Activity: Why do I Deserve to Be Happy?

Make a list of all of the reasons you deserve to be a priority, and deserve to be happy

1. _____

2. _____

3. _____

4. _____

5. _____

6. _____

7. _____

8. _____

9.

Activity: Emotional Interventions

It is very difficult to be miserable and happy at the same time. Think of times when you have helped yourself feel better, and times when you are NOT feeling these feelings. That will give you clues about what you can do to feel better.

Brainstorm at least three things that help you feel better when you are feeling:

Angry

　　1. _____

　　2. _____

　　3. _____

Resentful

　　1. _____

　　2. _____

　　3. _____

Depressed

　　1. _____

　　2. _____

　　3. _____

Anxious/Stressed

　　1. _____

　　2. _____

　　3. _____

Note: These things that you already do to help yourself feel better are your strengths. Build off of these as you start trying to deal with life on life's terms.

A partial list of things you can try to help yourself feel better is listed below:

✓ Emotional: Positive self-talk, acceptance, laughter (releases endorphins), journaling, keep a gratitude list

✓ Mental: Identify negative or all or nothing thinking, use positive self-talk, develop a plan to deal with the problem, take a break and relax for the day—focus on what is most important. Identify where you want to go and develop a plan to get there. This instills a sense of hope, optimism and…motivation. Identify the things in life that you do and do not have control over (i.e. what you can and cannot change) and how to deal with those things.

✓ Physical: Go on a walk/run etc. Physical activity can release endorphins and help people feel better. Generally, something that gets the legs moving is better for calming your initial emotional response. Get adequate rest. Try to avoid bingeing on comfort foods. You may have difficulty sleeping in early recovery or cannot tolerate "down time" for relaxation because you start thinking about or remembering "stuff." Learning to relax is vital to emotional recovery. Biofeedback is also very useful in helping you learn to calm your physical reactions to emotional stressors (i.e. anger, panic etc).

✓ Social: Talk it over with a friend. Do something with a friend that will distract you or cheer you up. Take a break from friends that stress you out or drain you.

✓ Environmental: Get some sunshine. This not only just makes people feel better, but it also helps reset the body's clock improving sleep. Make sure you have at least one small space that is relaxing to you—a sanctuary of sorts. Clean.

Activity: List of Feeling Words

People react differently to things based upon upbringing, current stress levels, and temperament. In the following exercise, think about what each word means and looks like to you. It is likely that you had never really stopped to think about the different shades of emotions or the richness different words could convey. When you are practicing your mindfulness, think about these words and the visual representations. This will help you better clarify what you are feelings, so you can then figure out why.

Word Family	Word	Color	Face or Picture
Happy	Happy		
	Elated		
	Content		
	Joyful		
	Excited		
	Hopeful		
Sad	Sad		
	Depressed		
	Dejected		
	Guilty		
	Hopeless		
	Helpless		

Bored	Bored		
	Blah		
Angry	Angry		
	Mad		
	Irritated/Agitated		
	Envious/Jealous		
	Resentful		
	Vengeful		
	Betrayed		
Anxious	Anxious/Worried		
	Scared		
	Stressed		
Confused	Confused		
Overwhelmed	Overwhelmed		

Unpleasant Emotions: Depression

Unpleasant emotions include depression, anger, fear, and grief. All of these feelings are your mind's way of trying to protect you or get you to do something to protect yourself. People often fail to realize that these feelings have a purpose and they can be interconnected.

Depression is your body and mind's way of shutting down due to system overload. There is not enough energy to continue the behaving and/or feeling in the current manner, or for some reason you perceive the situation to be overwhelming and feel hopeless and helpless. (Examples: chronic pain, sickness, chronic sleep deprivation, chronic stress, grief, watching any ASPCA commercial). Your body needs enough time between stressors to recover. When there is a long, ongoing stressor, it is similar to a leaky faucet…gradually draining your energy.

You encounter minor (if not major) emotional and physical stressors every day. If the body cannot rest, then it cannot divert the necessary energy to replenish the "happy chemicals." Consider trying to do a simple task such as dishes. Do you think it is more efficient to do it uninterrupted, or while you have a child that is wanting attention, dogs that are needing to be fed and a spouse that is trying to talk to you about your day. Your body experiences energy diversions in the same way. After it depletes its reserves of "happy" chemicals, it must make more. If it cannot do that efficiently, the end result is depression or distress.

You learned a lot about depression in the chapter on co-occurring disorders. The key is to recognize what your depression is trying to tell you, so you can move forward. Below are some common causes of depression. Your body is trying to tell you something…

Activity: Identifying Depression Messages

- ☐ I need rest
- ☐ I need to do something fun to get the endorphins goig
- ☐ I need more sunlight (more vitamin D)
- ☐ I need a hug
- ☐ I feel hopeless or helpless about…..

- ☐ I need better nutrition
- ☐ I am having "unacceptable" side effects from my medication
- ☐ I need to deal with or let to of an issue
- ☐ Other messages_____

_____

Once you figure out which of the messages your body is sending you, then you can start to figure out how to deal with them. Sometimes the answer will seem apparent, other times you may have to phone a friend. Either way, there are answers. If you figure out what needs to be done, but don't want to do it, well, that is another issue. Why don't you want to do what needs to be done? Are you afraid of failing? Do you not have enough energy? How can you deal with these things. Since depression is part of the grief process, we will look at this more closely in the section on grief. For now, if you are feeling depressed/blue/blah, try to identify why and make one simple change to start feeling better.

Activity: Hope and Strength

The key feelings underlying depression are hopelessness and helplessness. In the following activity, you will identify what each of these feelings means, what things you feel hopeless and helpless about, and make a plan to deal with them.

Hopelessness means believing that no matter what you do, or what happens things will never improve. Sometimes this is because you are focused on huge problems like world hunger, instead of smaller issues like hunger in your community. Other times you may be focused on things that are out of your control, in which case, you may not be able to fix it, so you will have to adjust your thinking about it.

1. I feel hopeless about: _____

    because _____

    I can deal with this by: _____

    _____

2. I feel hopeless about: _____

    because _____

    I can deal with this by: _____

    _____

3. I feel hopeless about: _____

    because _____

    I can deal with this by: _____

    _____

Helplessness can mean that you believe there is hope things can improve, but you do not know how or feel you have the tools. Strength is knowing what you can and cannot change, taking steps to do what you can and dealing with your feelings about the rest. For example: You may feel helpless to fix a relationship.

1. I feel helpless about: _____

   because _____

   I have the ability to control or deal with these parts of it: _____

   _____

   I can deal with my feelings about this by: _____

   _____

2. I feel helpless about: _____

   because _____

   I have the ability to control or deal with these parts of it: _____

   _____

   I can deal with my feelings about this by: _____

   _____

3. I feel helpless about: _____

   because _____

   I have the ability to control or deal with these parts of it: _____

   _____

   I can deal with my feelings about this by: _____

   _____

Unpleasant Emotions: Anger and Fear/Anxiety

Depression is your body saying, "I am out of gas," or "This is hopeless." Often the feelings that drained you energy were anger and/or fear which have run amuck. That is, you may be feeling angry or anxious about things that are either not worth getting upset about, or over which you have no control. Humans and other animals have something called a fight or flight response. When you are faced with a threat, you size it up and make a decision whether to get angry and fight or flee in fear. When either of these emotions is activated your body starts dumping stress chemicals (adrenaline, cortisol, thyroxine). These chemicals increase your heart rate and respiration and start dumping energy into your bloodstream to give you the fuel to do what needs to be done—fight or flee.

In theory this is a great system, but there are a couple of problems. First, these emotions are based in a very primitive part of your brain. In order to prevent unnecessary distress, you have to use your rational mind to determine whether this truly is a threat. The second issue is that energy has to come from somewhere. Your body diverts energy from cellular repair, digestion and your immune system in order to prepare you to fight or flee. Occasionally, this is not a problem; however, when you are constantly angry or anxious, your body has to constantly provide energy to fight or flee. Eventually, the fuel tank is empty, and with no energy left, you start feeling "depressed." Usually this starts with fatigue, difficulty making decisions and sleep problems. "But I am exhausted," you say? You are right, but like a soldier sleeping in a fox hole on the front lines, if your body still perceives a threat, it will likely try and avoid a deep sleep so you can spring to action at any moment.

In the big picture, if you are very anxious or angry AND depressed, the depression may be a sign that you are out of gas. Your body is shutting you down for a while until it can restock. Most of the time organisms will choose to flee instead of fight. It is the smarter evolutionary choice. When David faced Goliath, how likely was it (without divine intervention of course) that David would win in a fight with him? Unlikely. However, it was very likely that he would be able to successfully flee. Somewhere along the way, many humans started becoming control freaks, trying to control and fight things that are not controllable. Some people become depressed or simply irritable all the time, because they spend so much time focusing on things that are out of their control. Let's take a look at some of the basic fears.

Humans are meant to be social creatures. Just like some animals get terribly depressed if they do not have at least one friend, so do humans. This is why rejection and isolation are such basic fears. We don't want to be alone. We don't want to feel like nobody understands us. Sane, sober social supports are vital to mental health, as well as recovery. Since, in our society, failure can lead to rejection and isolation, then you can see why that is also a pretty basic fear. Finally, there is loss of control and the unknown. By definition you cannot control the unknown, because it is unknown. Therefore, both of these come back to the desire to control everything…

In the following activities, you will start to identify your anger and fear triggers, explore whether they are "rational" and develop ways to deal with them so they do not drain your energy and make you miserable. Dealing with these unpleasant emotions will be vital to your sustained recovery. That is not to say you will always feel great. There will be times things happen and you are legitimately angry, stressed or depressed. The key is to know how to minimize the impact of inevitable unpleasant events.

Activity: Nothing to Fear, but Fear Itself.

For this exercise, you will explore fear

Rejection

What does it mean to me? _____

_____

Why do I fear this? _____

_____

How can I deal with this fear? _____

_____

I have experienced this by _____

_____

_____

Cross off the things that have caused you to experience this fear which you have already let go, or decided weren't worth your energy.

Make a plan for how to deal with the ones that are left. _____

_____

_____

Loss of Control

What does it mean to me? _____

_____

Why do I fear this? _____

_____

How can I deal with this fear? _____

_____

I have experienced this by _____

_____

_____

Cross off the things that have caused you to experience this fear which you have already let go, or decided weren't worth your energy.

Make a plan for how to deal with the ones that are left. _____

_____

_____

Isolation

What does it mean to me? _____

_____

Why do I fear this? _____

_____

How can I deal with this fear? _____

_____

I have experienced this by _____

_____

_____

Cross off the things that have caused you to experience this fear which you have already let go, or decided weren't worth your energy.

Make a plan for how to deal with the ones that are left. _____

_____

_____

Failure

What does it mean to me? _____

_____

Why do I fear this? _____

_____

How can I deal with this fear? _____

_____

I have experienced this by _____

_____

Cross off the things that have caused you to experience this fear which you have already let go, or decided weren't worth your energy.

Make a plan for how to deal with the ones that are left. _____

_____

_____

_____

Activity: Exploring Anger and Fear Triggers

Angry

    1. I feel this way when: _____

        because: _____

        I can deal with this by: _____

    2. I feel this way when: _____

        because: _____

        I can deal with this by: _____

    3. I feel this way when: _____

        because: _____

        I can deal with this by: _____

        _____

Mad

    1. I feel this way when: _____

        because: _____

        I can deal with this by: _____

    2. I feel this way when: _____

        because: _____

        I can deal with this by: _____

    3. I feel this way when: _____

        because: _____

        I can deal with this by: _____

        _____

Irritated/Agitated

1. I feel this way when: _____

   because: _____

   I can deal with this by: _____

2. I feel this way when: _____

   because: _____

   I can deal with this by: _____

3. I feel this way when: _____

   because: _____

   I can deal with this by: _____

   _____

Envious/Jealous

1. I feel this way when: _____

   because: _____

   I can deal with this by: _____

2. I feel this way when: _____

   because: _____

   I can deal with this by: _____

3. I feel this way when: _____

   because: _____

   I can deal with this by: _____

   _____

Guilty

1. I feel this way when: _____

   because: _____

   I can deal with this by: _____

2. I feel this way when: _____

   because: _____

   I can deal with this by: _____

3. I feel this way when: _____

   because: _____

   I can deal with this by: _____

   _____

Resentful

1. I feel this way when: _____

   because: _____

   I can deal with this by: _____

2. I feel this way when: _____

   because: _____

   I can deal with this by: _____

3. I feel this way when: _____

   because: _____

   I can deal with this by: _____

   _____

Vengeful

1. I feel this way when: _____

   because: _____

   I can deal with this by: _____

2. I feel this way when: _____

   because: _____

   I can deal with this by: _____

3. I feel this way when: _____

   because: _____

   I can deal with this by: _____

   _____

Betrayed

1. I feel this way when: _____

   because: _____

   I can deal with this by: _____

2. I feel this way when: _____

   because: _____

   I can deal with this by: _____

3. I feel this way when: _____

   because: _____

   I can deal with this by: _____

   _____

Anxious/Worried/Stressed

1. I feel this way when: _____

    because: _____

    I can deal with this by: _____

2. I feel this way when: _____

    because: _____

    I can deal with this by: _____

3. I feel this way when: _____

    because: _____

    I can deal with this by: _____

    _____

Scared

1. I feel this way when: _____

    because: _____

    I can deal with this by: _____

2. I feel this way when: _____

    because: _____

    I can deal with this by: _____

3. I feel this way when: _____

    because: _____

    I can deal with this by: _____

    _____

Activity: Anger Meets Fear.

For the next 5 days, when you start feeling angry, irritated, resentful, anxious or worried identify which fears are coming up for you and why. Make copies of this page as needed.

Example: You start dating someone and you are spending a lot of time together. Now, when you are apart, or when he does not call when he says he will, you feel anxious.

Analysis: You may be fearing rejection (I thought he liked me. I wonder if I am not good enough?),failure (All my friends have great boyfriends and I cannot keep a guy interested), the unknown (I wonder if he is thinking about me or has moved on to someone else), loss of control (I cannot stand not knowing what is going on) and isolation (I haven't felt this way in a long time. If he leaves, I might be alone forever)

What happened? _____

What fears did it bring up? _____

Why did it bring those up? _____

_____

_____

Are these fears realistic and based in fact? _____

Use what you learned in cognitive restructuring to reframe those fears. _____

_____

_____

What parts are in your control? _____

_____

How else can you deal with these feelings so you can stop feeling angry or worried? _____

_____

_____

256

At the end of the week, review all of your entries. There should be at least one each day.

Are there any themes? _____

_____

_____

Do you have particular fears, like fear of rejection? _____

_____

_____

What do you need to do so you do not experience that fear so often? _____

_____

_____

Example self-statements

- ✓ Rejection: I am not going to be liked by everyone all the time. Someone else may have been more suited to the position.

- ✓ Isolation: I do not have to be alone, because I can choose to find common ground. It may take some work, but I can find people with similar values and interests.

- ✓ Failure: Failure only means that I tried and still had more to learn. I cannot be successful at everything.

- ✓ The Unknown/Loss of Control: I have made it this far, without controlling everything. The unknown is an exciting challenge. I do not have to face the unknown alone.

Unpleasant Emotion: Guilt

"Guilt" comes from an Old English word that meant "delinquency." Today Merriam-Webster's Collegiate Dictionary defines guilt as "feelings of culpability, especially for imagined offenses or from a sense of inadequacy; self-reproach." It's a revealing definition — **nowhere does it say that guilt is related to things you actually did wrong**.

Sometimes you should feel guilty (if you've done something morally wrong, committed a crime, or intentionally hurt someone), but holding onto that guilt serves no purpose. Guilt motivates you to make amends. Sometimes this can mean fixing it. Other times it can mean apologizing, and still other times you may only be able to learn from it and not do it again. If you're like most people, you walk around feeling guilty and not knowing what to do to make that guilt go away. That is not only bad for your mental and physical health, but it is also completely unfair to you.

Think about all of these different ways that guilt can impact you.

- ✓ Make you become over responsible, striving to make life 'right'. You may overwork, give too much of yourself, or be willing to do anything to try to make everyone happy.

- ✓ Make you over-conscientious. You may fret over every action you take as to its possible negative consequence to others, even if this means that you must ignore your needs.

- ✓ Make you over sensitive. You may become obsessed with the tenuous nature of all your personal actions, words and decisions.

- ✓ Immobilize you. You can become so overwhelmed by the fear of doing, acting, saying, or being 'wrong' that you eventually choose inactivity, silence, and the status quo.

- ✓ Interfere in your decision making. It may become so important to always be 'right' in your decisions that you are unable to make a decision lest it be wrong.

- ✓ Codependency. You honestly believe it is better to serve others first, unaware that 'guilt' can be the motivator for such 'generous' behavior.

- ✓ Make you ignore the full array of emotions and feelings available to you, your attention is always being with the negative.

- ✓ Mislead or misdirect you. As many irrational beliefs lie behind guilt, you may be unable to sort out your feelings. Be objective with yourself when you are experiencing guilt so that your decisions are based on sound, rational thinking.

- ✓ Be a motivator to change. Guilt and the discomfort it brings can be used as a barometer of the need for change and a way to move in a different direction in your life.

For the next few activities, make a list of those things about which you feel guilty. It could be something stupid you said recently, an act of cruelty you did to a sibling as a child, or a detrimental personal habit that has hurt your relationship with a loved one.

Activity: Guilt List

I feel guilty about:

1. _____

2. _____

3. _____

4. _____

5. _____

6. _____

7. _____

8. _____

9. _____

10. _____

Review your list and cross out those things which were not under your control.

Next cross out the things you have atoned for, but are still holding yourself hostage.

The things that are left are the ones you still need to deal with.

Activity: Learn to forgive yourself.

First, review the list the things you feel guilty about. Then ask, "How can I forgive myself and let it go?" You may need to do something to make amends, but often it's merely having the courage to say, "I'm sorry." Then do what it takes so you can honestly, finally forgive yourself. Continually beating yourself up is hurting nobody but you.

I can forgive myself by..

1. _____

2. _____

3. _____

4. _____

5. _____

6. _____

7. _____

8. _____

9. _____

10. _____

Activity: Set a no-guilt-allowed rule

Often you may not experience vacations, breaks, and other relaxing activities as stress-relieving because you feel guilty that you are not doing more productive things. Remind yourself that you are taking a break and doing it for a reason (improved health, decreased stress, etc.) so there is no reason to feel guilty. As soon as you hear yourself say, "I should be…" remind yourself why you are choosing not to do that. For more on this topic, google Stephen Covey's 7th habit: Sharpen the saw. You are much less effective when you are run-down. Write the mantra (what you will tell yourself and others) to remember this rule.

_____

_____

Activity: Recognize that guilt doesn't always mean that what you did was wrong.

For instance, if you're feeling guilty because you decided it was more important to relax with a book than to have coffee with your always-in-a-crisis friend, that means you're learning to set limits and take time for yourself. In cases like this, have the confidence to admit that you made the right choice.

Things I often feel guilty about that are not anything I am doing wrong are:

1. _____

2. _____

3. _____

4. _____

5. _____

I can learn to stop feeling guilty about these things by:

1. _____

2. _____

3. _____

4. _____

5. _____

Activity: Start A Guilt Journal.

Every time you feel guilty about something, write it down in your journal. Write the time, the day, what you feel guilty about. Go back and reread this journal every couple of weeks to find the trends in your guilt. This will provide clues to the source of your guilt that will enable you to better deal with its underlying roots.

Activity 6: Live in the present moment.

You cannot change the past, you can only learn from it and, possibly, fix something you did wrong.

I can do the following things to stay focused on what I can do in the present.

1. _____

2. _____

3. _____

4. _____

5. _____

Unpleasant Emotion: Grief

Grief is a label assigned to all of the emotions associated with dealing with a loss. The grief process actually occurs in phases: denial, anger, bargaining, depression and acceptance. Different people go through these phases in different orders, and often go through each phase more than once. You may have difficulty resolving grief because you are stuck in the anger or depression phase. Remember all feelings have an aspect of self-preservation. Many people fail to identify the fears (remember rejection, isolation, failure, the unknown, loss of control) underlying the anger in the grief process. Without coming to terms with these fears, it is much harder to "resolve" the loss. Once you have identified the source of your anger, grief or fear, then you can choose the most effective way to deal with it. The following exercise will help you explore different types of losses, the stages of grief, blocks to healthy resolution (such as unfinished business) and how to move through them.

Once you get past denial, you have to face some very scary realities, which brings us to the next phase, anger. Anger protects you against the six basic fears: Fear of failure, fear of rejection, fear of loss of self-control/respect, fear of isolation, fear of death, fear of the unknown. It protects you emotionally, physically and socially by keeping you from feeling afraid. It gets you out of threatening situations (ideally). It also alienates you from other people who could cause you to experience fear.

Activity: The Fear and Loss Connection

For each of the listed fears, identify one loss you have experienced related to it.

Rejection (loss of a friend, not getting a job etc...)
_____

I was angry because: _____

_____

I felt depressed because:_____

_____

I came to accept the loss by: _____

_____

_____

Isolation (loss of a friend, moving, addiction etc…) _____

I felt isolated because: _____

_____

I was angry because: _____

_____

I felt depressed because:_____

_____

I came to accept the loss by: _____

_____

_____

The Unknown and Loss of Control _____

I felt anxious about being out of control because: _____

_____

I was angry because: _____

_____

I felt depressed because: _____

_____

I came to accept the loss by: _____

_____

_____

Failure (Not succeeding at something, not getting a job etc…) _____

_____

This bothered me because: _____

_____

I was angry because: _____

_____

I felt depressed because: _____

_____

I came to accept the loss by: _____

_____

Activity: Types of Losses

Some losses are more theoretical. You cannot touch them. They are not things, however, these losses are just as important to grieve.

EXAMPLE:
- ✓ Loss of self-esteem can happen because of things you did in your addiction, or when you were experiencing mental health problems.
- ✓ You can deal with it by focusing on the good things about yourself and doing the next right thing from this point forward.

Self-Esteem

What is one thing that caused you to lose it _____

What parts of this are you angry about? _____

How can you deal with it. _____

_____

Innocence

What is one thing that caused you to lose it _____

What parts of this are you angry about? _____

How can you deal with it. _____

_____

Hope/Dreams

What is one thing that caused you to lose it _____

What parts of this are you angry about? _____

How can you deal with it. _____

_____

Faith

What is one thing that caused you to lose it _____

What parts of this are you angry about?_____

How can you deal with it. _____

_____

Social Support

What is one thing that caused you to lose it _____

What parts of this are you angry about? _____

How can you deal with it. _____

_____

Optimism/Hope

What is one thing that caused you to lose it _____

What parts of this are you angry about? _____

How can you deal with it. _____

_____

Self-Control

What is one thing that caused you to lose it _____

What parts of this are you angry about? _____

How can you deal with it. _____

_____

Activity: Moving Through Grief

Regardless of the type of loss, you will deal with it in roughly the same way. What things can you do to help yourself move through each stage of the grief process?

Denial (The goal is to help yourself understand it happened and you have to deal with it.)

_____

_____

Anger (Identify all of the reasons you are angry about it and start dealing with the anger)

_____

_____

Depression (Identify and deal with any feelings of hopelessness and helplessness that arise when you realize that you cannot get it back)

_____

_____

How do you know when you have reached acceptance? What is different?

_____

_____

_____

Acceptance is the ultimate goal, but it is not always final. For instance, while grieving the loss of a job you may get another job and come to believe that you are in a better place than you would have been. Nevertheless, if you have to interact with the person who got your job, and learn that he/she is not doing what you know you could have done, that anger may resurface and the grief process needs to be re-attended to.

Activity: My Losses

Name the loss: _____

What FEARS did this loss bring up? _____

How did you (or can you) move through the following stages:

     Denial _____

     Anger _____

     Bargaining _____

     Depression _____

Name the loss: _____

What FEARS did this loss bring up? _____

How did you (or can you) move through the following stages:

     Denial _____

     Anger _____

     Bargaining _____

     Depression _____

Name the loss: _____

What FEARS did this loss bring up? _____

How did you (or can you) move through the following stages:

     Denial _____

     Anger _____

     Bargaining _____

     Depression _____

Summary of Important Points about Emotions

Anger

- ✓ The average person experiences 15 anger situations per day

- ✓ Anger reveals information about your values and what you think is important.

- ✓ Exercise, venting and time-out are often good strategies to dissipate the adrenaline, but are not effective for coping with anger.

- ✓ Coping with anger requires people to recognize what caused the anger and modify that stressor or perceptions about that stressor.

- ✓ Good communication, fair fighting and self-awareness are all important components for anger management.

- ✓ People express anger in different ways. Some people hold it inside and develop physical problems, some people explode and some people are passive-aggressive.

- ✓ It is important for people to know their personal anger styles, triggers and most effective anger management skills.

Fear

- ✓ There are six basic human fears: Failure, rejection, the unknown, death, isolation and loss of control.

- ✓ Most of the time when people experience anger, if they look deeper they can find that this situation caused them to feel one of the six basic fears.

- ✓ The reason people experience this fear may be socially or individually prescribed. For instance, if one is not accepted, then he/she is isolated. Therefore if people do not do things to be accepted then they may spend their entire lives alone.

Grief

- ✓ There are five stages of grief: denial, anger, bargaining, depression and acceptance.

- ✓ People move through the stages at different rates and can return to any of the stages at any time.

- ✓ The usual grieving process takes at least a year.

- ✓ Losses which seem out of order or unnatural, such as the death of a child, may take up to two years to grieve.

- ✓ Death is not the only loss to be grieved.

Chapter 10: Coping Skills and Defense Mechanisms

Coping skills and defense mechanisms help you interpret and deal with situations, feelings and reactions. Both of these skills are crucial to ongoing recovery and happiness.

Coping involves either changing a situation, or the way you feel about a situation, in order to resolve negative feelings.

Defenses are things you do to try to block, suppress or avoid the situation without doing anything to resolve it or the feelings about it.

Sometimes it is neither the time nor the place to deal with an unpleasant emotion. (Screaming at your boss usually gets you fired.) In the short-term, defenses are very useful; however, a certain amount of energy is constantly required to block feelings and/or thoughts about the event until you cope with it. It can be compared to those skeletons in your closet. (Yes, we all have them) Defense mechanisms just shove the skeletons in the closet so you don't have to see them, think about them or deal with them. That is fine if there are just one or two skeletons. Over time all of them add up and you can hardly open the door without everything falling out, and it takes a ton of energy to keep the door shut and everything locked away in the closet. Coping skills, on the other hand, take those skeletons out, one by one, and let you start dealing with them.

Early recovery is really not the time to start sorting through your skeletons. During this time you are learning new skills for dealing with life on life's terms. You want to, first just avoid adding anything else to the pile. This starts with honesty. If you are honest with yourself and others about your needs, wants, thoughts and feelings, then you will not be adding to the pile. An added bonus is you will start developing that sober support system, paying more attention to your own needs and getting better, stronger and rejuvenated. Once you feel like you are stable in recovery, it will be time to start coping with those skeletons. The first step is to go through them and sort out the ones you have no responsibility for. What you are left with you can figure out how to deal with one by one.

First you will learn about defense mechanisms. These are like the duct tape and paperclips of the mental health world. They are not meant to be permanent fixes. They are meant to help you get through right now without freaking out. Then, at a more appropriate time, you can deal/cope with whatever got you upset.

Defense Mechanisms

Defense mechanisms are ways that you use energy to block or avoid dealing with an event. Most people initially use defenses to help them get through the initial adrenaline rush that happens when they get upset, because it is not always the most appropriate time or place to deal with the issue. However, this energy must be constantly maintained until you cope with the situation. Understanding your defense mechanisms can help you identify when something is upsetting, so you can make a mental note to deal with it later. Place a star beside the defense mechanisms you use with regularity, and on the lines provided, identify at least one time when you have used it.

Activity: Defenses

____Denial: Inability or refusal to accept that something is real

Examples: After becoming paralyzed a person continues to insist that before long she will be up and walking.   Not beginning a job search before graduation because you refuse to accept that college is ending.

1. _____

2. _____

3. _____

____Avoidance / repression: Also known as deliberate forgetting

Examples: After experiencing a traumatic event, a person may try to forget that it happened. When faced with very distressing feelings people may eat, or drink alcohol in order to make themselves feel better without actually having to deal with whatever is causing the feelings.

1. _____

2. _____

3. _____

___Suppression: Diverting unacceptable emotions into acceptable activities.
Examples: When someone gets very angry, they may go on a walk instead of dealing with the problem about which they are upset.

1. _____

2. _____

3. _____

___Withdrawal: Retreating emotionally and/or physically from others.
Example: After repeated frustrations, a person may become very passive and unemotional and may or may not try to interact with others.

1. _____

2. _____

3. _____

___Regression: Acting at a younger age
Examples: An adult throwing a temper tantrum. After becoming overwhelmed with the horrific state of society, a person may refuse to watch the news.

1. _____

2. _____

3. _____

___Acting out: Often expressed as anger or a temper tantrum, acting out pushes others away so you will not have to deal with the problem, and/or so no one will see you suffering.
Examples: When you feels threatened or hurt you may throw a tantrum due to inability to cope with present emotions.

1. _____

2. _____

3. _____

___Reaction formation: Acting the opposite of what you are feeling.
Examples: When someone feels angry or devastated, they may laugh. After viewing a murder scene, officers may make callous jokes so they do not have to feel the horror.

1. _____

2. _____

3. _____

___Dissociation: "Fly on the wall" your mind separates from your physical body.
Examples: Trauma victims who seem to "space out" and do not feel anything. Some people with eating disorders report getting so engrossed in eating, they do not remember what they ate,

1. _____

2. _____

3. _____

___Projection: Placing unacceptable feelings of one's own on other people
Examples: You may believe you are incompetent, but cannot admit, so you "project" those feelings to others. So, instead of calling yourself incompetent, you blame everyone else...

1. _____

2. _____

3. _____

___Displacement: Directing unacceptable feelings at a less threatening target.
Examples: After a bad day at work, you come home and are mean to your roommate.

1. _____

2. _____

3. _____

___Splitting: Viewing events as all-good or all-bad maintains an "us-them" mentality which keeps us from facing the fact that we all have inappropriate feelings and impulses and we are just one wrong choice way from being like them.

Examples: When you take a test, you either get an "A" or it is a failure. Instead of having to see any redeeming qualities in a criminal, you view them as totally bad.

1. _____

2. _____

3. _____

___Moralization: Being judgmental about people's actions to help oneself feel superior.

Examples: Spending a lot of time being judgmental of others to cover up your insecurities.

1. _____

2. _____

3. _____

How do defenses reduce stress? _____

_____

_____

_____

How do they increase stress? _____

_____

_____

_____

Coping Skills

A major part of recovery is developing appropriate coping skills. That is, you need to figure out how to deal with life on life's terms so you can let things go and move on. Holding on to guilt, resentment, anger and fear are only going to wear you down. Those emotions are supposed to prompt you to do something, not just stew on it.

Early onset of problems (substance abuse, depression, anxiety, trauma, etc.) or a lack of effective role models may have prevented you from developing age-appropriate coping skills. Additionally, previously developed coping skills may have been forgotten due to an increased reliance on an addiction to "cope.". You may also be continuing to use skills that were appropriate when you were a child, but are no longer appropriate or effective. Or, you may have appropriate coping skills available, but they may not be strong enough to deal with your current pain. A primary goal of coping skills training is to help you develop and effectively use skills to help you cope with life on life's terms without having to resort to negative alternative responses (using drugs, lashing out etc.). Don't get me wrong, it is hard work. It doesn't happen overnight, but if you practice and pick skills that work for you, they will become more second-nature.

Activity: To Cope or Not to Cope

In this activity, you will quickly examine the effects of not coping with something.

Give an example of a time when you were angry and either changed the situation or how you felt about the situation:

_____

_____

Now give an example of a time when you got angry that you "let it go" but held on to the resentment: _____

_____

_____

Initially, which one took more energy? Why? _____

_____

_____

Two weeks later, which one was taking more energy? _____

_____

_____

How does harboring resentment affect all of the other areas of your life?

Emotional: _____

Mental: _____

Physical: _____

Social: _____

Spiritual: _____

Activity: Coping Skills Inventory

Think about when you have coped with things in your past. Place a check mark next to ways you have coped with things that have worked, at least a little bit.

- ☐ Talked to someone

- ☐ Wrote it down

- ☐ Tried to look at the bright side

- ☐ Figured out how to solve the problem

- ☐ Prayed about it

- ☐ Realized it was out of my control and let it go

- ☐ Other: _____

- ☐ Other: _____

Managing Thoughts About The Problem

There are generally three problematic ways of thinking about problems.

- ✓ Negative: Why me? The world is awful. The sky is falling.

- ✓ Obsessive: Gotta know. Won't let it go.

- ✓ Hindsight: Shoulda, coulda, woulda

Imagine you have just come to work and found out you are being laid off. That is a pretty crappy situation, no doubt. However, it is unlikely that you can change it. Now you are upset/angry/devastated/scared/stressed….some combination of those. How do you deal with it?

If you have a negative thought pattern, you suddenly start thinking about all of the things that are going to happen as your world falls apart. But, how likely is it that you will not get another job, lose your house and your car and suddenly be living on the streets? Not very likely. You may have to downsize or get a roommate, apply for food stamps and cut out nonessential expenses for a period, but you will probably be able to find at least temporary work until you find another career. In the section on cognitive restructuring in the next chapter, you will learn in-depth techniques to help you cope with your negative thoughts..

If you have an obsessive thought pattern, likely you will start asking, why me? Why not so and so? Why is this happening? The best questions you can ask yourself are "Is it worth worrying about?" "What is my next step" And then….DO IT!

If you have a shoulda, coulda, woulda thought pattern, then you are probably second guessing everything you should have done to prevent and/or prepare for it. However, you didn't, so it is time to use that energy to make a plan, not beat yourself up over the past.

Activity: Managing Thoughts

Think back to a time in the recent past when something went wrong. List three examples. For each example, rewrite it using: Negative, Obsessive and Hindsight, and an optimistic or helpful way of thinking about the problem.

Problem #1: _____

A negative way of viewing this would be: _____

_____

An obsessive way of viewing this would be: _____

_____

A hindsight way of viewing this would be: _____

_____

An optimistic/helpful way of viewing this would be: _____

_____

Problem #2: _____

A negative way of viewing this would be: _____

_____

An obsessive way of viewing this would be: _____

_____

A hindsight way of viewing this would be: _____

_____

An optimistic/helpful way of viewing this would be: _____

_____

Problem #3: _____

A negative way of viewing this would be: _____

_____

An obsessive way of viewing this would be: _____

_____

A hindsight way of viewing this would be: _____

_____

An optimistic/helpful way of viewing this would be: _____

_____

Which thinking pattern did you regularly use? _____

How did this add extra stress to your life? _____

_____

_____

How can you remind yourself to use an optimistic viewpoint? _____

_____

_____

Problem Solving Steps

When you feel stressed, depressed, angry or scared, your body is telling you that it thinks there is a problem. So…lets problem solve.

✓ First identify what your goal is. If the problem were resolved, what would be different?

✓ Then brainstorm ideas that will help you achieve that goal. Write everything down. Not all ideas are practical, but write them down anyway, so they do not block your creativity.

✓ Review your list of solutions. Identify the top 3 that would probably help you resolve the problem and keep you headed toward your ultimate goal of happiness and sobriety.

✓ Identify which of one the 3 feels like the right thing to do in your head, heart and gut. Sometimes you cannot change a situation (or a person) you simply have to change how you feel and think about the situation or person.

✓ Make it happen.

Activity: Problem Solving

Now, revisit each of the 3 problems you identified above.

How does an objective thinking pattern reduce your stress levels? _____

_____

_____

_____

Practice optimism for a week, then write about how you felt once you started getting the hang of it.

_____

_____

_____

Decision making

Sometimes the most stressful thing about a situation is NOT making a decision. Constantly weighing the options and thinking about it. If you follow the problem solving steps, step 5 is where you have to make a decision. How you determine whether it feels right in your head, heart and gut is a matter of personal preference. Some people make pro and con lists. Some people pray to their higher power. Some people meditate. You may do one or more of those. Ultimately, you will be at peace with the fact that your decision makes sense and is the best thing for you to do at the given time (head honesty). You feel content, maybe even proud of the decision (heart honesty). You may be a little stressed (gut honesty) because solving problems usually is hard work and often pushes you out of your comfort zone. However, you know in your gut it is the correct decision.

Activity: Decision Making

Identify 2 things you have had to make a decision about.

Problem #1: _____

Did your decision feel right in your head, heart and gut? _____

If not, why not. _____

_____

If so, why so. _____

_____

Problem #2: _____

Did your decision feel right in your head, heart and gut? _____

If not, why not. _____

_____

If so, why so. _____

_____

Planning for emergencies

Unfortunately, emergencies are inevitable. If you tend to be a more spontaneous type of person, this might not bother you as much. As a very structured person, I not only have a plan B, I also have a C and a D. In early recovery, your mind and body are working overtime to recover. You are learning new coping skills, which can be exhausting. Therefore, it is good to have an emergency plan in place, so you do not have to try to come up with things when you are in crisis.

Activity: Planning for Emergencies

Brainstorm all the potential emergencies

Kids

    1. Sickness _____

    2. Childcare _____

    3. Transportation _____

    4. Teen Drama _____

Financial

    1. Unexpected Bills_____

    2. Job Loss _____

    3. Holidays _____

Health/Medical

    1. Doctor Bills_____

    2. Prescriptions _____

    3. Health Insurance Premium Increases _____

    _____

Transportation (Lack of)

    1. To work _____

    2. Kids to school_____

3. Groceries _____

4. Medical Appointments _____

Now identify how you are going to deal with them

Kids

1. Sickness _____

2. Childcare _____

3. Transportation _____

4. Teen Drama _____

Financial

1. Unexpected Bills _____

2. Job Loss _____

3. Holidays _____

Health/Medical

1. Doctor Bills _____

2. Prescriptions _____

3. Health Insurance Premium Increases _____

_____

Transportation (Lack of)

1. To work _____

2. Kids to school _____

3. Groceries _____

4. Medical Appointments _____

Coping With Persistent Problems

Some problems, like anxiety, depression, addiction, chronic pain, PTSD and physical problems in yourself or others you care about can be persistent. It is important to learn how to deal with these issues without letting them wear you down. As you read about before, making sure to get enough good, quality sleep; eating a nutritious diet and having a few good social supports can mean the difference between relapse and recovery.

Activity: Coping with Persistent Problems

Make a list of your persistent problems, those things that serve as a regular stressor in your life, and ways to minimize their impact.

Examples:

> **Persistent problem:** Boss that is overbearing, micromanaging
> **Ways to manage:** Get plenty of rest. Set clear boundaries about work vs. off time. Create a template for the daily & weekly reports
>
> **Persistent problem:** Chronic neck and back pain or tension
> **Ways to manage:** Get plenty of rest. Ensure sleeping, living and working areas are ergonomically sound. Stretch frequently. Take relaxation breaks throughout the day. Take medications as prescribed.

Persistent Problem _____

Ways to minimize its impact _____

_____

Persistent Problem _____

Ways to minimize its impact _____

_____

Persistent Problem _____

Ways to minimize its impact _____

_____

Assertiveness Training and Refusal Skills

When you first heard the terms assertiveness training and refusal skills, you probably thought about addiction recovery. While these skills are very useful in addiction recovery and prevention, it is also important to be able to be assertive and refuse requests that are not healthy or would overwhelm you and trigger a relapse of any mental health problems such as depression or anxiety. Some examples of this include asking for space or personal time, asking for help, or saying no when you are too busy or too tired.

You may feel guilty telling people no or setting boundaries. Unfortunately, like persistent problems, constant demands on your time and attention by other people can also be draining. It is okay to just say "no." You do not need to provide an explanation. You may find it easier to compromise. For example, if your friend wants you to go out, tell her you are too tired tonight, but make plans for another day, or invite her over to your house to watch a movie. It is also okay to have different preferences and desires than other people. Maybe your friends all want to go see a scary movie, but you don't like scary movies. It is okay to say you don't want to go. Assertiveness means calmly and objectively stating your opinion. If your friends are not used to that, they may try to push you. The important thing is to hold firm without getting upset. Once people realize that you say what you mean and mean what you say, they will start respecting it. Dr. Seuss said "Say what you mean and mean what you say, because those who matter don't mind and those who mind don't matter." Refusal skills are part of assertiveness. It takes practice, but both of these are essential to developing healthy relationships.

Activity: Assertiveness Training and Refusal Skills

Think back to a time when you wanted or needed something but didn't ask for it.

What did you want or need? _____

Why didn't you ask for it? _____

How could you use assertiveness or refusal skills to get what you needed? _____

_____

What is the scariest thing about being assertive? _____

_____

How can you deal with that fear? _____

_____

Enhancing social support networks

Social support is incredibly important to living a happy, healthy life. Nobody can be everything to everyone all of the time. Social supports help you be the best at what you are best at, encourage you when you are tired and assist you when you are overwhelmed or spread too thin.

What you need in a social support network varies based on your temperament, lifestyle, and frankly, what is going on in your life at any given moment. Sometimes you may need to revisit this activity. The first part will have you think, in general, what you need in a social support network. The second part will ask you to fine tune that and identify what you need right now, and from whom you can get it.

Activity: Enhancing social support networks

What do I need in a social support network (in general)? _____

_____

_____

Who in my life would be a good person to include in my social support network? _____

_____

_____

What do I need in a social support network (right now)? _____

_____

_____

Where can I find good people to include in my social support network? _____

_____

_____

There are many ways to do help yourself cope with things better, from the biological to the behavioral. Several biological methods of coping are to get adequate sleep, exercise and eat well. (Gee, who'd have thunk it?) These strategies allow your body to efficiently produce the neurochemicals involved in helping you feel happy and calm--serotonin, acetylcholine and dopamine. If you have the feel good chemicals in stock, you have gotten enough sleep so you can concentrate and function efficiently, and you are healthy, and well nourished, then you have already eliminated 60-80% of the potential vulnerabilities for problems. Another way to alter the neurochemicals is by taking medications. Sometimes, especially after a long period of addiction, nutritional and "natural" interventions may not work fast enough to help you stay sober. If this is the case, you can talk with your doctor about trying a short course (6-24 months) of a medication. Other coping methods can be used to help you change how you *feel* about a situation by changing how you **think** about the situation, or change the situation all together. Behavior modification can be used to eliminate a behavior that is causing distress or used to increase the frequency of other coping skills like cognitive restructuring, journal writing, social facilitation or time management.

As stated before, coping skills either change the situation or change the way a person feels about a situation. These activities require a significant amount of mental energy, but this "stress" on your mental reserves is short-lived. Defenses, on the other hand, constantly require energy (remember, like shutting the door to the overfilled closet).

If you have reservations about applying a coping skill, ask yourself "what about this am I uncomfortable with?" You will probably find that the way you are trying to apply it does not fit with your learning style or temperament. If you have trouble modifying it, ask for suggestions. For example: People who are strong "Perceivers" can benefit from some time management, but will not do well if they try to manage time through rigid schedules and strict deadlines. They will be more successful with weekly to-do lists.

Chapter 11: Relationships

Remember Maslow's hierarchy. First you need to get your physical health well and be safe from physical and emotional harm. The next step is to start developing your relationships. Relationships can be your greatest buffer against (or cause of) stress, therefore, it is helpful to understand what a healthy relationship looks and feels like. Because of your past, you may have difficulty setting boundaries and/or trusting people. That is okay. It will take time for you to work through the lessons you learned from your dysfunctional relationships in the past, and learn how to trust not only other people, but also yourself. This will probably be uncomfortable at first. You may decide you need to distance yourself from certain people. Other people may not be healthy or helpful for you, but, for whatever reason, you feel you cannot distance yourself. It will be up to you to figure out what you want or need out of these relationships and how to navigate them. You will learn a lot more about this in this chapter, but to get you jump started, complete the activities below.

Activity: Hello to Me

In your past you have probably denied your feelings, felt misunderstood and, at times, felt abandoned. Before you can have healthy relationships with other people, you need to develop a relationship with yourself.

To be a good friend to myself, I need to:

1. _____

2. _____

3. _____

4. _____

5. _____

6. _____

7. _____

8. _____

9. _____

Getting in Touch—Lessons Learned from Your Family of Origin

Being a good friend to yourself, is a start, but you also need to have healthy relationships. Most people have no idea what a healthy relationship looks like or how to create one. The next few activities will help you examine what you have learned about relationships (good and bad), and how to start improving your current relationships. Not all people with mental health or addiction issues come from broken or dysfunctional families. In fact, most people come from families that have some healthy characteristics.

Healthy Relationships

Healthy relationships require you to have a significant amount of knowledge about themselves and others. Carl Rogers suggested that all healthy relationships are built upon four core elements:

- ✓ Unconditional positive regard---discuss how you would do that

- ✓ Respect--- give the person your attention--fully, no tv, take the phone off the hook

- ✓ Genuineness--people know when you are just saying what you think they want to hear. If you have a gut feeling about something, be tactful, but share it

- ✓ Empathy-- the ability to walk a mile in that person's shoes

Since then, many theorists have described what a "healthy relationship" is. The following list is a synopsis of current thoughts on the subject.

Requirements of Healthy Relationships

- ✓ Expressing open affection and loving thoughts
- ✓ Sensitivity to feelings of others/ Relating to others with warmth and compassion
- ✓ Being sharing and open with your feelings
- ✓ Trust and honesty
- ✓ Listening, hearing and understanding others
- ✓ Being accepting and uncritical/ Ability and willingness to show respect for others
- ✓ Ability to care deeply for oneself and another individual
- ✓ Being contentious and dependable
- ✓ Encouraging growth in myself and others

Activity: Healthy Relationship Characteristics

Review the list below to see which healthy characteristics your family had.

☐   Self worth is high among all members.

What does this mean? _____

_____

I can do the following to improve this in my current relationships: _____

_____

☐   Communication is direct, clear, specific and honest and feelings are expressed

What does this mean? _____

_____

I can do the following to improve this in my current relationships: _____

_____

☐   Rules are human, flexible and can be changed.

What does this mean? _____

_____

I can do the following to improve this in my current relationships: _____

_____

☐   Each person is involved in the community and/or neighborhood and/or has other friends

What does this mean? _____

_____

I can do the following to improve this in my current relationships: _____

_____

☐ Each person has goals and plans to get there, and is supported by the family.

What does this mean? _____

_____

I can do the following to improve this in my current relationships: _____

_____

Since you are learning about a strengths-based perspective, I had to start with that. Those characteristics are also what you need to work toward in order to have healthy relationships in the present. Now you will turn your attention to some of the not so healthy relationship patterns you have learned.

Growing Up in an Addicted Family

As you have learned so far, much of how you interpret events and the world is impacted by your past. A large part of this past is your family. Not only did you learn random things, but you also learned about yourself, relationships, how to cope. In a healthy family, you learn to love yourself, because you are you. You learn healthy communication skills and how to identify and deal with emotions. Addicted and borderline families teach you to not talk about yourself or your feelings because they are not important; not trust yourself or anyone else and not to feel feelings because they are overwhelming and/or irrelevant.

People in addicted families often take on certain roles. Each of these roles has a place in helping the person with the addiction maintain the addiction. Unfortunately, you are likely recreate these dysfunctional relationship patterns at work and in your social relationships. The following information on each role, is provided so you can see how the significant people in your life have played a part in, or been affected by the addiction. If you came from a family in which there was someone with an addiction, you may also recognize yourself in some of these roles. You need to to identify who fills which roles for you and begin fixing those relationships.

There are several key players in the addicted family
✓ The Addict.
✓ The Hero.
✓ The Mascot.
✓ The Lost Child.
✓ The Scapegoat.
✓ The Caretaker (Enabler)

The person with the addiction is the center, and though the key to alcohol and drug addiction recovery, not necessarily the most important in family recovery. Family recovery means setting boundaries and limits. If the addict chooses recovery, then that is wonderful. The family can recover without the addict in it. However, in the addiction the "world" revolves around this person, causing the addict to become the center of attention.

As the roles are defined, the others unconsciously take on the rest of the roles to complete the balance after the problem has been introduced. Recovery many times focuses on the addict to the exclusion of the rest of the family who also developed dysfunctional behaviors and feelings along the way.

Activity: Addiction and the Addict

If you grew up in an addicted family, what was it like when the addict would use?

_____

_____

_____

_____

How did you feel? _____

_____

_____

What did you learn from the addict? _____

_____

_____

How does what you learned still impact you today? _____

_____

_____

What do you need to start doing differently? _____

_____

_____

How can you deal with the addict in a healthier way? _____

_____

_____

Activity: Addiction and The Hero

The Hero is the one who needs to make the family, and role players, look good. They ignore the problem and present things in a positive manner as if problems within the family did not exist. The Hero is the perfectionist and finds something(s) at which to excel—academics, football, music... Not only does this make the family look good, it also takes the focus off of the addict. The underlying feelings are fear, guilt, and shame. Sometimes the hero believes that if he or she were perfect, the addict would get better.

Who was the hero in your family? _____

Who in your life is currently the hero?_____

How did you feel about the hero in your family of origin and why? _____

_____

_____

How do you feel about the hero in your current family and why? _____

_____

_____

What was the benefit of this behavior to the hero? _____

_____

_____

What would be better alternate behaviors? _____

_____

_____

How can you deal with the addict in a healthier way? _____

_____

_____

Activity: Addiction and The Mascot

The Mascot's role is that of the jester who often makes inappropriate jokes about those involved (including themselves). Though they do bring humor to the family roles, it is often harmful, hurtful and passive aggressive. Although the use of humor helps some people survive intolerable situations, the inability to "turn it off" and communicate genuinely can cause difficulties in coping and relationships. The underlying feelings are embarrassment, shame, and anger.

Who was the mascot in your family?_____

Who in your life is currently the mascot? _____

How did you feel about the mascot in your family of origin and why? _____

_____

_____

How do you feel about the mascot in your current family and why? _____

_____

_____

What was the benefit of this behavior to the mascot? _____

_____

_____

What would be better alternate behaviors? _____

_____

_____

How can you deal with the mascot in a healthier way? _____

_____

_____

296

Activity: Addiction and The Lost Child

The Lost Child is the silent, "out of the way" family member, and will never mention alcohol or recovery. Quiet and reserved, the lost child is careful to not make problems. The Lost Child gives up or ignores self needs and makes efforts to avoid any conversation regarding the family's problems. The lost child just wants to "fly under the radar" until he or she can escape the family. The underlying feelings are guilt, loneliness, neglect, shame and anger.

Who was the lost child in your family?_____

Who in your life is currently the lost child? _____

How did you feel about the lost child in your family of origin and why? _____

_____

_____

How do you feel about the lost child in your current family and why? _____

_____

_____

What was the benefit of this behavior to the lost child? _____

_____

_____

What would be better alternate behaviors? _____

_____

_____

How can you deal with the lost child in a healthier way? _____

_____

_____

Activity: Addiction and The Scapegoat

The Scapegoat often acts out in front of others. They will rebel, make noise, and divert attention from the person who is addicted and their need for help in addiction recovery. The Scapegoat covers up or draws attention away from the real problem through constant crises ranging from eating disorders and drug use to school or legal difficulties. The underlying feelings are shame, guilt, and emptiness

Who was the scapegoat in your family?_____

Who in your life is currently the scapegoat? _____

How did you feel about the scapegoat in your family of origin and why? _____

_____

_____

How do you feel about the scapegoat in your current family and why? _____

_____

_____

What was the benefit of this behavior to the scapegoat? _____

_____

_____

What would be better alternate behaviors? _____

_____

_____

How can you deal with the scapegoat in a healthier way? _____

_____

_____

Activity: The Caretaker (Enabler)

The Caretaker (Enabler) makes all the other roles possible. He or she tries to keep everyone happy and the family in balance, avoiding the issue. The enabler makes excuses for all behaviors and actions, and never mention addiction recovery or getting help. The Caretaker (Enabler) presents the picture of a family without problems to the public. The underlying feelings are inadequacy, fear, and helplessness.

Who was the enabler in your family?_____

Who in your life is currently the enabler? _____

How did you feel about the enabler in your family of origin and why? _____

_____

_____

How do you feel about the enabler in your current family and why? _____

_____

_____

What was the benefit of this behavior to the enabler? _____

_____

_____

What would be better alternate behaviors? _____

_____

_____

How can you deal with the enabler in a healthier way? _____

_____

_____

Activity: My Family Roles

Which family roles are you currently using/filling and what do you need to do to heal that part of yourself.

Role 1: _____

What can I do now? _____

_____

Role 2: _____

What can I do now?_____

_____

Role 3: _____

What can I do now? _____

_____

Role 4: _____

What can I do now? _____

_____

Role 5: _____

What can I do now? _____

_____

Growing Up in a Borderline Family

Borderline personality disorder has many traits in common with addiction including being impulsive, having low self-esteem, fear of being alone and intense anger. Even if there was not someone in your family with a true diagnosis of Borderline Personality Disorder, many of these traits were probably present, and you may feel many of these feelings even today. This chapter is designed to help you understand how messages you got when you were growing up cause you to react the way you do in relationships now. Once you are able to understand why you feel or react a certain way (remember feelings cause reactions) then you can start making more logical, healthy choices.

Characteristics of the Borderline Family

The main features of borderline personality disorder (BPD) are instability in relationships, self-image and emotions, and a tendency to be very impulsive. Unfortunately, many people who grow up in a family where one or more people are borderline causes them to develop borderline symptoms themselves. If you grew up in a borderline family, your parent (and maybe you) will have several of the following issues:

- ✓ Frantic efforts to avoid real or imagined abandonment (Please don't leave me. I can't live without you)

- ✓ A pattern of unstable and intense interpersonal relationships characterized by alternating between extremes of love and hate. (I love you. I hate you)

- ✓ Identity disturbance, such as a significant and persistent unstable self-image or sense of self (I will be whoever you want me to be.)

- ✓ Impulsivity in at least two areas that are potentially self-damaging (e.g., spending, sex, substance abuse, reckless driving, binge eating)

- ✓ Recurrent suicidal behavior, gestures, or threats, or self-mutilating behavior

- ✓ Emotional instability (e.g., intense episodes of depression, irritability, or anxiety usually lasting a few hours and only rarely more than a few days)

- ✓ Chronic feelings of emptiness (I feel dead inside. I am worthless.)

- ✓ Inappropriate, intense anger or difficulty controlling anger (e.g., frequent displays of temper, constant anger, recurrent physical fights)

- ✓ Transient, stress-related paranoid thoughts or severe dissociative symptoms (Everybody hates me. People are always doing things to hurt me)

In the next few pages, you will learn about the purpose of these symptoms, how it impacts the child and significant others involved with a person with these symptoms.

NOTE: I refer to these as symptoms, because these behaviors, thoughts and emotions can all be addressed and treated. They served a purpose at one time. Now you can develop new, healthier skills to serve the same purpose.

Activity: What I Learned from Borderline Behaviors

<u>Your caregiver would make frantic efforts to avoid real or imagined abandonment</u>

Function: The person has no concept of who he or she is. He or she only knows how to exist as a role, such as being someone else's boyfriend/girlfriend/parent etc. The addicted parent may have lost touch with his or her roles, and be completely lost in the addiction

Take Away Messages for Children:

I cannot leave. It is my responsibility to take care of my parent.

Describe what happened in your family to teach you this.

_____

_____

_____

How is this message still negatively impacting you today?

_____

_____

_____

Replace this "take away message" with a healthier message.

_____

_____

_____

302

If I acted differently, she would not be so upset all of the time.

Describe what happened in your family to teach you this.

_____

_____

How is this message still negatively impacting you today?

_____

_____

_____

Replace this "take away message" with a healthier message.

_____

_____

She hates me. I cannot do anything right, but she will die if I leave.

Describe what happened in your family to teach you this.

_____

_____

How is this message still negatively impacting you today?

_____

_____

Replace this "take away message" with a healthier message.

_____

_____

Your caregivers relationships are unstable and intense, and alternate between extremes of loving or hating a person or idealizing one person and despising another (the golden child vs. the black sheep).

Function: When people are acting in ways the borderline or addicted person wants, then he or she feels safe. When they don't, he or she fears abandonment and becomes defensive. This defensiveness often looks like--- I will hate you and hurt you before you can leave me.

Take Away Messages for Children:

Things are all or nothing, black or white, good or bad. If I am who my parent wants me to be, then I will be loved; otherwise, I am hated, not worthy of love. The world is very inconsistent and unpredictable. One day I am loved, the next day, hated

Describe what happened in your family to teach you this.

_____

_____

How is this message still negatively impacting you today?

_____

_____

_____

Replace this "take away message" with a healthier message.

_____

_____

_____

I have little control over what happens, how others treat me or if I am lovable.

Describe what happened in your family to teach you this.

_____

_____

How is this message still negatively impacting you today?

_____

_____

_____

Replace this "take away message" with a healthier message.

_____

_____

_____

Her perspective is right. Mine is wrong. If I would only listen to her things would be okay.

Describe what happened in your family to teach you this.

_____

_____

How is this message still negatively impacting you today?

_____

_____

_____

Replace this "take away message" with a healthier message.

_____

_____

_____

Her needs come first. When she is doing something for me, it is likely that she is doing it to satisfy her own needs or validate herself.

Describe what happened in your family to teach you this.

_____

_____

_____

How is this message still negatively impacting you today?

_____

_____

_____

Replace this "take away message" with a healthier message.

_____

_____

_____

Your caregiver had an identity disturbance, or a difficulty describing his or herself, interests or aspirations.

Function: This is more of a symptom than a function. People who define themselves by who they are to other people often have difficulty just describing themselves. They compare themselves to external expectations and have no sense of what they want or need. This also means that if someone in the borderline or addicted person's life does not do what he or she wants, it causes feelings of helplessness which may lead to lashing out.

Take Away Messages for Children:

I cannot do anything right. I am damned if I do and damned if I don't.

Describe what happened in your family to teach you this.

_____

_____

How is this message still negatively impacting you today?

_____

_____

_____

Replace this "take away message" with a healthier message.

_____

_____

_____

I am not lovable unless I do what she wants. My wants, needs, thoughts are not valid.

Describe what happened in your family to teach you this.

_____

_____

How is this message still negatively impacting you today?

_____

_____

_____

Replace this "take away message" with a healthier message.

_____

_____

_____

Other people are not trustworthy. What is said one day may be different the next.

Describe what happened in your family to teach you this.

_____

_____

How is this message still negatively impacting you today?

_____

_____

_____

Replace this "take away message" with a healthier message.

_____

_____

_____

What we present to the world is often not related to who we are.

Describe what happened in your family to teach you this.

_____

_____

How is this message still negatively impacting you today?

_____

_____

Replace this "take away message" with a healthier message.

_____

_____

_____

<u>Your caregiver was impulsive in at least two areas that are potentially self-damaging (e.g., spending, sex, substance abuse, reckless driving, binge eating)</u>

Function: This one is easy---distraction from the Hell that is inside his or her head. Unfortunately this comes with a lot of blaming—"Look what you made me do…"

Take Away Messages for Children:

If I ….she would be happier and take better care of herself.

Describe what happened in your family to teach you this.

_____

_____

How is this message still negatively impacting you today?

_____

_____

_____

Replace this "take away message" with a healthier message.

_____

_____

_____

If only I were a better person she wouldn't do these things or have these problems.

Describe what happened in your family to teach you this.

_____

_____

_____

How is this message still negatively impacting you today?

_____

_____

_____

Replace this "take away message" with a healthier message.

_____

_____

_____

It is my fault she _____

Describe what happened in your family to teach you this.

_____

_____

_____

How is this message still negatively impacting you today?

_____

_____

_____

Replace this "take away message" with a healthier message.

_____

_____

_____

<u>Your caregiver had recurrent suicidal behaviors, gestures or threats, or self-mutilating behavior.</u>

Function: Gets attention. Controls other people's behavior. Provides an alternate focus for the pain/misery. Most often these gestures are preceded by an argument of some sort. Again, the message in the behavior is "Look what you made me do."

Take Away Messages for Children:

I am bad. If I were better, she would not have these problems. It is all my fault.

Describe what happened in your family to teach you this.

_____

_____

How is this message still negatively impacting you today?

_____

_____

_____

Replace this "take away message" with a healthier message.

_____

_____

_____

Negative reactions of others are my fault and I must fix it.

Describe what happened in your family to teach you this.

_____

_____

_____

How is this message still negatively impacting you today?

_____

_____

_____

Replace this "take away message" with a healthier message.

_____

_____

_____

I am completely responsible for other people's thoughts, feelings and actions. ("You made me....")

Describe what happened in your family to teach you this.

_____

_____

_____

How is this message still negatively impacting you today?

_____

_____

_____

Replace this "take away message" with a healthier message.

_____

_____

_____

Your caregiver had frequent and unpredictable mood swings

Function: Again, this is more of a symptom of feeling helpless and terrified. When things are going well, the borderline person is happy. When things start to unravel, so does she.

Take Away Messages for Children:

It is better not to get too excited of feel good, because it may trigger a violent or nasty response.

Describe what happened in your family to teach you this.

_____

_____

_____

How is this message still negatively impacting you today?

_____

_____

_____

Replace this "take away message" with a healthier message.

_____

_____

_____

It is easier not to celebrate, because it is quickly followed by criticism of humiliation.

Describe what happened in your family to teach you this.

_____

_____

_____

How is this message still negatively impacting you today?

_____

_____

_____

Replace this "take away message" with a healthier message.

_____

_____

_____

I notice the subtle cues so I have some warning about what is coming

Describe what happened in your family to teach you this.

_____

_____

_____

How is this message still negatively impacting you today?

_____

_____

_____

Replace this "take away message" with a healthier message.

_____

_____

_____

I never know from what hour to the next what I am in for.

Describe what happened in your family to teach you this.

_____

_____

_____

How is this message still negatively impacting you today?

_____

_____

_____

Replace this "take away message" with a healthier message.

_____

_____

_____

Your caregiver has chronic feelings of emptiness

Function: This is another symptom. When you only feel okay if someone is telling you that you are okay, then without constant praise and validation, you feel empty or lost.

Take Away Messages for Children:

Don't talk, don't trust, don't feel.

Describe what happened in your family to teach you this.

_____

_____

_____

How is this message still negatively impacting you today?

_____

_____

_____

Replace this "take away message" with a healthier message.

_____

_____

_____

I am responsible for making you feel whole

Describe what happened in your family to teach you this.

_____

_____

_____

How is this message still negatively impacting you today?

_____

_____

_____

Replace this "take away message" with a healthier message.

_____

_____

_____

I am responsible for your self-image

Describe what happened in your family to teach you this.

_____

_____

_____

How is this message still negatively impacting you today?

_____

_____

_____

Replace this "take away message" with a healthier message.

_____

_____

_____

<u>Your caregiver has under expressed or overexpressed anger (e.g., frequent pouting, displays of temper, constant anger, recurrent physical fights, sarcasm or withdrawal)</u>

Function: Anger is a protective behavior. It takes back power when the person feels helpless. It pushes people away when the person feels threatened. It diverts attention when the person feels exposed.

Take Away Messages for Children:

I hurt her/prevented her from being happy. It is my responsibility to fix it.

Describe what happened in your family to teach you this.

_____

_____

How is this message still negatively impacting you today?

_____

_____

_____

Replace this "take away message" with a healthier message.

_____

_____

_____

She feels entitled (or worthless depending on the day), so I owe it to her to make sure I don't let her down.

Describe what happened in your family to teach you this.

_____

_____

_____

How is this message still negatively impacting you today?

_____

_____

_____

Replace this "take away message" with a healthier message.

_____

_____

_____

She is not in control and cannot be held accountable for her actions

Describe what happened in your family to teach you this.

_____

_____

_____

How is this message still negatively impacting you today?

_____

_____

_____

Replace this "take away message" with a healthier message.

_____

_____

_____

_____

Anger is dangerous and should not be expressed

Describe what happened in your family to teach you this.

_____

_____

_____

How is this message still negatively impacting you today?

_____

_____

_____

Replace this "take away message" with a healthier message.

_____

_____

_____

It is unacceptable to disagree with her

Describe what happened in your family to teach you this.

_____

_____

_____

How is this message still negatively impacting you today?

_____

_____

_____

Replace this "take away message" with a healthier message.

_____

_____

_____

I cannot trust my own judgment and feelings

Describe what happened in your family to teach you this.

_____

_____

_____

How is this message still negatively impacting you today?

_____

_____

_____

Replace this "take away message" with a healthier message.

_____

_____

_____

If I am perfect and do everything the way he or she wants I may not be subject to the drama or criticism

Describe what happened in your family to teach you this.

_____

_____

_____

How is this message still negatively impacting you today?

_____

_____

_____

Replace this "take away message" with a healthier message.

_____

_____

_____

Activity: Reparenting

In order to recover from the effects of an unhealthy parent, it is vital to reparent yourself. That means reprogramming the tapes in your head to play messages which can help you be happy and healthy. Below is a list of the basic components to raising a happy, healthy child. For each one, write the messages from your childhood that you internalized and currently tell yourself. Then, in the right column, write alternate, positive statements that you will start using instead.

I learned that life was unpredictable and I needed to be hypervigilant because: _____

_____

_____

In order to feel safe and secure I need to: _____

_____

_____

Growing up, I was regularly undermined and told I couldn't succeed which taught me _____

_____

_____

To provide myself support and encouragement in my future, I will: _____

_____

_____

Growing up I regularly experienced rejection by: _____

_____

_____

Now I can give myself respect and acceptance by: _____

_____

_____

Growing up, my thoughts and feelings were regularly invalidated by: _____

_____

_____

Now I can give myself voice and validation by:_____

_____

_____

Growing up learned that people were unpredictable and unreliable because:_____

_____

_____

I can develop consistency in my own moods and expectations by: _____

_____

_____

Growing up I learned that love always had conditions or strings attached by: _____

_____

_____

Now I can learn to love unconditionally by: _____

_____

_____

Now that you have identified some of the most harmful behaviors and messages, you have probably come to the realization that life isn't fair and you did not have the childhood you deserved and wanted. As frustrating or depressing as it is to admit to that, it is important not to justify or minimize your feelings, or take responsibility for your parent's behavior. You have every right to be angry. The big question is what you are going to do with that anger. The past cannot be changed. The addicted or borderline parent is probably not willing to change (unless she has already done so by her own choosing). Confronting the borderline or addicted parent probably will not get the reaction you are hoping for. Hopefully, you are starting to more clearly see which parts of your current unhappiness are within your control, and which parts were caused by a dysfunctional environment and things that were not in your control. Now it is up to you to start creating the life you want.

Part of that life, regardless of whether or not you are in recovery, involves developing healthy, mutually fulfilling relationships. As humans, we are not designed to be hermits. In recovery this is even more true. Because the addicted-self lives within your head, you are already essentially outnumbered…so you need reinforcements. Easy peasy right? Not so much. Not any relationship will do. You need people in your life who are sane. I chose the word sane instead of normal, because normal is all in how you see things. Sane, on the other hand, means someone who is relatively psychologically healthy, and can be part of a give and take relationship (not just a taker). Sober, in this context, means someone who is generally able to deal with life on life's terms without having to escape or numb the pain with addictive behaviors. It does NOT necessarily only limit you to people who don't drink or drug. Start by identifying who already exists in your support network.

Activity: Identifying your sane, sober social support network

Supporters	Neutral	Underminers

Pick one or two people on that list with whom you will share your recovery goals and needs. It is vital that you accept that you cannot do it alone. Inside your head dwells your addicted self and your sober self. You need a neutral third party to help you quiet the addiction, tolerate your feelings and deal with life on life's terms.

Co-Dependency

So you have identified some supportive people, now you need to take a look at the quality of your relationships. Co-dependent relationships are just as toxic as any other addiction. In these relationships, you ignore your own needs, wants and feelings to make the other person happy, especially to avoid being .... Alone. Because of the lessons learned in your family of origin, you may have developed some codependent patterns to help you feel worthy of love, or to simply cope with the negative behaviors of your parents.

Activity: Co-Dependency Worksheet

_____ I devote a lot of time to that relationship and little time to other relationships

Why? _____

_____

How can I deal with those fears/issues? _____

_____

What can I do that would be healthier? _____

_____

_____ I often feel jealous or have feelings of possessiveness

Why?_____

_____

How can I deal with those fears/issues? _____

_____

What can I do that would be healthier? _____

_____

_____ Even though I am not happy in the relationship, I stay in it

Why?_____

_____

How can I deal with those fears/issues? _____

_____

What can I do that would be healthier? _____

_____

_____ Pleasing that person is extremely important to me

Why? _____

_____

How can I deal with those fears/issues? _____

_____

What can I do that would be healthier? _____

_____

_____ I tend to conform to what I believe that person wants, or doesn't want me to do

Why? _____

_____

How can I deal with those fears/issues? _____

_____

What can I do that would be healthier? _____

_____

_____ I avoid expressing my feelings if they are different from that person's

Why?_____

_____

How can I deal with those fears/issues? _____

_____

What can I do that would be healthier? _____

_____

_____ I feel anxious or panic when I am apart from that person

Why? _____

_____

How can I deal with those fears/issues? _____

_____

What can I do that would be healthier? _____

_____

_____ I try and make myself indispensable to that person

Why? _____

_____

How can I deal with those fears/issues? _____

_____

What can I do that would be healthier? _____

_____

_____ I devote a lot of time and energy into taking care of that person

Why? _____

_____

How can I deal with those fears/issues? _____

_____

What can I do that would be healthier? _____

_____

_____ I want to be around that person all the time, or as much as possible, even if that means neglecting other areas of my life.

Why? _____

_____

How can I deal with those fears/issues? _____

_____

What can I do that would be healthier? _____

_____

_____ I often feel angry and taken advantage of in the relationship

Why? _____

_____

How can I deal with those fears/issues? _____

_____

What can I do that would be healthier? _____

_____

_____ I often feel like doing the opposite of what the person wants me to do

Why? _____

_____

How can I deal with those fears/issues? _____

_____

What can I do that would be healthier? _____

_____

_____ I fall in love quickly and fall apart when the relationship ends

Why? _____

_____

How can I deal with those fears/issues? _____

_____

What can I do that would be healthier? _____

_____

_____ I tend to jump from one relationship to another with little time in between

Why? _____

_____

How can I deal with those fears/issues? _____

_____

What can I do that would be healthier? _____

_____

_____ Sometimes I start another relationship before my current relationship ends

Why? _____

_____

How can I deal with those fears/issues? _____

_____

What can I do that would be healthier? _____

_____

_____ The more involved I become in a relationship, the more fearful and needy I feel

Why? _____

_____

How can I deal with those fears/issues? _____

_____

What can I do that would be healthier? _____

_____

Knowing these things about yourself will help you form healthier, more mutually fulfilling relationships. It will also help you spot unhealthy tendencies in your significant others. These tendencies may be a cause for caution in your relationships.

Self-Esteem: Your Relationship with Yourself

Self-esteem is simply the way you feel about yourself. In order to form healthy relationships it is important to first be okay with yourself. It is the product of your evaluation of your real-self compared with their ideal-self. Everyone has an ideal-self. This is who you believe you should be. (Remember, "shoulds" almost always add unnecessary stress.) You form this concept of the ideal-self at an early age based upon conditions of worth. That is, as a child, praise was given not for who you were, but what you were able to do or how you were able to act. As a result, you formed schemas or ideas about what a "good girl" or "good boy" should be. Due to children's immature reasoning, many things are overgeneralized and made into global, stable and internal attributions, creating an unrealistic ideal-self. For instance, many girls grow up to believe that they must be successful: partners, mothers and business-women. This is called the superwoman stereotype. Little boys may believe they must always be: strong, successful, good partners and primary providers. In reality, that is nearly impossible for either gender to do. Your real-self is who you are with all of your inherent imperfections. To improve self-esteem, you must change the way you feel about a situation (i.e. change your feelings about your self-evaluation) or change yourself (either the real-self or the ideal-self).

Suggestions for Improving Self-Esteem

- ✓ Make a list of positive affirmations and add one new one each day

- ✓ When you find a fault in yourself, remind yourself of three positive qualities

- ✓ Do not minimize your accomplishments. Take credit where credit is due.

- ✓ Surround yourself with people who are positive and encouraging

- ✓ Instead of complaining about faults, take positive action

- ✓ If there is something you feel "bad" about that is impossible to change, then add a new, positive quality.

- ✓ Do a good deed every day

- ✓ Make changeable, specific attributions for negative events

- ✓ Patience-- changes do not happen overnight

- ✓ Accept your fears and work with and through them. Nobody is perfect.

- ✓ Evaluate whether you hold yourself to a higher standard than you hold everyone else. Do you think you are that much better than everyone else, or do you just need a reason to beat yourself up?

Activity: Self Esteem Worksheet

Describe your ideal self.

_____

_____

_____

_____

_____

List all of the personal attributes you have of which you are proud

_____

_____

_____

List all of the good/nice things you have done for other people in the past month

_____

_____

_____

_____

What is your biggest fault?_____

Why is this a fault? _____

_____

In what ways does this keep you from being who you want to be?

_____

_____

_____

What can you do to correct this problem? _____

_____

_____

Abraham Maslow said that there are basic needs we must fulfill (food, shelter, safety) before we can devote the energy to creating healthy relationships with ourselves and others. How well are you fulfilling these needs and what could you do to better fulfill them.

Biology--food, shelter, health_____

_____

_____

Safety/security (this includes safety from the negative voices in your own head)

_____

_____

Love and belongingness _____

_____

_____

Activity: Hope, Health and Happiness

As your self esteem improves, you will likely develop some of the following characteristics of healthy, happy people. Place a check next to those characteristics that describe you.

1. Highly efficient perception of reality and the ability to take multiple perspectives and be objective

2. Acceptance of strengths and weaknesses in self and others

3. Naturalness and spontaneity: flexible and comfortable with themselves

4. Commitment and dedication

5. Independence and interdependence

6. Appreciation for the present moment: random acts of kindness, "stop and smell the roses"

7. Creativity

8. Brotherly love: genuine desire to help the human race

9. Democratic character

10. Integrity: strong sense of personal ethics

11. Resistance to enculturation (peer / sociopolitical influences)

12. Sense of humor

13. A sense of being at peace with oneself and one with the world

How can you further develop each of these characteristics in yourself?

1. _____

2. _____

3. _____

4. _____

5. _____

6. _____

7. _____

8. _____

9. _____

10. _____

11. _____

12. _____

13. _____

What things did your family do to help you develop a healthy self-esteem when you were growing up?

1. _____

2. _____

3. _____

4. _____

5. _____

What things did your family, friends or significant others do to hinder your self-esteem?

1. _____

2. _____

3. _____

What things can you do to improve your self-esteem?

1. _____

2. _____

3. _____

Boundaries

Boundaries are another important part of relationships, both with yourself and others. By knowing and maintaining your boundaries, you are respecting and caring for yourself and developing healthier relationships with others. We all have personal boundaries that define who we are, and determine how we are interact and relate to the world, physically, emotionally and spiritually. Boundaries help you understand where you end and others begin, express who you are and allow others to do the same. One of the primary causes of conflict and difficulties in relationships is unhealthy boundaries. Physical boundaries define your need and rights to personal space and safety. Emotional boundaries define your emotional needs and rights including your rights to your own thoughts and feelings.

Overly rigid boundaries compromise your ability to form intimate relationships, because you will not make yourself vulnerable in any fashion. It is like being surrounded by a giant, ten foot thick iron wall. On the other extreme, a lack of boundaries means you cannot experience yourself as separate from others. You feel your feelings as well as everyone else's and define yourself according to everyone else's definition of who you are. In essence you are a human chameleon. Healthy boundaries allow you to feel your feelings without having to impose them on others and without the need to be validated by others.

Activity: Boundaries

Which best describes your boundaries?

☐ Compliant: Feels guilty or controlled by others. Can't set boundaries. Can't say "no" or assert thoughts, feelings or needs.

☐ Controller: Aggressively, intentionally and/or manipulatively violates other people's boundaries. "You will think and act how I want you to, or I will (leave, withhold affection, throw a temper tantrum…)"

☐ Nonresponsive: Sets boundaries to avoid the responsibility of loving or caring for another. "Do it yourself"

☐ Avoidant: Sets boundaries against receiving the care of others. "I don't need your help"

How are these boundaries working for you? _____

_____

How could you better respect the feelings, thoughts and needs of yourself and other people?

_____

336

Activity: Relationships Inventory

Rank your typical relationships on the following dimensions:

1. Suspicion	1	2	3	4	5	Trust
2. Abuse	1	2	3	4	5	Affection
3. Domination	1	2	3	4	5	Companionship
4. Jealousy	1	2	3	4	5	Confidence
5. Secrecy	1	2	3	4	5	Openness
6. Self-centered	1	2	3	4	5	Sharing
7. Dependence	1	2	3	4	5	Independence

For the dimensions which you circled 1,2 or 3, ask yourself why you tend to be that way in relationships.

Are you afraid of being hurt? _____

Why? _____

How can you deal with this? _____

_____

Afraid of being alone? _____

Why? _____

How can you deal with this?_____

_____

Is it "baggage" from other relationships that you are holding everyone else hostage for? _____

Why? _____

How can you deal with this?_____

_____

Are some dimensions worse in certain types of relationships such as with significant others or same-gender friends? _____

Why?_____

How can you deal with this? _____

_____

How can you improve in each dimension?

1. _____

2. _____

3. _____

4. _____

5. _____

6. _____

7. _____

How do these characteristics (Trust, Affection, Companionship, Confidence, Openness, Sharing, Independence) impact your recovery and happiness?

1. _____

2. _____

3. _____

4. _____

5. _____

6. _____

7. _____

Activity: Relationship Myths

True or False?

_____ If we become involved, I will lose my individual identity

_____ If you really knew me you would not care about me

_____ You will leave me if you find out that I am not perfect

_____ Being vulnerable usually results in getting hurt

_____ We should never argue or criticize each other

_____ Anything that goes wrong is my fault

_____ You are perfect

_____ In order to be loveable, I must be happy all of the time

_____ We will trust each other totally, automatically and immediately

_____ We will do everything together

_____ If you really cared, you would learn to anticipate my every need, wish, desire

_____ If we really love each other, we will stay together forever

_____ You will never take me for granted

_____ I will always be supportive and non-critical

_____ If we disagree, I must be wrong

_____ We both have the same needs

_____ If you do not approve of something I do, say or believe, then I should change

The above True/False statements represent relationship myths. For the ones you checked true write a reason why this may be considered a relationship myth.

_____

_____

_____

_____

_____

Activity: Relationships Needs Assessment

When beginning a relationship you must accept that you and your partner are individuals.

List the 5 most important qualities you have which you are not willing to change.

1. _____

2. _____

3. _____

4. _____

5. _____

List the 5 most important qualities you look for in a partner or friend, on which you will not compromise.

1. _____

2. _____

3. _____

4. _____

5. _____

Things to consider putting in the above lists: Goals, values, parenting styles, ideas about money management, love of children or animals, lifestyle etc.

Developmental Stages

Another issue that affects the quality of relationships is each person's developmental level. As people mature, they actually begin to think differently. Different things matter. Their perspectives change, and they begin to form their own opinions and values. The next section aims to help you improve your communications with others so you can be compassionate, nurturing and develop healthy relationships.

It is important to be aware of "where" people are developmentally when you talk with them for many reasons. First, you will understand some of the things they are going through and why they are reacting the way that they are. You will also understand what things might be important to them, and how to best approach conversations to make the most of your (and their) time. For instance, when talking to an adolescent, it may be more useful to approach a conversation about career choice from the perspective of what they can accomplish and how that career would help them demonstrate to the world who they are. That same conversation would be more effective with a young adult, if it were presented from the perspective of how it would help them support their family and fulfill their current goals. Simply understanding this can help you more effectively relate to your children and everyone else in your world.

Below you will find descriptions of each of the developmental stages. According to Erickson, at each stage you have a skill to learn. If you do not learn it, then it becomes a stuck point. For example, if your parents were not attentive and did not meet your needs, when you were an infant and toddler, then you may never have learned to trust your own feelings, intuition ("Spidey senses"). Part of the recovery process is going back and learning what you did not learn. You will recognize a lot of the goals as some of the characteristics of healthy relationships that you learned about earlier.

Overview of the Stages

- ✓ Hope: Trust vs. Mistrust (Birth-2 years)
- ✓ Will: Autonomy vs. Shame & Doubt (2-4 years)
- ✓ Purpose: Initiative vs. Guilt (4-5 years)
- ✓ Competence: Industry vs. Inferiority (5-12 years)
- ✓ Fidelity: Identity vs. Role Confusion (13-19 years)

Activity: Developmental Stages

Hope & Trust vs. Mistrust (Birth – 2 years): Existential Question: Can I Trust the World?

The first stage of Erikson's theory centers around your basic needs being met by your parents when you were an infant, and this interaction leading you to trust or mistrust not only other people, but also your own thoughts and feelings. If your parents exposed you to warmth, consistency, and dependable affection, your view of the world is one of trust. If your parents failed to provide a secure environment and to meet your basic needs; a sense of mistrust will result. For example, if you were given a bottle every time you started to cry, regardless of if you were tired, cold, scared, wet or hungry, then you likely learned not to listen to your body's cues, but to just eat or drink to self-soothe. If your caregivers were consistent sources of food, comfort, and affection, you learned that others are dependable and reliable. If they were neglectful, or abusive, you learned that the world is an undependable, unpredictable, and possibly a dangerous place. Development of mistrust can lead to feelings of frustration, suspicion, withdrawal, inability to effectively identify feelings, wants and needs, and a lack of confidence.

When you were growing up, were your needs adequately met?   Yes   No

How can you learn to trust yourself and your thoughts and feelings?

_____

_____

How can you create warmth, consistency, and affection in your life now?

_____

_____

How can this help you relate with or understand the little ones in your life?

_____

_____

What are some the needs for the infant/young child?

_____

_____

Autonomy vs. Shame and Doubt (2–4 years) Existential Question: Is It OK to Be Me?

As you began to explore your surroundings, your parents still provided a strong base of security from which you could venture out. Children at this age like to explore the world around them and they are constantly learning about their environment. Highly restrictive parents, however, are more likely to instill in the child a sense of doubt, and reluctance to attempt new challenges. As they gain increased muscular coordination and mobility, toddlers become capable of satisfying some of their own needs. They begin to feed themselves, wash and dress themselves, and use the bathroom. If caregivers encourage self-sufficient behavior, toddlers develop a sense of autonomy—a sense of being able to handle many problems on their own. If caregivers demand too much too soon, refuse to let children perform tasks they are capable of, or ridicule attempts at self-sufficiency, children may doubt their ability to handle problems.

When you were growing up, were you encouraged to be independent? Yes   No

How can you develop the confidence that you can handle life on life's terms?

_____

_____

How can you prevent yourself from taking on too much?

_____

_____

Who can support and encourage you now?

_____

_____

How can this help you relate with or understand the toddlers in your life?

_____

_____

What are some the priorities (motivators) in the toddler's life?

_____

_____

Initiative vs. Guilt (4–5 years) Existential Question: Is it OK for Me to Move, and Act?

Initiative adds to autonomy the quality of undertaking, planning and attacking a task for the sake of just being active and on the move. The child is learning to master the world around them, learning basic skills and principles of physics. Things fall down, not up. Round things roll. They learn how to zip and tie, count and speak with ease. At this stage, you wanted to begin and complete your own actions for a purpose. Guilt is a confusing new emotion. You may have felt guilty over things that logically should not cause guilt, for example, when your initiative did not produce desired results.

The development of courage and independence are what set preschoolers, ages three to six years of age, apart from other age groups. You may have also developed a sense of frustration for not being able to achieve a goal as planned and may engage in behaviors that seem aggressive, such as throwing objects, hitting, or yelling.

If parents and preschool teachers encouraged and supported your efforts, while also helping you make realistic and appropriate choices, you developed initiative- independence in planning and undertaking activities. But if, instead, they discouraged the pursuit of independent activities or dismissed them as silly and bothersome, you may have felt guilty about your needs and desires.

How did you deal with failure and frustration when you were growing up?

_____

_____

What can you learn from your failures?

_____

_____

How can you effectively deal with frustration?

_____

_____

What can you do to enlist encouragement and support for your efforts?

_____

_____

344

How can you support and encourage others?

_____

_____

How can this help you relate with or understand the kindergarten age children in your life?

_____

_____

What are some the priorities (motivators) in the kindergartener's life?

_____

_____

Industry vs. Inferiority (5–12 years) Existential Question: Can I Make it in the World of People and Things?

Children at this age are becoming more aware of themselves as individuals. They work hard at being responsible, being good and doing it right. They are also now more able to share and cooperate. At this stage, children are eager to learn and accomplish more complex skills: reading, writing, telling time. They also get to form moral values, recognize cultural and individual differences and are able to manage most of their personal needs and grooming with minimal assistance. During this stage, children might express their independence by talking back and being disobedient and rebellious.

Erikson viewed the elementary school years as critical for the development of self-confidence, because it provides many opportunities for children to achieve the recognition of teachers, parents and peers by producing things- drawing pictures, solving addition problems, writing sentences, and so on. If you were encouraged to make and do things and were then praised for your accomplishments, you likely began to demonstrate industry by being diligent, persevering at tasks until completed, and putting work before pleasure. If you were instead ridiculed or punished for your efforts or if you found you were incapable of meeting your teachers' and parents' expectations, you may have developed feelings of inferiority about your capabilities.

Were you encouraged to make and do things when you were growing up? If so, how?

_____

_____

Are you able to be diligent, work on tasks until completed, and put work before pleasure.?

_____

_____

What things do you feel inferior or less capable to do?

_____

_____

What can you do to help yourself when you want to quit or give up?

_____

_____

How can this help you relate with or understand the elementary aged children in your life?

_____

_____

_____

_____

What are some the priorities (motivators) in the young child's life?

_____

_____

_____

_____

_____

Identity vs. Role Confusion (Adolescence, 13–19 years) Existential Question: Who Am I and What Can I Be?

The adolescent is newly concerned with how they appear to others. As they make the transition from childhood to adulthood, adolescents ponder the roles they will play in the adult world. Initially, they are apt to experience some role confusion—mixed ideas and feelings about the specific ways in which they will fit into society—and may experiment with a variety of behaviors and activities (e.g. tinkering with cars, baby-sitting for neighbors, affiliating with certain political or religious groups). The adolescent seeks leadership and someone to inspire him. Gradually the adolescent develops a set of ideals. The goal is to achieve a sense of identity regarding who they are and where their lives are headed. This marks the transition from childhood to adulthood. Role confusion involves not being sure about themselves, their values or their place in society. This can lead to feelings of ambivalence and inferiority.

Who inspired you when you were growing up? _____

Who inspires you now, and why? _____

_____

_____

How do you fit in to society?

_____

_____

What skills and strengths do you have?

_____

_____

What are some the priorities (motivators) in the teenager's life?

_____

_____

How can this help you better relate to the teenagers in your life?

_____

_____

Intimacy vs. Isolation (20–39 years) Existential Questions: What is Love? Can I Love?

Young adults are still eager to blend their identities with friends. They want to fit in. Yet, they are afraid of rejections such as being turned down or their partners breaking up with them. Rejection is painful and some people cannot bear the pain. To deal with this, intimacy has a counterpart: Distantiation: the readiness to isolate and if necessary, to destroy those forces and people whose essence seems dangerous to your own, and whose territory seems to encroach on yours." Once people have established their identities, they are ready to make long-term commitments to others. They become capable of forming intimate, reciprocal relationships (e.g. through close friendships or marriage) and willingly make the sacrifices and compromises that such relationships require. If you were and/or are unable to form these relationships a sense of isolation may result; arousing feelings of darkness and angst.

How do you deal with rejection? _____

_____

How do you make friends?

_____

_____

In what ways are your relationships give and take?

_____

_____

How can you make sure that your relationships maintain a balance of give and take?

_____

_____

What are some the priorities (motivators) in the young adult's life?

_____

_____

How can this help you better relate to the young adults in your life?

_____

_____

Care: Generativity vs. Stagnation (40–64 years) Existential Question: Can I Make My Life Count?

Generativity is the concern of guiding the next generation. During middle age the primary developmental task is one of contributing to society and helping to guide future generations. When people make a contribution during this period, perhaps by raising a family or working toward the betterment of society, a sense of generativity, or productivity and accomplishment results. In contrast, people who are self-centered and unable or unwilling to help society move forward develop a feeling of stagnation, a dissatisfaction with their relative lack of productivity.

Central Tasks/Priorities/Motivators of Middle Adulthood

Describe how you do or will do each of the following

Express love through more than sexual contacts.

_____

_____

Maintain healthy life patterns.

_____

_____

Help growing and grown children to be responsible adults.

_____

_____

Create a comfortable home.

_____

_____

Be proud of accomplishments of self and mate/spouse.

_____

_____

Adjust to physical changes of middle age.

_____

_____

Use leisure time creatively.

_____

_____

How can this help you better relate to the older adults in your life?

_____

_____

Putting it Together

Throughout this book you have developed skills and tools to help improve your physical health, mood, coping skills and relationships. There was a lot of information. Review what you have read and written, and identify the 10 most important points for you to remember and work on in the upcoming year.

1. _____

2. _____

3. _____

4. _____

5. _____

6. _____

7. _____

8. _____

9. _____

10. _____

Appendix 1: Treatment Plan

Instead of (the behavior you are trying to get rid of) _____ ,

I want to start _____

> *Be specific. Include goals that are positive (wanting to increase, improve, do more of something), and not just negative goals (stop, avoid, or decrease a behavior).*
>
> *For example:*
>
> - *Instead of using drugs, I want to start learning how to deal with life on life's terms.*
> - *Instead of getting into fights and arguments, I want to start being able to control my temper.*

My main reasons for making this change are _____

_____

_____

_____

What are the likely consequences of action or inaction? _____

_____

_____

_____

Which motivations for change are most compelling? _____

_____

_____

_____

The first steps I plan to take in changing are:

- ✓ To learn about (i.e. addiction, depression, relationships, healthy living)_____

  by _____ reading books _____ talking to a therapist/doctor _____ watching videos

- ✓ To learn about this as it applies to me (my relationships, my addiction, my depression etc.) by _____ talking to someone _____ journaling _____ self-help books/worksheets

- ✓ To start by making the following three changes

  1. _____

     When _____ How _____

  2. _____

     When _____ How _____

  3. _____

     When _____ How _____

Triggers for returning to the old behaviors and ways to avoid, eliminate or cope with them:

  1. _____

     Eliminate or avoid by:_____

  2. _____

     Eliminate or avoid by:_____

  3. _____

     Eliminate or avoid by:_____

Some things that could interfere with my plan are_____

_____

_____

Alternative, healthy behaviors to deal with distress and discomfort._____

_____

_____

How will I stick with the plan despite these particular problems or setbacks?_____

_____

_____

Other people could help me in changing in these ways:_____

_____

_____

Rewards to keep me motivated _____

_____

_____

I will know that my plan is working if_____

_____

_____

Appendix 2: Mood Journal

Rate each of the following dimensions using a 1-4 scale 1= very low; 2= moderately low 3= okay 4=great. Add notes beneath the chart to explain anything.

Day _____

	6am	8am	10am	Noon	2pm	4pm	6pm	8pm	10pm
Depression									
Anxiety/Stress									
Anger/Irritability									
Cravings									
Energy/Sleepiness									
Concentration									

How many hours did you sleep last night? _____   Was it quality sleep? Yes   No

If not, why? _____

Notes: _____

_____

_____

_____

_____

_____

Additional Resources

Videos and worksheets can be found at
http://RecoveryandResilience.org/JTR

Upcoming titles in our series include:

- Journey to Recovery:Tips for Dealing with Depression

- Journey to Recovery: Practical Tips for Understanding and Coping with PTSD

Made in the USA
Lexington, KY
29 February 2016